BRANDING

GOVERNANCE

BRANDING

GOVERNANCE

A Participatory Approach to the Brand Building Process

Nicholas Ind
and
Rune Bjerke

John Wiley & Sons, Ltd

Other Wiley Editorial Offices

John Wiley & Sons Inc., 111 River Street, Hoboken, NJ 07030, USA

Jossey-Bass, 989 Market Street, San Francisco, CA 94103-1741, USA

Wiley-VCH Verlag GmbH, Boschstr. 12, D-69469 Weinheim, Germany

John Wiley & Sons Australia Ltd, 42 McDougall Street, Milton, Queensland 4064,
Australia

John Wiley & Sons (Asia) Pte Ltd, 2 Clementi Loop #02-01, Jin Xing Distripark,
Singapore 129809

John Wiley & Sons Canada Ltd, 6045 Freemont Blvd, Mississauga, ONT, L5R 4J3,
Canada

Wiley also publishes its books in a variety of electronic formats. Some content that
appears in print may not be available in electronic books.

Library of Congress Cataloging-in-Publication Data

Ind, Nicholas.
        Branding governance : a participatory approach to the brand building process /
Nicholas Ind and Rune Bjerke.
        p.   cm.
        Includes bibliographical references and index.
        ISBN 978-0-470-03075-2 (cloth)
    1. Product management.   2. Brand name products.   I. Bjerke, Rune.   II. Title.
        HD69.B7I527 2007
        658.8′27 – dc22

                                                        2007004231

British Library Cataloguing in Publication Data

A catalogue record for this book is available from the British Library

ISBN 978-0-470-03075-2 (HB)

Typeset in 11.5/15pt Bembo by SNP Best-set Typesetter Ltd, Hong Kong
Printed and bound in Great Britain by TJ International Ltd, Padstow, Cornwall, UK
This book is printed on acid-free paper responsibly manufactured from sustainable
forestry in which at least two trees are planted for each one used for paper production.

To our sons
Jonathan and Evan Mathias

CONTENTS

TABLES AND FIGURES

INTRODUCTION

THE PHILOSOPHY OF THE BOOK AND THE CONCEPT OF PARTICIPATION

This book is about how to build value in the lives of customers. Once the word 'customers' is mentioned, the immediate assumption is that a book on marketing is bound to follow. In the case of this book, that is only partly true. *Branding Governance* is about brand-building but our premise is that branding as it is currently practised is both limited and flawed. It is limited in the sense that it is largely seen as the preserve of marketers who tend to focus on the external environment and turn their back on the internal – a vestige of a marketing communications led, Fast Moving Consumer Goods (FMCG) dominated era. It is flawed because of its tendency to be seller-centric; to focus on what the organisation can sell. Our argument is that brand building is too important and complex to be left just to the marketing department.

Rather, it requires an organisation-wide engagement that reaches across boundaries where leaders determine a clear and inspirational vision, which they, together with employees, nurture and develop through day-to-day actions that build human capital and deliver customer value. It is about realising what Peter Drucker claimed was the raison d'être of organisations – to endeavour consistently to make human progress. *Branding Governance* is concerned with an organisation-wide (and in our view participatory) approach to the process of planning, structuring, executing and measuring brand policy. Consequently, it stretches across such areas as leadership, organisational culture, marketing, human resources and evaluation to develop brand building capability. It is a book that breaks down the boundaries of specialisation that exist in the perspectives of writers and academics and in the way organisations are structured. It recognises that while departmentalisation might be valuable to the organisation, customers benefit from a seeming seamlessness of experience that suggests organisational unity. The principle of such a participatory approach to branding is that customers and other external audiences as well as managers and employees are all active participants in defining and developing the brand. This implies that the relationship that exists between employees and customers must be one of respect and authenticity.

For many organisations there is some distance to travel to attain such an authentic customer unity. A whole populist genre of criticism has emerged (Klein 2000, Korten 2001, Ehrenreich 2002, Hertz 2002, Schlosser 2001, Bakan 2004) that has attacked the duplicity and manipulation of organisations, while the media has highlighted some negative practices such as monopolistic behaviour, developing world labour practices and environmental disregard at traditionally well thought of businesses such as Microsoft, Nike and Exxon. The negative actions of organisations derive from a narrow view of shareholder value and a misuse of power. This should not be so surprising: Adam Smith, the icon of free trade, conservative thinking, pointed out in *The Wealth of Nations* (1776) – appropriately published in the year of American independence – that corporate power is often likely to be abused,[1] while Bakan (2004) argues that the dysfunctional nature of the publicly owned business (at least in its North American construction), which separates ownership from management, has a legal necessity and cultural accountability to put the interests of shareholders first rather than any broader responsibility to society.[2]

When companies face moral dilemmas over delivering shareholder value or a more balanced view of the long-term interests of all stakeholders, they should legally choose the former. Tirole (2006) begins by citing Berle and Means (1932), finding that the separation of ownership and control can lead to management abuse, and goes on to argue that 'corporate insiders need not act in the best interests of the providers of the funds'. These views do not mean that the actions of the corporation are necessarily bad: as Kant argues with the example of a shopkeeper in *Groundwork of the Metaphysics of Morals* (4: 397), there can be a coincidence between honest behaviour and economic well-being because of the recognition of the importance of building a positive reputation and trust (something which Nike in particular has been keenly aware of in trying to repair the public damage to its image caused by the association of the company with words such as 'sweat shop') – but as Smith, Bakan, Berle and Means, and Tirole suggest, the potential for abuse is always present.

Equally marketing can either be valuable when it engages and informs, or corrupting when it dissimulates and manipulates. As Naomi Klein points out in *No Logo* (2000) marketing techniques are clearly used in corrupting and increasingly intrusive ways to sell products and services through such mechanisms as the sponsoring of schools by commercial organisations, to the use of individuals as advertisements. When almost anything can be – and is – marketed, the tendency is to greater exaggeration. As marketing noise increases, the pressure is on to shout louder; to be noticed; to be heard. The consequence is that as marketing becomes less effective, ironically marketers try to do more of it. Mitchell (2000) says:

> the source of marketing ineffectiveness and waste, therefore, lies in its seller-centric preoccupations. Marketers say the acid test of good value is find out what your customer wants and need and give it to them. When it comes to marketing communications, this is the one thing marketers do not do. Marketers seem to believe that the only people who do not need to practice what marketing preaches is . . . themselves.

This often leads to a gap between brand promise, as defined through advertising and other mechanisms, and the reality of brand delivery. The end result of this marketing mediated world is a diminution of trust in institutions and business organisations.

While the description of business above might seem gloomy, we remain optimistic. We believe it is possible to restore confidence and credibility. There is nothing about the way things work now that determines they have to work in the same way in the future. There is no natural law that defines the continuance of past practice. The philosophers, Gilles Deleuze and Félix Guattari, write (2003), 'there is no good reason but contingent reason; there is no universal history except of contingency'. We also note that in Europe, where there is a different legal and cultural framework, there is a better balance to meeting the needs of different stakeholders. In a debate held at the Royal Society of Arts in London in April 2005, partly as a response to an editorial in *The Economist* that proclaimed in very Smithsian terms 'the selfish pursuit of profit serves a social purpose', John Drummond of Corporate Culture argued in Druckerian tones:

> in my view the primary purpose of business is not profit, it is to create the products and services that people value. If they do this successfully shareholder value follows. What that means at its most successful is showing consumers the difference my product or service makes to your life.[3]

The balanced view has also been espoused by Macrae (2003), who argues for transparent trust-flow mapping and recognition for the need of congruity between the attitudes and values of those working inside the organisation with those purchasing, utilising and consuming products and services.

THE PARTICIPATORY BRANDING PHILOSOPHY

> There is nothing which requires more to be illustrated by philosophy than trade does.
>
> *Samuel Johnson*

Many of the classics of branding and marketing literature (Kotler and Armstrong 1987, Aaker 1996, Kapferer 1997, Keller 2003) have a dominantly external focus. They reflect an era concerned primarily with products rather than services in which there was a long love affair with advertising as the prime determinant of brand image. Yet most Western economies have long been service dominated such that in France 73% of the economy is service based and even in Germany – the largest export economy in the world – it is 68% (2004). Equally in the UK, it is retailers rather than manufacturers that predominate: Tesco, for example, has a 30% plus market share (2005) of supermarket retailing, profits of £2 billion and accounts for one pound in every eight spent in shops. While employee engagement and commitment is important in product-based companies (Pfeffer 1998), in services the behaviour of employees is the prime determinant of value creation. Employee willingness to engage with customers 'has a significant impact on customer loyalty more so than many traditional marketing tools' (Thomson and Hecker 2000) and it is brand-aligned individuals who are particularly effective in generating service innovations.[4] It is the importance of employees and services that has led to the recognition of intangible assets as a determinant of value and to the emergence of the concept of intellectual capital. As Edvinsson and Malone (1997) argue, 'the core of the so-called *knowledge economy* is huge investment flows into human capital as well as information technology' (p. 12) and as Drucker predicted (1993), 'the competitive advantage of tomorrow lies in the application of knowledge'.

Just as services have come to dominate over products, advertising has become a less credible tool in defining brands.[5] While the proclamation 'we are immune to advertising. Just forget it', from the iconoclastic authors of *The Cluetrain Manifesto* (Levine et al. 2000) was an over-statement, the growing sophistication of consumers (a factor long observed by the Henley Centre for Forecasting), the excesses of some advertising campaigns and the growth in importance of other elements in image formation have undermined advertising's stature. In its place a different perspective on brand building has emerged that stresses the importance of employees in communicating and delivering both product and service brands and in creating value for customers (Reichheld 1996, de Chernatony 2001, Ind 2001, Pringle and Gordon 2001).

This book identifies with the emphasis on employees but it goes further than previous texts in prescribing an organisation-wide approach to delivering value to customers and other audiences. Often this idea of value gets narrowly defined: financiers see value in economic terms; customer relations people see it in terms of loyalty; public relations managers think of reputation; and marketers see awareness, image and purchase intentions. However, by merely concentrating on one notion of value it is possible to destroy overall customer value: spending heavily on advertising might boost saliency, but it can also undermine cash flows if it does not lead to increased sales, while a focus on short-term profit margins might play well with some financial audiences, but might undermine standards of service delivery and customer loyalty, which require long-term thinking to develop. Also we would argue that all the above definitions of value fall into Mitchell's trap of seller centricity. True customer value is the value – whether it be convenience, efficiency, enrichment, excitement, status – that the customer attaches to the relationship they have with the brand. It is determined by the actions of managers and people inside the business, but its relevance is external. The challenge here is that most organisations are not wholly focused on customers, nor are they joined together on the inside. The balkanization of most organizations leads to a lack of integration between such areas as marketing and finance, HR and operations. Silo thinking positions areas of specialisation as departments or as functions and inhibits communication, reduces innovation and stimulates conflict. Interesting connections are missed and the customer becomes a mere spectre rather than an active presence inside the organisation.

If we try to imagine this organisational picture visually, the immediate image is one of a series of boxes representing departments or functions[6] – with tenuous horizontal links between each. Some boxes connect with the outside world of the customer (who sits outside the structure) to whom, as a result of a planned strategy, things are done. In much management thinking and literature,[7] with its scientific predilections, this is a world of linear causality. Management books use such phrases as 'laws of' and 'rules of', which suggest a 'relation of universal determinations'.[8] A strategy is set, enacted and results occur; 'laws' determine cause and effect. However, as anyone who has tried to implement a strategy knows, things never work as planned – there is always emergence. The strategy itself will be based on dated and abstracted market research that does not reflect the present situation; competitor actions continually change the operating environment; engineering or product development will be unable to deliver the intended design or service and political infighting creates delays. Testing is 'always temporally determined' in that research can never catch up with itself (Ronell 2005). And as Mintzberg, Ahlstrand and Lampel (1998: 17) argue:

> it has to be realized that every strategy, like every theory, is a simplification that necessarily distorts reality. Strategies and theories are not reality themselves, only representations (or abstractions) of reality in the minds of people.

This is not to suggest that we dispense with strategy, but merely to recognise that linear causality is a myth. Setting and implementing strategy is messy and much closer to evolutionary biology and morphogenesis than scientific determinism.

To cope with the messiness of strategy and to align the organisation so that everything connects with customers, we are going to challenge the concept of linearity. We will argue that linearity is inappropriate for the free flow of knowledge within the organisation and its connections to customers, and that linearity is ill-suited to the speed and flexibility required to deliver value to the seeming irrationality of customer needs. It is not possible simply to create an input and expect some slavish Pavlovian response from a customer – this is why we are continually surprised by product successes and failures. Managers ought to know this intuitively and it has been written about for both a populist audience (Gladwell 2000) and a specialist one – the Nobel prize winning economists, Kahneman and Tversky's demonstration, through their Prospect Theory, that investors do not behave in a purely rational way, but rather make choices asymmetrically. In place of linearity we use as the basis of our thinking an assemblage – an idea developed by Gilles Deleuze in conjunction with Félix Guattari. There is an irony to this in that Deleuze was a critic of capitalism and in particular of advertising and marketing which he accused, among other wrong-doings, of appropriating a certain kind of capitalist-friendly philosophy that is able to 'provide communication with an ethic' (Deleuze and Guattari 1991: 99). However, we may also note that Deleuze is used as a reference and inspiration in organisational development (Carter and Jackson 2004) and by the philosopher, Manuel Delanda as a point of departure for the analysis of organisational structure and the idea of economies of agglomeration (Delanda 2003, 2004).

One of the primary appeals of Deleuze as a source is that he is a philosopher of 'becoming'. The importance of 'becoming' lies in its recognition that the world – and we within it – is in a constant state of change. Even though we try to grasp what is going on around us and pin it down as part of our need to make sense of things, in truth we are playing with something that is ungraspable. We like the comfort of abstractions[9] and categorisations ('we think the universal explains, whereas it is what must be explained' (Deleuze and Guattari 1991: 49)), but identities are not fixed. Rather they are changeable, because the world itself is fluid and dynamic. Identities morph because they are subject to forces behind, below and around them. In Deleuzian thinking we would not be able to set a strategy at the beginning that had a final pre-determined, end-point, but rather we would have to recognise that there is a range of possibilities that never truly close, and which are partly defined by determinism and partly by chance. This still suggests that strategies should be planned, but it also means that managers and employees have to recognise emergence and have the adaptability to change in tune with the ever-becoming or the 'restlessness of negativity' (Nancy 2002: 68) – the constant challenge to the given order of things.

This book is a demonstration of the fluid identity of things: the idea that mutation points create difference and variation. This approach has been adapted to different circumstances. It is used in software development as a way of iteratively exploring possibilities, computerised jazz music (GenJam) and architecture as a mechanism for breeding urban environments. Deleuze uses the idea to reconsider how connected elements synthesise to produce an effect in an assemblage. Now, we will take the assemblage and yet again rework its identity to make it relevant to organisations by developing the idea that managers have to understand real customer needs and connect them with the organisational infrastructure in an evolving world of connectivity. The organisation, like GenJam, will have to explore possibilities rapidly and to encourage the flow of ideas that engage internal and external audiences. Rather than just accept repetition of events as an organisational norm, managers need to recognise that 'difference inhabits repetition' (Deleuze 1968: 97). There is always difference to be discovered if we look hard at the everyday experiences of employees and customers. And it is in discovering 'difference' that questioning and learning take place – but only if the organisation is attuned to its external audiences and capable of sharing knowledge internally. This is the role of the assemblage.

INTRODUCING THE ASSEMBLAGE MODEL

In this opening chapter we will merely introduce the nature of assemblage thinking – its full development and applications will be discussed in the chapters that follow. Here it should be noted that it is both a way of thinking and a means of modelling – it can be presented graphically. The assemblage can be used both as a descriptive device to appraise what has happened as well as scope the range of strategic possibilities. In the case of the latter, if the assemblage is used as a live tool it can help keep the organisation aware of change and able to react rapidly to emergent trends. It should also be recognised that all organisations are already assemblages in that they are operative machines that connect internal systems with external stakeholders. Our argument is that a rigid and largely static approach often creates imperfect machines that are unable to achieve effective connections either internally or externally. This is what Drucker (1993) believed when he argued that the idea of organisational permanence was a myth and that organisations would have to become more flexible and adaptive. One of our goals in this book is to improve the performance of the organisational machine.

An assemblage describes the collection of a series of elements into a single context. It can be used to describe everything from a pendulum to a bicycle to an organisation (Wise 2005). In the case of the last there is considerable complexity, because the assemblage must contain all the relevant elements both inside the organisation (for instance, leadership, organisational culture and human resources drivers such as commitment, satisfaction and innovation orientation) and outside (stakeholder attitudes and behaviour) where it connects with the environment. The important, defining characteristics of a fluid, brand connected assemblage are as follows.

1. It is always fluid and becoming: 'they are a bit of becoming in the pure state' (Deleuze and Guattari 1980: 326). We may not always be aware of the speed and nature of change, but this is because we tend to look at the surface of things (extensive properties) rather than the underlying intensities. In other words we tend to concentrate on what we can observe rather than digging underneath to see the hidden drivers of change; what we should be looking at are movements and at the relations of speed and slowness in the assemblage.

2. We can never be sure of what the organisation is capable. There is always opportunity and potential contained within a structure. This may be unrealised because of the constraints imposed by culture or leadership or perceived boundaries or, indeed, by the structure itself. In Deleuzian terminology, what the organisation does is to territorialise concepts. This means it begins to accept the way things are, rather than questioning, and to accept as true a certain way of behaving. The great virtue of territorialisation is that it provides stability, but the downside is that it reduces the capacity to

innovate. To balance creativity and stability, elements within the organisation (but not the whole at one time) need to be de-territorialised to align behaviour with the hidden drivers of change. De-territorialisation allows for changing the structure and adding to and taking away of elements as a means of uncovering value and building relationships with customers in new kinds of ways. De-territorialisation also requires a willingness to challenge the past and the constraints imposed by corporate memory: 'Becoming is an antimemory' (Deleuze and Guattari 1980: 324).

3. In the previous description of an organisation (the archetypal structure chart) the emphasis is on the boxes (functions/ departments) and the vertical lines. In the brand assemblage, the emphasis is more on the horizontal lines and the connections between the boxes rather than the boxes themselves. In this way of thinking it is the interaction between parts that creates the potential for action and innovative ways of thinking. The assemblage reduces the importance of silos in the organisation and instead stresses the communication and unity derived from the connecting lines. This does not suggest that the assemblage can be reduced to its connections nor that the connections are pre-ordained: 'machines are productive in unpredictable and often novel ways . . . even when they are connected in a particular way they are capable of other connections and other functions' (May 2005: 125). It does suggest that managers pay attention to the way an organisation is fused.

4. In assemblage thinking the organisation needs to redefine its boundaries and to open up the inside to the outside. This suggests that the customer is not a box that sits outside the organisation, but is an integral part of its thinking; it is part of the machine (see Figure 1.2). This does not simply imply the cliché of 'getting close to your customer', but rather a

sense of oneness, or entrainment, with the customer. Here customers are part of the process of product development, suppliers of ideas and challengers of direction, not passive recipients of marketing communication.

5. Assemblages, like all organisations, are populated by individuals who share some sense of collectivity. It is individuals who determine the structure of the assemblage and who possess the power to change it. Yet the ability of individuals to effect change is constrained or facilitated by the nature of leadership and the organisational culture. The most productive assemblages are those that balance 'freedom and order' (Schumacher 1974) and enable individuals to express their creativity and initiative in delivering customer value.

The assemblage model creates the opportunity to chart relevant choices – based on the degrees of freedom the organisation has, which are in turn defined by consumer experience and expectation, the organisational structure and the elements of branding governance: leadership, organisational culture, marketing, human resources and evaluation. What this means in terms of practical application is that we can, through analysis, draw a picture of the organisation as it currently exists. However, this image needs to be fluid (and becoming), so we also need to be able to define the key factors (attractors) that will determine fundamental change in the assemblage. This is of course easier to map on a computer, than in a book, but we will show the operation of organisational assemblages.

The implications for managers of assemblage-based thinking are several. While many managers are educated to believe in linearity and what Deleuze and Guattari call 'arborescent systems' based on logical connections and hierarchy, the operating reality of most organisations is untidy. The managerial response to this is to try and turn this messiness into some kind of order –

to make it manageable. This is important if there is to be focus to the organisation's activities, but there are challenges to overcome.

First, 'in a multilinear system, everything happens at once' (Deleuze and Guattari 1980: 328). It is impossible to manage a complex system, such as a business organisation, if we imagine it statically. We have to recognise that it will change all the time and consequently communication systems (those lines connecting the boxes internally and externally) need to work as effectively as possible and bring the elements of the assemblage together.

Secondly, attention needs to be paid to understanding and involving customers and other audiences. This is not just about doing more market research, but rather building a partnership with customers; of being attentive to the subtle changes of intensity and speed at all the points the organisation touches others.

Thirdly, it requires a willingness to challenge accepted ways of doing things – 'to create is to resist' (Deleuze and Guattari 1991: 110). If an organisation is going to be a genuine innovator it needs to be continually searching for new ideas. Working against this need is the conservatism of the organisation.

Last, a focus on partial measures of performance tends to sustain silo thinking and can work against value creation. We advocate that measurement systems are linked together so that they relate to overall strategy and provide a true picture of the performance of the whole assemblage. This enables effective brand governance because it focuses measurement metrics on the relationship between investment and performance and helps to pinpoint any weaknesses in the assemblage. Overall the relevance of the assemblage is that it is designed to integrate the core elements of leadership, organisational culture, marketing, human resources management and evaluation with the needs and wants of customers to build a brand of relevance and power.

CONCLUSION

In this introduction we have set out the standard we will follow in the rest of this book. The core of our argument is that to deliver sustained performance the orientation of all businesses should be about building value in the lives of customers. The ability to build this value relies on a close and fluid connectivity with customers and the internal alignment and engagement of employees, teams, units and managers and advisors. In our view, it is the identification of internal audiences with the organisational cause and the meaning and purpose that people find in their day-to-day work that determines customer perceptions of value. However, most organisations currently have barriers to building value, not least of which is a lack of unity. The organisational machine often does not connect as deeply as it should with customers and also resists internal connections. Our goal is to demonstrate that just as managers have constructed disjointed machines, it is possible to rework them to deliver unity through an integrated approach that brings the customer to the fore and links together disciplines that often operate independently. One key mechanism for achieving this transition is to alter management thinking away from a belief in linear causality to the messiness of the assemblage. The challenge here, which will be addressed in subsequent chapters, is that management is brought up to believe in order and control. This ordering needs to be maintained but another layer of thinking needs to be added that recognises the reality of constant change and the value of difference (Deleuze 1968). Or as Denison and Mishra (1995) argue managers need to be to willing to try to manage both stability traits (mission and consistency) and flexibility traits (involvement and adaptability) – something that effective organisations do without relying on simple trade-offs (Denison 2000).

If there is an underlying theme in this book, it is that borrowed from evolutionary biology. To survive and develop, species need variation and evolution; they need difference to adapt to their environment. If there is no mutation, species would die out. Equally businesses need difference: new products and services; new thinking; new ways of doing things; all of which must make the organisation more relevant to its environment. Without change businesses go the way of the dodo.

NOTES

1. 'People of the same trade seldom meet together, but the conversation ends in a conspiring against the public, or in some diversion to raise prices.' However, Smith also goes on to argue that merchants should think of themselves not society: 'By pursuing his (the merchant's) own interest he frequently promotes that of society more effectually than when he really intends to promote it. I have never known much good done by those who affected to trade for the publick good' (Smith 1998: 292).
2. 'The corporation, like the psychopathic personality it resembles, is programmed to exploit others for profit. That is its only legitimate mandate' (Bakan 2004: 69).
3. RSA Economist Debate: Companies that put time and money into corporate social responsibility are digging their own grave. Held at the RSA, London, 7 April 2005.
4. Tesco here is a prime example. Its success as a brand has been driven since the mid 1990s by a series of small employee generated service innovations under the banner of 'every little helps'.
5. Yesawich, Pepperdine, and Brown/Yankelovich Partners National Travel Monitor, 2001: research study into consumer trust of sources of information in which US adults recorded a trust figure of only 3% for messages received through advertisements.
6. One large international automotive company once described this structure as a series of vertical chimneys that could not (or would not) communicate horizontally.
7. For example, read Porter (1980) as a philological exercise and you can see how there is a clear cause and effect pronounced in the language.
8. Hegel's *Philosophy of the Mind: Part III of the Encyclopedia of Philosophical Sciences* (1830) quoted in Nancy (1997: 68).
9. As Nancy (1996) points out, the very use of the word 'we' is an abstraction.

PART I

TWO CONCEPTS OF BRAND BUILDING

INTRODUCTION

This book has two parts. In the first we outline the two core approaches to brand building (the outside-in perspective and the inside-out perspective), while in the second we develop the concept of a participatory approach to branding and show how it can be applied to all the core facets of an organisation. Our objective in these first two chapters is to create a counterpoint to what will follow – for if a fully participative approach is to have meaning, its antecedents need to be understood. We need to know wherein lie the faults of traditional brand thinking to appreciate the value of a different approach. For those brought up on a diet of classic marketing and branding books, there might be some questioning of the need to challenge a way of thinking that seems to work. Yet, as will become clear in the text, there is strong evidence to suggest that some of the core beliefs about branding and the way it should be practised are becoming obsolete – consequently, branding needs to be re-thought. The rethinking we have been doing is based around the core premise of participation: the idea that the successful brands of the future will touch and engage their employees, customers and shareholders in an active way. This sense of participation draws on the principles of marketing (which are not so often reflected in practice) and of some writers in the internal branding arena. But we have also drawn inspiration and examples from organisational development, philosophy, anthropology and sociology. These disciplines draw on different principles and there is a danger in mixing them together, but we have found that the new angles they provide encourage creative thinking and offer a conceptual base for our arguments.

In Chapters 1 and 2 we hint at some of the solutions to making branding relevant in the future, but our primary concern here is to present the core ideas of the market-led and inside–out perspective and to challenge some of their basic premises; to indicate the strengths of the thinking, but also point out the weaknesses, some of which seem to have been inherent, but some of which have emerged as the nature of business and society has changed. We should also point out what we are *not* trying to do here, which is to give a full description of the marketing and internal branding process. There are other books that already do that, including other texts we have written. If our purpose was to be comprehensive in looking at alternative definitions of brands and branding, for example, we could have devoted a whole chapter to the subject. However, here we deal with it in one section and consider just a few of the different ideas. Thus we have been selective and have focused on just a few of the core principles of the two perspectives that are relevant to the ideas of participation that we will develop in subsequent chapters.

Consequently in Chapter 1 our areas of discussion are the importance of becoming close to customers, the limitations of market research in achieving closeness, the advocacy of a more entrained approach to closeness, using customer knowledge to define a brand, the problems of a marketing-led approach to brand definition and the challenge of communicating the brand in a cohesive way. In Chapter 2 we look at the idea of citizen employees, the development of an internal orientation to brand definitions, the problems of methodology in choosing the right values, the advocacy of a participative approach, the importance and benefits of employee engagement and how to connect employees and customers to achieve entrainment. As becomes immediately obvious, although we present the market-led and inside–out as distinct perspectives there are clear overlaps in thinking and practice. Yet there is still a fundamental divide in approach with the former placing emphasis on external marketing mechanisms as a means to build brands and the latter placing emphasis on employees as ambassadors for the brand. What will become apparent later in the book is that the participative approach takes the important elements from the outside–in (market-led) and the inside–out school and fuses them together in an organisation-wide, customer-value delivering perspective.

THE OUTSIDE-IN PERSPECTIVE

OUTLINE: 1960 ONWARDS

In this chapter and the one that follows we set out the key perspectives on brand building. In Chapter 1 we outline the traditional outside–in led view of branding which has held sway in literature for the last 45 years – at least since Theodore Levitt published his now famous article, 'Marketing myopia' (1960) in which he argued for a customer value led view of how organisations should define themselves. In this and subsequent writings Levitt contended that marketing should be concerned with identifying and catering to customer needs. Levitt suggests that marketing is concerned with viewing 'the entire business process as consisting of a tightly integrated effort to discover, create, arouse and satisfy customer needs'. This might seem like sound thinking, but we will argue that there are problems with the outside–in view both in its basic philosophical premise and in the way it is executed. Inevitably these two problems are linked: the problems are due to marketing's fundamental belief in 'unidirectional control' (Kotler, Jain and Maesincee 2002), its adherence to a sales orientation, in spite of Levitt's diagnosis (Mitchell 2000), the lack of a tightly integrated organisational effort and the reliance on advertising. In reality, marketing has too often failed what Drucker (1998) claimed it should do, which is to bring the outside world inside the organisation and to use that knowledge as the 'foundation for strategy and policy'.

In Chapter 2, we outline the inside–out view of brand building which argues that it is employees through their assumptions and behaviour that define the brand experience for customers. This line of thinking challenges the Levitt viewpoint because it argues that organisational competence and knowledge are vital elements in the marketing process. It counters the oft-cited example of the outside–in approach: the buggy whip manufacturer that could have resisted obsolescence when the car was invented by redefining itself as being in the transportation business by suggesting the transition to automotive supplier would be extremely difficult if the company lacked the knowledge to produce anything but buggy whips.[1] The inside–out view argues that as well as understanding changing needs, the organisation has to understand itself. This perspective has an equally long heritage, deriving as it does from organisational development and another defining publication: Douglas McGregor's *The Human Side of Enterprise* (McGregor 1960) which challenged the scientific management of F.W. Taylor and replaced it with Theory Y's principle of integrating individual and organisational goals. This strand of thinking travels through organisational theorists to Edgar Schein's *Organisational Culture and Leadership* (1985) and to a meeting with branding writers (Ind 1997, de Chernatony 2001, Ind 2001, Pringle and Gordon 2001) who have synthesised views on the working of the organisation with a customer orientation. Our perspective, which will be developed in the subsequent chapters, brings together the market and inside out views, but also goes beyond them to argue that all the core elements of the organisation – leadership, organisational culture, marketing, human resources and finance – need to be aligned to deliver relevant value to customers and to build the brand.

THE NATURE OF BRANDS AND BRANDING

In 1960, alongside Levitt and McGregor, E Jerome McCarthy introduced the 4Ps of marketing and the American Marketing Association (AMA) produced its glossary of marketing terms, including this on brand: 'a term, symbol or design . . . intended to identify the goods or services of one seller . . . and to differentiate them from those of competitors'. The AMA definition doesn't extend the idea of brand much beyond that of its use to identify cattle, but since then writers, associations, advertising agencies and marketers have defined and redefined the terminology. Ries and Trout (1986) extended the definition to argue that the effect of a brand is to create a distinctive positioning in the mind of the customer. De Chernatony and McDonald (1998: 20) also developed the meaning by setting out what makes for a successful brand:

> an identifiable product, service, person or place, augmented in such a way that the buyer or user perceives relevant, unique added values which match their needs most closely. Furthermore, its success results from being able to sustain these added values in the face of competition.

There are alternatives to this last definition, but it does contain the essentials of identifiability, augmentation, customer orientation and competitive sustainability. If we structure de Chernatony and McDonald's definition we can see how the different elements of the successful brand interrelate. Internally the brand is defined

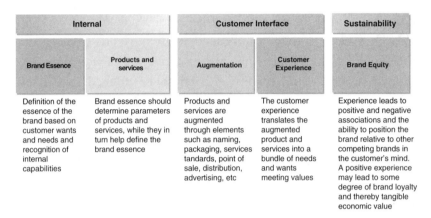

Internal		Customer Interface		Sustainability
Brand Essence	Products and services	Augmentation	Customer Experience	Brand Equity
Definition of the essence of the brand based on customer wants and needs and recognition of internal capabilities	Brand essence should determine parameters of products and services, while they in turn help define the brand essence	Products and services are augmented through elements such as naming, packaging, services tandards, point of sale, distribution, advertising, etc	The customer experience translates the augmented product and services into a bundle of needs and wants meeting values	Experience leads to positive and negative associations and the ability to position the brand relative to other competing brands in the customer's mind. A positive experience may lead to some degree of brand loyalty and thereby tangible economic value

Figure 1.1 Branding model based on de Chernatony and McDonald's definition (1998)

by an understanding of customer needs and wants that determines the approach to product and service development. At the interface with customers the augmentation of the product through such mechanisms as advertising and packaging is converted into the perception of relevant values that leads to brand equity.

While the definition works well, it does lack in one sense: if brands belong to customers, this remains an organisation-centric view. If we turned the definition on its head we might argue that for the individual a successful brand is 'the product, service, person or place I consider, buy and use in preference to others that meets my aspirations, hopes and needs'. Of course, the challenge is that a brand manager must think from the organisational perspective and work with the process of branding to deliver the brand to the customer. This indicates the role of branding as a concept of transformation: it is the thing that changes products and services into something of perceived added value in the minds of customers. It effects this transformation through the meeting of emotional and functional wants and needs. This is, of necessity, an imperfect process because a customer is not always able to define wants and needs precisely (and in any case they are always changing) and the organisation has to be capable of understanding and interpreting customer values, attitudes and behaviour and then communicating the brand offer and delivering on its promises (Feldwick 1991). Achieving a distinct positioning is much to do with the ability to execute consistently and effectively (Ind 2001, Godin 2005). This is where Ries and Trout's idea (1986) of desired positioning can come unstuck because what the organisation tries to communicate is not necessarily what the customer takes out – a dissonance can emerge between the brand identity and the brand image. This dissonance can either be due to a failure to deliver what is claimed and consequently what the customer experiences or a failure to communicate effectively.

Communication dissonance occurs partly because of narcissism and seller centricity (Drucker 1998, Mitchell 2003), but also because branding is an editing process. Branding is concerned with a synopsis not the whole story, and inevitably in creating a synopsis things are lost. Even though consumers are sometimes interested to see behind the façade of the brand, the full diversity of what constitutes the brand, such as its history, the details of its performance, the design of its products, the manufacturing process and the thinking behind it, have to be edited if communication is to be viable. This process enables the brand to fulfil its role as a signifier, so that the essence can be communicated: it makes more sense to talk about a pair of Puma shoes than

> those sports trainers that have a strong design element, are made by a German company that was set up by the brother of the founder of adidas, are used by the Jamaican track team and have a symbol of a large cat.

We only do the latter when we forget or don't know a brand name or when a pop star perversely dispenses with his name and adopts a symbol instead (subsequently he had to append 'the artist formerly known as Prince'). A brand communicates its story in truncated pieces of communication. As Alan Mitchell (2003: 39) writes, the naming, matching and connecting aspects of brands are vital for the effective functioning of economies and companies: 'If we did not have brands, we would have to invent them.'

The fact that brands and branding have becomes so pervasive in our lives can partly be attributed to this signifier function, but it is also due to people's need to define themselves through patterns of consumption (Rokeach 1973, Schwartz 1992, Nunnally and Bernstein 1994, Thyne 2001). The use of brands by consumers to define their position and personality is both the driver of purchase behaviour and the opportunity for manipulation and the cause of post-purchase disappointment and anxiety. This anxiety is not created by brands *per se*, but rather by the 'anxiety of "Social Being"' (Nancy 1996) and the challenge of choice (Rosenthal 2005). Nonetheless branding is an effective exploiter of modernity and people's need for placement, in a world of displacement (Debray 2000) and fuel for a way of thinking that too often equates consumption with meaning (commodity fetishism): 'the spectacular commodity in all its forms consists essentially in the imagery (imaginaire) that it sells as a replacement for authentic imagination' (Nancy 1996: 49). Something Klein (2000) echoes when she argues that brands absorb cultural ideas and then present them as their own by nudging 'the hosting culture into the background' and then making 'the brand the star'.

While we believe it is important to understand the dangers of branding – that it can be manipulative and socially disruptive – we would also argue that branding can be useful and also enjoyable. The key is to put branding in its place – not in the negative sense of putting it down, but in determining its appropriate role as a deliverer of authentic value to customers. We can criticise its social purpose but we should also recognise its potential virtue as a conveyer of information and deliverer of experience. As consumers we may sometimes over-estimate the meaning a brand will give us in our lives, but there is still a pleasure in owning an Apple computer, an Audi car or a pair of Puma train-ers or using Amazon to buy a book. Indeed the better we feel these brands understand us and our lifestyles, the greater the reward of ownership. It is to this issue that we will now turn.

UNDERSTANDING CUSTOMERS

There is an adage in marketing – indeed it may be *the* adage – that it pays to be close to the customer. The rationale for this is that the organisation is more likely to develop a beneficial rela-tionship with the customer if there is mutual understanding. Equally the likelihood of dissonance between identity and image emerging is reduced. For a small business closeness is often intui-tive: for example, a shopkeeper in a local community is close both in terms of physical proximity and customer knowledge and is able to adapt offers accordingly. However, for a larger business 'close' implies a metaphorical closeness based on an understanding of how current and potential customers think and behave. To become close does suggest a communion between the customer and the organisation in an almost intimate way with both sides willing to open up to each other. Close indicates transparency and reciprocity. The way organisations have tried to become close has been primarily through the vehicle of market research.[2]

It can be argued that much of the success of modern brands is attributable to the insights gained from researching customer attitudes and behaviour. Research has been used as a key driver in transforming many organisations from being production led to customer oriented. By using quantitative and qualitative research methods, businesses have been able to track purchase behaviour, assess attitudes to a brand, determine levels of awareness, pre-ference, satisfaction and loyalty and test new product ideas and communication. The use of research has long been a dominant feature of fast-moving consumer goods companies (Procter &

Gamble, Unilever) but it is now used in all spheres of life from sports brands to politics. The value of market research, when well used, is that it (a) helps provide an understanding of the customer and their changing lifestyles; (b) enables managers to challenge preconceptions about the nature of customer relationships; (c) can provide an understanding of the relative strengths and weaknesses of the brand; (d) can reduce risk by limiting the range of viable options and testing concepts and communication; (e) provide an internal currency by which ideas can be sold internally and decisions assessed. Not surprisingly, brand managers and commentators are supportive of the value of research. However, we have reservations about research as a means of getting close to customers and about the way organisations use research to aid decision-making.

THE CHALLENGE OF RESEARCH

In the early 1990s the renowned police chief, William Bratton, arrived to take over the New York Transit Police. At the time there were more than 5000 people living in the subway system, 170,000 people evading the fare every day and New Yorkers considered it the most dangerous place in the city. Yet senior managers, who commuted to work and travelled round the city in cars provided for them, never met these problems. They relied on crime research (that showed only a small percentage of serious crimes were committed on the subway) to reassure themselves that everything was running smoothly and that there were no serious concerns with the management of the system. To destroy this complacency, Bratton took away his officials' cars and made them commute by subway and use it to attend meetings, which he would specifically arrange in the evenings when the journey was at its most intimidating. This experience helped convert managers rapidly to the need to change (Chan Kim and Mauborgne 2003b).

The writers of this story, of what they called 'Tipping Point Leadership', might also have recognised the remoteness of managers in a BBC television fly-on-the-wall documentary series that started in 1999 called *Back to the Floor*, where leaders of such organizations as Heathrow Airport, Burger King, Carnival Cruises and J Sainsbury undertook operational grassroots jobs for a short period where they had to confront the daily problems of complaining customers and unreasonable bosses. In each case, the experience was a real revelation for the individual and a moment of catharsis for them. In one instance – the Managing Director of J Sainsbury – the lack of customer understanding contributed to their departure from the organisation. Larry Keeley from the strategic consultancy, the Doblin Group,[3] observes that

> what they're managing (executives) in their heads is an abstraction – something they remember from their one day out in the field in 1968. Or an abstract understanding of what they think they want a programme to achieve.

Shotter (2005: 128) also reinforces the challenge and the solution. Using Wittgenstein's later philosophy as an inspiration he notes that one of the things we should do is to gather concrete examples: 'only if we walk the shop floor, go out into the field, etc., will we as managers get a sense of the real complexities "out there" – the concrete complexities out of which new relations can emerge'.

What these examples illustrate are some of the difficulties of using research. How is it that the managers of the New York Transit Police could ignore the problems of the subway system? How is it that managers of well-known brands that spend significant sums on research could know so little about their customers? The fundamental issue is that to replace the day-to-day contact with customers, research must abstract – which is why we talk about the abstraction of *the* customer. Unless the company in question is a business-to-business organisation with only a

limited number of contacts, organisations must group and categorise customers. If we accept the specific individuality of people,
this categorisation will inevitably be flawed because it groups
people together as if their actions were a communal act rather
than a set of separate 'identical instances of the same act' (Sartre
1960: 262). Yet such is the widespread faith in measurement and
systems[4] there is a tendency to mistake the abstract for the real:
as soon as managers start seeing numbers, they tend to stop seeing
people. There is a belief that objective, logical knowledge is
superior to aesthetic knowledge (Gagliardi 2006: 567). Spinoza
(1677) argues that people are deceived when they start to categorise and universalise the particular: 'how easily we are deceived
when we confuse universals with singulars, and beings of reason
and abstractions with real beings'.

While market research can be valuable for informing
decisions, the argument is that we should not over-rely on it
nor mistake data for reality. It is at best an approximation
based on the past (Ronell 2005) and inevitably predicated on
assumptions. Also managers can universalise behaviour without
always questioning the intensive processes below the surface
(Deleuze 1968). This is a particular problem if we are trying to
use research as part of an innovation process. Writing about
research in the automotive industry, one journalist noted, 'being
customer-driven is certainly a good thing, but if you're so customer-driven that you're merely following yesterday's trends,
then, ultimately, customers won't be driving your supposedly
customer-driven products' (Flint 1997). Generally, research asks
people to rationalise their thinking and to judge how they will
behave, which presupposes that people are thinking consciously
(rather than thinking striking them) and acting rationally when
they make purchase decisions. Equally if the requirement is to
think about new to the world ideas, we are asking people to
imagine possible futures in which wants and needs are not fully
formed.

While we should recognise the limitation of abstraction, probably a larger challenge in the quest to get close to the customer is the way organisations misuse market research. There are several factors at play here.

1. Organisations have so much information at their fingertips that research simply forms part of the wallpaper of the organisation: always there but hardly noticed. A movement in customer awareness might excite some interest in the market research department, but it probably has limited impact on senior managers.

2. Large amounts of customer knowledge never migrate beyond the marketing department. This is largely because of the problem of departmentalisation, whereby the marketing department that is most often the commissioner of research, retains control of the knowledge rather than sharing it with other managers who might use it or with people who interact regularly with customers and would value its insights. This barrier to knowledge flow is exacerbated by other possessors of information who also exhibit tendencies to hoard data,[5] leading to insular rather than connected knowledge – a problem neatly summarised by the ex-head of HP, Lew Platt, 'if HP knows what HP knows, we would be three times as profitable'.

3. The problem of context: although trend and comparative research gives a picture of what data might mean, historically research providers have tended to deliver raw material rather than interpret it. This has created the opportunity for misjudgment and misuse by research commissioners.

4. Research is used internally for business case or political reasons, in which instance there can be highly selective use of data. There might be nothing intrinsically wrong in this, but it implies a tendency to look for yes/no answers rather than using the material as a departure point for decision-making

or an inspiration for innovation. As Mintzberg argues, 'while hard data may inform the intellect, it is largely soft data that builds wisdom' (Mintzberg et al. 1998, p. 71).

5. The research may well be predicated on a sense of knowing what the answer will be: 'it does not pose what we might call an innocent question' (Ronell 2005). This tendency colours the interpretation of the research and potentially obscures what might be wondrous.

There are several interesting examples of the misuse of research, but the launch of the Volvo Cross Country (Ind and Watt 2004) serves to make the point. This car was developed by the Swedish car maker (now owned by Ford) as a hybrid vehicle, designed to reach a new type of younger customer who might want the practicality of an estate car with the off-road appeal of a sports utility vehicle (SUV). This was a new approach toward the end of the 1990s. Part of the insight for the new car came from extensive research that was undertaken to understand the lifestyle of the potential customer. This helped to steer the brief and the decisions made in the development of the car. However, Volvo management felt the need for the reassurance of research in its largest market, the USA. The model of the car was tested in clinics and a clear-cut negative response was delivered: the research participants had never seen a vehicle like this and couldn't put it into any existing category. As a consequence the project was closed down. However, six months later, Subaru successfully launched a new vehicle, the Outback, directly into this supposingly non-existent sector. Volvo quickly restarted its own project and rushed the Cross Country onto the market. Sara Öhrvall, who was the concept development manager of the project, says, 'People without knowing it were looking for this alternative. These people thought a jeep impractical and too expensive and a normal estate car too boring. The Cross Country was on the spot: a perfect balance between design features and functional features.'

Volvo is a good example of an organisation with a clear focus on customers, but often organisations are narcissistic, and marketing, in spite of its supposed outward focus, can be in reality an inward-looking process (Mitchell 2003). Mitchell reinforces the point that the root cause of this is that marketers concentrate on what comes out of the organisation's operations and what they can sell, not on understanding buyers and the value that could be created in their lives. The failings of traditional market research are part of the reason for the lack of genuine customer orientation, but also corporate cultures encourage narcissism by erecting boundaries between those inside the organisation and customers outside. To get close to the customer we would argue that the proper use of market research is to help break down the boundaries and to bring a real customer presence inside the organisation. Research can also bring the customer to a wider internal audience if knowledge is shared across the organisation and used as a tool to destroy the silos that prevent horizontal communication. The goal here is to build a structure that has the potential to achieve organisation/customer synchronicity or entrainment.

The idea of entrainment will be developed and explored in the chapters to follow but we will define the overall concept briefly here. Entrainment[6] derives from the work in the seventeenth century of the Dutch scientist, Christiaan Huygens, who found that when he placed two pendulum clocks on a wall near each other and swung the pendulums at different rates, they would eventually end up swinging in at the same rate due to their mutual influence on one another. Scientists have since discovered that entrainment is prevalent in systems of oscillation, while musicians and dancers have recognised its ability to connect notes and actions in an assemblage of unity. In a business context, entrainment means the organisation is focused on building value for the customer not via abstracted thinking that see numbers and categories, but through a union of interest based on a dynamic relationship:

'we' always expresses a plurality, expresses 'our' being divided and entangled: 'one' is not 'with' in some general sort of way, but each time according to determined modes that are themselves multiple and simultaneous. (Nancy 1996: 65)

What entrainment means in practice for organisations is a change of perspective so that the customer is seen as an insider. It implies that 'we' means something. This represents a real challenge, because how can we truly know what others think and believe?

To create a sense of 'we', there has to be a continuous dialogue and participation both among employees and with customers based not on a power relationship but one of mutual interest. It suggests the importance of listening (Lévy 1997) and engagement and the emergence of the brand. It suggests the importance of 'co-': co-creation, co-operation, co-ordination. This does not negate the value of market research, but it does indicate that it has limits. Closeness cannot be achieved through abstraction. It necessitates presence.

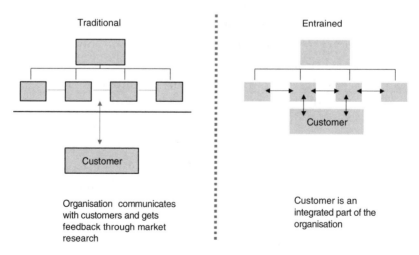

Figure 1.2 Traditional and entrained structures

USING CUSTOMER KNOWLEDGE
TO BUILD BRANDS

Assuming that there is some degree of customer connectivity and understanding of customers' needs and wants, the E Jerome McCarthy approach suggests that the next important phase is to align the ubiquitous 4Ps (product, promotion, price, place) with the needs of the market. The rationale for this is that to communicate in a marketplace with a huge variety of messages a brand needs clarity. If the product, the way it is promoted, the pricing policy and the channels it is sold through lack coherence or point in different directions, customers will struggle to categorise the brand and position it relative to other offers. Although customers have some tolerance for deviation, too much inconsistency is uncomfortable and heightens risk (Sjödin 2006). As a mechanism to achieve more unity, organisations and their advisors have developed articulations of what a brand stands for. Descriptors of brands are diverse and include such variants as Brand Pyramid, Brand Anatomy, Brand Platform, Brand DNA, Brand Essence and Brand Values. In the two examples below, we can see how such ideas are articulated. In Figure 1.3, the energy and aluminium supplier Hydro has a mission statement and five values that equate to five behavioural and communication traits. Combined with the organisation's institutional talents,[7] these ideas together form what is referred to as the Hydro Way. The Hydro Way is designed to deliver a broadly consistent image to internal and external audiences, including employees, customers, politicians, the media and environmental groups.

In Figure 1.4 there is another way of defining the brand that derives from Gad (2001), which is known as the Brand Code. In this example it has been applied to the Nordic software services company, Visma.

Essentially the purpose of these creations has been to build customer-oriented statements (often based on knowledge derived

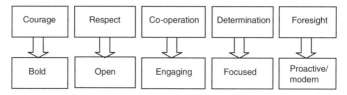

Mission: to create a more viable society by developing natural resources and products in innovative and efficient ways

Courage	Respect	Co-operation	Determination	Foresight
Bold	Open	Engaging	Focused	Proactive/ modern

Hydro's mission and values provide a platform for all internal and external communications, which must be consistent in terms of messaging as well as visual expressions in the building of one international brand

Figure 1.3 Brand mission and values: Hydro

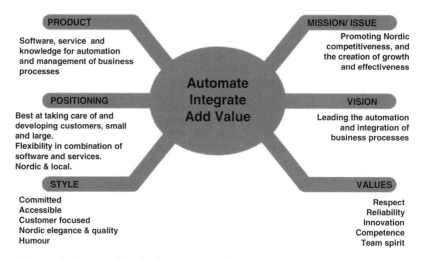

PRODUCT
Software, service and knowledge for automation and management of business processes

MISSION/ ISSUE
Promoting Nordic competitiveness, and the creation of growth and effectiveness

Automate Integrate Add Value

POSITIONING
Best at taking care of and developing customers, small and large.
Flexibility in combination of software and services.
Nordic & local.

VISION
Leading the automation and integration of business processes

STYLE
Committed
Accessible
Customer focused
Nordic elegance & quality
Humour

VALUES
Respect
Reliability
Innovation
Competence
Team spirit

Figure 1.4 Brand code for Visma software. (Reproduced by permission of Visma and with thanks to Thomas Gad.)

from market research) that summarise in a concisely, differentiated way what the brand stands for and how the brand should address its potential market (and hopefully what the market takes out as well). As well as forward-looking visionary-type statements, brands are also constructed around what are known as values: the words, collectively agreed by the managers of the brand, that define its (seemingly) immutable needs. By referring to these needs as *values* their status is heightened, indicating their likely longevity and the dangers of transgression or compromise. If managers explore, dynamically, the meaning of the brand concealed within the values and deliver it through their actions, the status of the values is enhanced. However this is not always simple, not least because values are statements of excess. They ask for more than can be delivered: it will not be possible to adhere completely to all the values for all time in every circumstance. Yet if the values are no more than conveniences, to be ignored at the first sign of difficulty, they will cease to have relevance. This indicates the obligation of managers to work with and to test the values, to elevate their importance in decision-making, and to accept the responsibility to resolve dilemmas with imagination and integrity.

The great virtue of a brand statement is that it has the potential to provide greater consistency over time and across different presentations so that a customer can form a clear picture of what is being offered and what the benefits of use are, relative to other purchase alternatives. Generally people are looking to transform the cues they receive from different channels of communication into something they can understand (Murdoch 1994) and be confident in. According to Douglas (1966): 'the more consistent experience is with the past, the more confidence we can have in our assumptions.' (p. 46). The value for the customer in this process is that the brand shorthand is aligned to their needs and wants, which can speed up decision-making, enhance relevance, reduce anxiety and provide reassurance. The benefit for the organisation is in having a standard around which the attributes of the brand can be rallied, a basis against which brand judgments can be made and boundaries for defining the limits of brand innovation. When the process works well, the research inputs from genuine customer understanding enable the organisation to develop statements that provide a focus for all forms of communication. However it cannot, and should not, deliver absolute consistency for the customer.

Consistency is only relative. If, for example, we put ourselves in the role of a customer of a bank or an airline, how is our image of the brand formed? It might be through advertising, the look of environments, the website, the signage and all of those things that could be to a larger degree controlled by the organisation, but it is also concerned to a large extent with our interactions with people. How someone answered the phone, how they talked to us, how they dealt with our problems, are all important determinants of image[8] that cannot be dictated in an absolute sense by the organisation. There is no rule book that can deal with every eventuality. In fact, as customers, we enjoy the sense that people step outside the rules to deliver us an individualised service. The importance of employees is particularly powerful in the case of service brands but it also applies to packaged goods and online brands as well.[9] The level of direct interaction with company employees may reduce and the importance of packaging, place, online interaction and point of sale may increase, but it is still the assumptions about the brand statement and its meaning that drive the decision-making of employees – especially those involved in marketing.

GIVING BRAND VALUES MEANING

The inside–out view of brand building is the subject of the next chapter, but we will make some observations here, because they serve to point out the limitations of a purely outside-in view. One of the benefits of working through a definition of the brand is that it is a cathartic process in itself. It encourages organisational members to think closely about the nature of the brand and its points of differentiation from competitors. Even though this self-descriptive process is inevitably a simplification[10] the process of reduction – of taking the complex idea of a brand with all its nuances and reducing it to its essential features encourages people to make choices and to provide the brand with focus. This is important, because the short-handing of the brand in terms of communications to the consumer requires things to be stripped away. Not everything about the brand can be said – indeed with the competition for people's time and interest, very little can be said. However on the negative side there are dangers in the process of articulating the brand.

1. The prime movers in brand definitions are marketing depart-ments and their agencies. This is natural as marketing is the core discipline involved in the management of the brand but the delivery of the brand goes beyond the marketing depart-ment into human resources, operations, logistics, retail and customer service. If these disciplines are not actively involved in the process of definition there is the potential limitation that the brand will not be relevant to them. It almost certainly means that people from these disciplines will feel less engaged with the brand idea and less committed to delivering it.[11]

2. While the internal barriers within an organisation discourage horizontal communication, many marketers have a myopic view of the brand in any case which does not stretch far beyond marketing communications. As McGovern and Quelch (2004), argue:

> gone are the days when marketing consisted solely of clever promotions and attention-getting advertising copy. Talented CMOs must excel in these areas, but also be experts in market research, target market segmentation and distribution channel management and be comfortable with finance, technology and other functions. (p. 5)

In some organisations, where the dominant culture is perhaps engineering or logistics or scientific research, the role of marketing is limited by other functions that diminish its value.[12] Both viewpoints lead to a lack of connection, with other departments and disciplines and a focus on advertising, PR, packaging and direct marketing as the key determinants of brand image. Roy Gardner, CEO of Centrica (owners of British Gas among others), argues,

> the problem is that marketers traditionally have not been very fluent in the language of finance. As a result, they have been less than able to translate their activities into the quantitative language of the boardroom. Therefore in many companies, the marketing function has become marginalised within the power hierarchy.[13]

This challenge is also part of the reason why the nature of measurement that marketing departments engage in, such as awareness and preference, is marketing communications biased rather than oriented towards business performance.

3. Leaders of large organisations do not generally come from marketing disciplines, yet if the brand is to have meaning for managers and employees, leaders need to be explicitly supportive of the brand. This is because, if leaders recognise the importance of the brand to the organisation and demonstrate commitment, it is an important signal to organisational members that the brand matters. Also it is leaders who in the process of overseeing organisational direction either give weight, or not, to the brand in terms of budget allocation and strategic relevance. When leadership support is missing, marketers can do little. They might have control over the dominion of marketing communication, but the ability to influence the brand in a more comprehensive way in terms of developing the human capital behind the brand, is lost.

4. While simplification of brand complexity is inevitable it is also problematic. There is a limited lexicon of words available to the definer and, as Kapferer argues, market research

encourages homogeneity because of the common usage of the same lifestyle studies of behaviour (Kapferer 1997). This has the potential to create internal cynicism towards the brand and, as Kapferer also argues, a sameness in advertising execution. Sometimes in an attempt to get around the lack of distinctiveness, companies and their agencies take part in flights of fancy. Rather than basing the brand definition on real insight into the organisation the desire for differentiation leads to the insertion of words that have little connection to what the organisation is or is able to deliver. This process of invention leads to advertising campaigns that communicate a point of difference, but cannot be sustained by organisational reality.

COMMUNICATING THE BRAND

While simplification of the brand can provide focus, it is important that the nuances of the brand are not lost to the organisation. Rather than striving for pure, but perhaps unsustainable, differentiation in a brand definition, marketers should also be thinking about the capacity for brand delivery, for it is in action that difference is achieved and that the nuances of distinctiveness are conveyed. The approach to brands that stresses delivery is aligned with that of realism – the idea that it is our experience of things that determines language and meaning. Therefore, when we describe a brand as 'creative', we have a set of expectations of what that might be, based on our previous experience of things that are creative. When the marketing department is considering a new advertising campaign or reviewing the packaging, it should be asking itself how to imbue the brand with creativity. If it is successful, it might also be true that the customer takes out the idea of creativity from the packaging or advertising. If over time 'creative' is explored in many different ways by the organisation in terms of innovative products and services, it (and also the customer) will begin to acquire a deeper understanding of what 'creative' distinctively and explicitly means.

This is the sort of distinction that the writer and semiotician, Umberto Eco draws when he refers to dictionary and encyclopaedic knowledge (Eco 1997). In the case of the former, the understanding of 'creative' would be constrained by the definition of the word. However in the case of the latter, experience among a community counts for more than linguistics and the encyclopaedic knowledge of creativity for the organisation grows (becomes) fuller through exploration and action – which in turn suggests the importance of knowledge capture and sharing. Indeed we might argue that brand definitions are not really definitions at all until they acquire contextual meaning by being adopted by individuals. In other words, a number of brands might proclaim they stand for creativity, but this remains a concept until employees and then customers, experience it through both intended and unintended consequences. This is not to suggest that people will understand creativity in the same way, because as we argued at the outset individuality works against neat categorisations, but past consistent experiences and feelings create an expectation of cause and effect: think 'Apple' and 'Innovation', 'Volvo' and 'Safety', 'Alessi' and 'Design'.

Achieving this cause and effect is nonetheless difficult. Of the 4Ps we have discussed, the only P that marketing has a clear control over is promotion and even that may be subject to debate if marketing budgets are dispersed to different geographies, business units or functions. The other Ps – product, price and place – will tend to involve others, including finance, logistics, research and development, engineering and sales. If marketing has a strategically strong role it may have the power to influence decision-making in these other areas, but it will remain a process of negotiation that is dependent on the depth and quality of brand understanding and commitment in the organisation and also the ability of marketers to influence the integration of the brand into the organisational fabric. When corporate cultures are more brand-resistant, even effective marketing analysis is no guarantee of the ability to align and deliver the 4Ps. The power of other organisational viewpoints can work against integration and undermine brand building, so that it is equated only with promotion.

The challenge for marketing is suggested in Figure 1.5 (below). Not only does the marketer struggle to achieve some sort of clear and consistent picture in the customer's mind through marketing communication, but somehow she has to influence other departments to recruit the right employees and develop them in alignment with the brand, ensure that the product and service experience is of the appropriate quality, safeguard future brand investments and oversee the channel strategy. Even if all of this is achievable in an idealised world, cohesion is undermined by employee actions and customer dialogue. Although

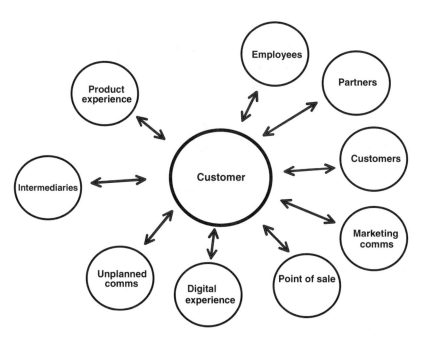

Figure 1.5   Factors influencing customer perceptions

organisations still maintain their boundaries they are increasingly transparent: 'quite suddenly, business finds itself transparent in ways inconceivable a decade ago. I don't think most marketing people have really caught up with the implications of this' (Moore 2003).

One thing that transparency emphasises is what marketing should always have known: it is the customer who has the power in the brand relationship. Yet we see that organisations often forget this and consequently rely on unidirectional control. This leads to an emphasis on the external brand equity as defined by marketing communications – and specifically advertising (Aaker 1996, Keller 2003) – as a means of influence and a tendency to underplay the other factors. Advertising has dominated the agenda of marketing directors and the textbooks of marketing because of its entertainment value, its profile, its strongly visual presence and its controllability. It can be emotionally engaging, but it is an 'at' form of communication. It is a medium of distance in that it clearly distinguishes the boundary between the organisation and its customers. It asks for observation (and sometimes engagement), but not participation. Its spectacle sets it apart. All of this works against the goals of participation and relationship building.

For example, whereas once, Coca-Cola used advertising and promotions as the main mechanism to build its brand, it increasingly seeks other methods that deliver a closer connection. Indeed, recognising that the traditional 30-second television spot can no longer deliver anything like the audience it once did, Coke President Steven J. Heyer has stated, 'the days of mass, homogenous marketing are behind us'. As a consequence Coca-Cola has been cutting its advertising budgets and investing instead in such entrainment type concepts as Coke Red Lounges in an attempt to achieve a closer bond with its customers (Business Week 2004). Primarily this is about a change of approach, but the opportunity for company/consumer dialogue and involvement has opened up the organisation to the outside and created the opportunity, partly through the Internet, for greater connectivity. Now employees can talk directly to customers, customers can blog with each other and customers can actively engage with the organisation if they want.

Online organisations such as Amazon, e-Bay and Wikipedia and the whole Open Source Movement thrive on an intensive sense of community, because they enable people to achieve a Maslowian sense of self-realisation and the plaudits of their peers. These online brand builders have largely eschewed traditional forms of marketing communication. Instead their power has grown through a transparent approach and word of mouth engagement. For example Wikipedia is a demonstration of what writer, Pierre Lévy, calls 'collective intelligence'. Wikipedia is a non-profit-making organisation that provides an online encyclopaedia. Rather than relying on a panel of experts to explain ideas, Wikipedia's entries are produced by enthusiasts. These entries are then argued over, questioned and corrected by subsequent contributors. There is no central controlling body over content (although sometimes calm and reflection will be urged on contributors when a subject generates too much heat) and everything grows organically. The army of contributors to its 1.4 million English language entries (October, 2006) and even larger non-English entries receive nothing for their efforts, except for the glow of anonymous achievement. If no one is really controlling Wikipedia and indeed no one is controlling the huge volume of individual blogs that comment on, praise and criticise brands, it becomes clear that there is a movement away from the conventional wisdom of management that suggests the brand can be controlled. Rather stabilisation comes from a culture that encourages participation – from a willingness to contribute and share (Morner 2003: 269). Our judgment is that in future, the only real control will be in having an authentic, participative brand. That means bringing the customer inside the organisation and aligning the whole organisation to create relevant value to the customer. Organisations can either see the loss of control to customers as a threat or they can seize the opportunity to build active networks of engagement and become truly entrained.

CONCLUSION

This chapter has argued that some of the shibboleths of marketing need to be questioned. It is not sufficient simply to rely on the abstraction of market research to get close to the customer. Organisations also have to try and bring customers inside and to involve them in the process of creating relevant value. This has several implications: the borders of the organisation need to be challenged, employees need to be encouraged to engage with customers and communications need to flow across internal boundaries. These are partly structural issues, but they are much more to do with attitude. Are managers confident enough to be transparent? Are employees willing to get involved? Is their sufficient humility to recognise good ideas coming outside of established elites? Are leaders willing to challenge the authority of internal fiefdoms? In the later chapters of this book, we will put forward strategies for dealing with these issues.

We have also set out the argument that an outside–in focus is insufficient because it fails to take account of the importance of an integrated approach to brand building. If the challenge is to align the whole organisation to deliver customer value, marketers must look inside as well as outside. They have to persuade others to take on the role of value delivery and to develop the meaning of the brand, the potential of which will otherwise never be fully explored. A brand is not value words on a page or a logo or an advertisement, but is rather a concept that becomes meaningful for customers through consistency of experience. In the next chapter we will show how important employees and human capital can be in creating that experience.

NOTES

1. Levitt's suggestion was that the buggy whip manufacturer should diversify into fan belts and air cleaners.
2. The estimated annual turnover of the market information industry was $17.5 billion in 2004 – up from $6 billion in 1990.
3. Interview with author, 2000.
4. Dostoyevsky writes in *Notes from Underground*: 'But man is so partial to systems and abstract deduction that in order to justify his logic he is prepared to distort the truth intentionally' (Dostoyevsky 1864: 31).
5. Kotler (1984) identifies six pertinent complaints about market research, one of which is 'marketing information is so dispersed throughout the company that it takes a great effort to locate simple facts' (p. 188).
6. *Entrainment* is the process whereby two connected oscillating systems, having similar periods, fall into synchrony. The system with the greater frequency slows down, and the other accelerates. Christiaan Huygens a notable physicist, coined the term entrainment after he noticed, in 1666, that two pendulum clocks had moved into the same swinging rhythm, and subsequent experiments duplicated this process. The accepted explanation for this is that small amounts of energy are transferred between the two systems when they are out of phase in such a way as to produce negative feedback. As they become more in phase, the amounts of energy gradually reduce to zero. In the realm of physics, entrainment appears to be related to resonance. (from www.wikipedia.org)
7. Hydro define institutional talents as those skills shared by everyone in the organisation: an ability to source business, a drive to optimize; an instinct to commercialize; a passion for social commerce.
8. Research by MORI and MCA (1999) among consumers found that 'staff attitudes and behaviours have a significant impact on customer loyalty, more so than many traditional marketing tools . . . unfortunately, consumers say that staff currently are not up to the challenge

and in many cases are actually damaging relationships with them'. Cited in Thomson and Hecker (2000).

9. Although most customers never interact directly with Amazon employees, company founder Jeff Bezos proclaimed, 'our goal is to be the Earth's most customer-centric company' – something Amazon attempts to deliver through rigorous employee recruitment and development procedures and a customer focus to software development and service delivery.

10. David Seidl in writing about the ideas of the social systems theorist Niklas Luhmann argues that 'for Luhmann self-descriptions are inevitably *self-simplifications* . . . The organisation's complexity cannot be represented in a text.' In spite of this he goes on to point out this is inevitable, because systems must be more complex than the described system (Seidl 2003: 138).

11. A research project by tompeterscompany! among 700 business professionals in the US (2002) discovered that 75% of employees don't support their company's branding initiatives and that 90% don't understand how to represent the brand effectively.

12. Research by Research International in the UK and US among 1000 employees and managers (2004) uncovered the following views about marketing: 'advertising and promotions are seen as by far the most important marketing activity. There is general agreement that internal brand building is the least important'; 'Marketing is not seen as contributing significantly to the strategic development of companies'; 'The main issue that emerges from comparing marketing with other corporate functions and professions is general low prestige and low expectations' (The Economist 2004).

13. Marketing Magazine (2004), discussing the results of a piece of Chartered Institute of Marketing research that showed that only four FTSE100 companies have board level marketers.

CHAPTER 2

THE INSIDE–OUT
PERSPECTIVE

THE BEGINNINGS OF
INSIDE–OUT THINKING

In this chapter we will explore the basis of the inside–out perspective as a vehicle for building brands. The core thinking behind the approach derives from the field of organisational development (OD) and in particular its focus on enabling organisations to develop cultures that facilitate renewal through participation. The OD strand, in contrast to the scientific management approach stresses the importance of human relations and the psychology of individuals as employees and managers in a work context. Although the basic assumptions underlying scientific management have been continually challenged by organisational thinkers and writers, many of its components remain, not least in the adherence of management to militaristic metaphors and a belief in command and control.[1] This line of thinking has been typified by the Positioning School of Strategy (Mintzberg et al. 1998), that suggests in its language and processes a belief in strategy as a planned process. In particular the work of management writer Michael Porter has a strong belief in causality and a rationalist approach to performance. In *Competitive Strategy* (1980) Porter puts forward the view that the attractiveness of an industry and organisational performance is determined by such factors as high barriers to entry, non-substitutable products, market share, buyer power, supplier power and competitive rivalry. Porter's control based model, however, has been challenged on its lack of emphasis on the challenge of implementation, the over emphasis on analysis and its predictive accuracy. In particular, Cameron and Quinn (1999) found that many high performance organisations such as Southwest Airlines and Wal-Mart did not align with the Porter model. Instead they suggested the key performance characteristics related to organisational culture and commitment in the form of shared values and norms, a strong sense of socialisation, a clear identity and employee commitment to it and a vision of the future. The Cameron and Quinn approach suggests that performance is defined by the attitudes and behaviour of those in the organisation, which is what Mintzberg et al. argue when they write, 'successful strategy is one that committed people infuse with energy: they *make* it good by making it real – and perhaps making it themselves' (1998: 116).

The work of Mintzberg et al. and Cameron and Quinn connect with organisational development theorists who have long questioned the idea of control and command and emphasised the importance of work fulfilment (Herzberg, Mausner and Snyderman 1959) motivation at work (Maslow 1943) and participation (Argyris 1970). Also writers from the inside–out school of branding have realised that by enhancing employee engagement with the organisation's values, employees could be stimulated to act as brand builders through their interactions with customers and other stakeholders. This conjunction of OD and branding raises some ethical questions about the extent to which employees should be encouraged (or perhaps, manipulated) to identify with the organisational ideology (Whetten and Godfrey 1998), but it also creates opportunities for enhanced job satisfaction and a greater sense of involvement.

CITIZEN EMPLOYEES

In scientific management people tend to be dehumanised: workers are seen as part of the machinery of production. This approach is also similar to social systems theory, such as Niklas Luhmann's autopoietic organisation which is a closed and self-referential entity, denuded of people – *Vollmenschen* (Luhmann 2003: 32): 'Luhmann wants to wipe out every trace of the subject (the person) in his theory' (Thyssen 2003: 222). These lines of thought ignore the specific competences and motivations of individuals and their potential to contribute new and innovative ideas to the organisation. In a dominantly product-based economy, such thinking is perhaps more understandable, but in OECD countries, services dominate, such that the average contribution in terms of employment and GNP is over 70% (2005).[2] Sectors such as telecommunications, transport, wholesale and retail trade, finance, insurance and business services are the fuel of growth. This means business success and innovation are primarily linked to human resources: the skill, power and energy level of people as expressed through leadership style, organisational culture, knowledge management, creativity, innovation orientation and capability, human resources policies and the ability of individuals to build relationships with stakeholders. Not surprisingly the OECD argues that there is a need for a stronger, more innovative and dynamic service sector that can provide growth and deal with the growing globalisation of services and rapid technological change and that the focus should be on factors 'internal to a firm like the organisation of work, the motivation and skills of workers and the company culture' – a point that academic and business research endorses by demonstrating the link between organisational culture, employee motivation, customer satisfaction and company performance.

The challenge here is that organisations traditionally have not made the links between employee engagement and customer satisfaction explicit. Instead they have distinguished between external stakeholders as a source of value and internal audiences as a controllable source of productivity. Stakeholders have been listened to and employees managed. As Chan Kim and Mauborgne (2003a) argue, 'the entire shape of the modern company reflects a fundamental distrust of its members'. This may in part be due to the tendency of employees and managers to ascribe different motivations to each other. For example, research by Chip Heath (cited in Morse 2003) suggests that managers are not as good at understanding employee motivation as they think they are. Managers tend to think that employees are motivated by extrinsic rewards such as pay and less by intrinsics such as a desire to contribute to the organisation. Heath's research shows this is misguided (Morse 2003). This mirrors Herzberg's view (2003) who has observed that managers have not understood that there are two sets of human needs: the built in drive to avoid pain and the ability to experience psychological growth. The factors that contribute to job satisfaction are primarily to do with the latter and consist of achievement, recognition, the work itself, responsibility and growth or advancement. The factors that contribute to dissatisfaction are primarily the former hygiene elements that can be categorised as interpersonal relationships, supervision, company policy, working conditions, salary, status and security. The idea that people can either be satisfied or dissatisfied is not accurate. They are not opposites. They relate to different needs. To achieve self-actualisation, employees need to have their work enriched by motivational elements, such as removing controls (while retaining accountability), granting additional authority and providing direct feedback. Trying to achieve actualisation through hygiene factors is to misunderstand people's relationship to their jobs. To create value for stakeholders, managers need to recognise the desire of most employees to engage with the organisational cause. That requires trust.

An interesting example of the transformation of an individual's attitude by focusing on actualisation is the story of an employee at New United Motor Manufacturing, Inc. (NUMMI). Originally this automotive plant in Fremont, California was a General Motors factory, but in 1984 it became a joint venture between GM and Toyota. NUMMI has been much written about because it introduced Toyota's production system and a team-based way of working to the US automotive industry and in so doing transformed productivity at Fremont. Also due to its location the corporate culture borrows from the ethos of Silicon Valley (see Chapter 3) which is adaptive and collaborative. The culture in return is reflected in the organisational values: teamwork, equity, involvement, mutual trust and respect, and safety. The employee's story, which is cited in Cameron and Quinn (1999), was about a plant worker who had been at the facility for more than twenty years. He was asked to describe the difference he experienced between the plant while it was managed by GM and the plant after the joint venture was formed. This employee said that prior to the joint venture, he would go home at night chuckling to himself about the things he had thought up during the day to mess up the system. He'd leave his sandwich behind the door panel of a car, for example.

'Three months later the customer would be driving down the road and wouldn't be able to figure out where that terrible smell was coming from. It would be my rotten sandwich in the door', he chuckled to himself. Or, he would put loose screws in a compartment of the frame that was to be welded shut. As the customer rode in the car, (s)he would never be able to tell exactly where that rattle was coming from because it would reverberate throughout the entire car. 'They'll never figure it out', he said.

'Now,' he commented, 'because the number of job classifications has been so dramatically reduced, we have all been allowed to have personal business cards and to make up our own titles. The title I put on my card is "Director of Welding Improvement".' His job was to monitor certain robots that spot-welded parts of the frame together. 'Now, when I go to a San Francisco Forty-Niners game, or a Golden State Warriors game, or go down to a shopping mall, I look for Geo Prisms and Toyota Corollas in the parking lot. When I see one, I take out my business card and write on the back of it: "I made your car. Any problems, call me". I put it under the windshield wiper of the car. I do it because I feel personally responsible for those cars.'

This reformed saboteur illustrates the change that is possible by focusing on building employee engagement. In looking at the nature of organisational membership, some writers (Manville and Ober 2003, Gratton 2004) see this in terms of citizenship and argue that employees should be regarded as citizens. This suggests a democratic ideal akin to that argued for by Lévy in his concept of collective intelligence (1997). The citizenship strand of thinking goes back to Katz (1964) who looked at the nature of organisational membership and drew conclusions about the potential of people to integrate their ideals with those of the organisation. Deriving inspiration from Katz, Organ (1988: 4) defined the ideal of organisational citizenship as 'individual behaviour, not directly or explicitly recognised by the formal reward system, and that in the aggregate promotes the effective functioning of the organization.' Podsakoff et al. (2000) further explored the idea and drawing on the extensive literature in the area, defined seven dimensions of citizenship: helping behaviour; sportsmanship; organisational loyalty; organisational compliance; individual initiative; civic virtue; self development. These categorisations have a connection to the Athenian style practices of citizen governance that Manville and Ober (2003) put forward, although they do not specify corporate examples. In contrast, Gratton (2004) is specific – she believes that companies such as BP, McKinsey, SONY, Unisys, Goldman Sachs, AstraZeneca, and BT are already democratic enterprises and handle their employees more like citizens. Gratton (2004) argues that there are six tenets to the concept of democracy in the organisational sphere:

1. The relationship between the organisation and the individual is adult-to-adult.
2. Individuals are seen primarily as investors actively building and deploying their human capital.
3. Individuals are able to develop their natures and express their diverse qualities.
4. Individuals are able to participate in determining the condition of their association.
5. The liberty of some individuals is not at the expense of others.
6. Individuals have accountabilities and obligations both to themselves and to the organisation.

According to Gratton (2004), democratic enterprises are ranked as the most admired, the best to work for and the most profitable.[3] This is because citizenship encourages.

1. individuals to become autonomous, lively and responsive;
2. citizens (as managers) to be committed and purposeful, thus influencing their colleagues to be be committed and purposeful;
3. openness – which can enable the integration of diverse business initiatives and cultures.

These modern ideas of citizenship and democracy may not be quite what Athenian thinkers believed. Aristotle, for example, was not concerned with individual freedom. In the *Politics*, he argues: 'One should say not that a citizen belongs to himself, but that all belong to the *polis*: for the individual is part of the *polis*.' In the *Republic*, Plato is plainly opposed to 'a society in which men are allowed to do whatever they like'. He goes on to argue that the individual 'must train the mind not even to consider acting as an individual or to know how to do it'. The Athenian approach to democracy stresses the social whole, not the individual. The sort of personal freedom from organisational control that we now anticipate is not derived from the ancient world but from nineteenth-century thinkers such as Benjamin Constant and John Stuart Mill and others (Berlin 2005: 287–321).

The sort of participatory citizenship we perceive confers responsibility, but it also creates a greater sense of freedom. Echoing the philosopher Karl Popper's argument that it is the responsibility of individuals to improve institutions (1945/2002), Koestenbaum and Block write (2001) 'our institutions are transformed the moment we decide they are ours to create'. To deliver the ideal of citizenship, managers have to move beyond the abstract categorisation of employees as passive receivers to an emphasis on participation and involvement (Ind 2001, Manville and Ober 2003) with the potential for real empowerment where the power of the manager is diminished as that of the employee increases.

Citizenship links explicitly to the management of seemingly conflicting principles: freedom and order. Manville and Ober (2003: 64) see this in terms of defining what it means to be a free individual *and* a member of a community of individuals. They go on to argue that 'it is a matter of surfacing and rearticulating core values and putting those values into action'. In this chapter we look at the importance of values in channelling the thinking and behaviour of managers and employees by creating a sense of engagement with the organisation and its ideology: 'something that any company strives for' (Manville and Ober

2003: 121) and then using that engagement to determine practices that are important to organisational performance (Whetten
and Godfrey 1998: 260) and in making meaning material (Debray
2000: 73).

THE VALUE OF VALUES

In inside–out thinking, values assume a dominant position,
because they have the potential to provide a focus for how people
inside the organisation relate to each other and to the outside
world. Values specify expected ways of thinking and behaving
and provide a framework against which decisions can be judged.
In some senses this is constraining. It cuts off actions outside the
framework which perhaps opportunistically might be of value, by
stressing the longer-term benefit of organisational cohesion. At
Toyota this way of thinking is enshrined as a key principle.
Toyota has a 4P model (philosophy, process, people and partners,
problem-solving) at the base of which is the philosophy that
management decisions must be based on a long-term perspective,
even at the expense of short-term financial goals (Liker 2004).

We could ask whether it might be possible to have a 'value-
less' organisation? The answer is probably, no. Organisations can
lack a dominant set of values if central control is weak and the
structure is heterogeneous and decentralised. Yet, even then the
decentralised parts of the organisation would have either explicit
or implicit values based on the beliefs of managers and the
dominant elements of the cultures. We could say in this context
that there is less cohesion in the values than in an organisation
that is more tightly structured, but the values are still there. The
very act of defining an organisation, whether it has been in
existence for ten days or ten years and whether its values are
focused on profit maximisation or some Aristotelian virtues,
involves some setting of ideological boundaries that define for

both managers and employees the meaning of organisational membership (Whetten and Godfrey 1998: 264). Indeed Debray (2000: 94) argues that belief is based on collectivity and the sense of belonging to an ideological cause: 'an individual's belief is not an individual phenomenon. It is a collective personality working through the individual.' This is why we would argue that values are not created but uncovered in an environment (Ind 2001). Values are within the fabric of the organisation and the ways of doing things whether they are defined or not. Indeed some organisations have strong value sets without making things explicit: Quiksilver has an implicit idea of its values, while it took Patagonia some forty years to define its beliefs and Nike twenty years.

Whether the organisation has multiple layers of values or not (some have corporate, behavioural, employer and separate brand values, while others make do with one over-arching set), their importance in brand building lies in the potential to influence the sort of people that work for the organisation and the way they behave towards stakeholders. Thus brand building is clearly connected with human resource policies. Values determine emotional perceptions about what is appreciated and preferred in the organization. According to Bang (1998) organisational values reflect national and local culture, the dominant values in an industry and the personal values of the organizational members, while Sadri and Lees (2001), argue that an effective organizational culture will be managed by employees' values and their coherence with corporate values and the corporate environment. This suggests that values determine norms (the way of dealing with events) and vice versa:[4] in other words, the shared values of a group of people determines the way they look at and tackle a problem, while the way of tackling a problem impacts on the dominant values. New employees' will adjust to norms and values, and over a period of time potentially adopt them as their own. For example, the employee citizens of the

Norwegian architectural practice, Snøhetta are very aware of living and realising the company values of 'respect', 'openness' and 'caring' in their day-to-day work. These operationalised values serve as an organisational cultural platform that encourages people to try out new ways of thinking about different architectural solutions, to dare to fail and to support each other through challenges.

The debate for an organisation is which values to adopt. In the previous chapter we looked at values as a shorthand, but the question remains as to what the shorthand should be. In simple terms the organisation should define a set of values that are true to the organisation, meaningful to employees and relevant to customers. We could also add that it is valuable if the values contain a tension, such as Volvo Cars do with their contrarian values of 'safety' and 'excitement'. If the values are simply comfortable and supportive of existing practices they may lack the dynamism to drive the organisation forward. When there is a tension in the values, people are forced to search for the meaning of the words and the implications for day-to-day actions. Tension stimulates dialogue and learning. In the inside–out school, the emphasis tends to be more on the truth and internal meaning while the outside–in school emphasises aspiration and relevance for customers. The ideal is a fusion of these two because it drives tension. We can see this precisely in the Volvo example, where 'safety', while of relevance to customers, is most important because of a long-term organisational commitment to the principle, while 'excitement' is something relatively new to the organisational culture, but of clear importance to the customer.

Drawing on the principle of values-tension and the ideas of management writer, Peter Koestenbaum, about the nature of leadership (Koestenbaum and Block 2001), we would argue that values should be true *and* yet visionary, ethical *and* courageous. Something Schein (1985: 17) echoes when he states that values that are congruent with underlying assumptions can create unity and provide a source of identity and mission, before he adds the caveat about the importance of distinguishing between currently existing and aspirational values. The rationale behind Koestenbaum's requirements is:

- *true*: values need to be credible within the organisation and to reinforce those behaviours that have made it successful
- *visionary*: organisations need to have forward momentum and to grasp future opportunities in support of the business strategy and the likely needs of customers
- *ethical*: organisations need to recognise that they have broader and longer term responsibilities to employees, customers and society rather than just meeting the immediate needs of shareholders
- *courageous*: to be seen as distinctively different by stakeholders, organisations need to think through their points of uniqueness and to challenge accepted norms.

The issue of internal versus external orientation can also be seen in organisations that choose to focus their values on Aristotelian virtues such as generosity, friendliness, honesty, honour and related moral value types akin to Schwartz's (1992) list of values that include *social justice, social recognition, equality, honour* and *honesty*, and those that concentrate on benefit values such as refreshing, fun, togetherness, simple or exciting. Here we could draw the distinction between corporate values, which are more likely to be the former and to steer internal behaviours and brand values, which are customer benefit focused. There is nothing wrong in making this distinction, but having separate corporate and brand values does provide the occasion for value overload and the potential for confusion as to when and how the values should be used in decision-making.

Some researchers link values to motivational factors because they represent the end state of being: *inner harmony, freedom, social power, exciting life, sense of belonging* (Rokeach 1973, Schwartz 1992, Nunnally and Bernstein 1994, Thyne 2001). Schwarz's listing (1992) is useful here and serves to show that values can be used (1) to segment and understand consumers and employees; (2) for differentiating and positioning an organisation or a brand in terms of developing a personality; (3) as guiding principles for managers in terms of how to govern a business and how to deal with people; and (4) in identification with elements of the organisational culture. The terminal values are seen as the "end state" of being, whereas the instrumental values are meant to be the tools (instruments) to "get there" (reach/fulfil the meaning of the terminal values).

Table 2.1   Value universe by Schwartz (1992) and cited in Bjerke et al. 2005

Terminal values:

1. Equality: *equal opportunity for all*
2. Inner harmony: *at peace with myself*
3. Social power: *control over others, dominance*
4. Pleasure: *gratification of desires*
5. Freedom: *freedom of action and thought*
6. A spiritual life: *emphasis on spiritual not material matters*
7. Sense of belonging: *feeling that others care about me*
8. Social order: *stability of society*
9. An exciting life: *stimulating experiences*
10. Meaning in life: *a purpose in life*
11. Politeness: *courtesy, good manners*
12. Wealth: *material possessions, money*
13. National security: *protection of my nation from enemies*
14. Self-respect: *belief in one's own worth*
15. Reciprocation of favours: *avoidance of indebtedness*
16. Creativity: *uniqueness, imagination*
17. A world at peace: *free of war and conflict*
18. Respect for tradition: *preservation of time-honoured customs*
19. Mature love: *deep emotional and spiritual intimacy*
20. Self-discipline: *self-restraint, resistance to temptation*

Table 2.1 *Continued*

21. Detachment: *from wordly concerns*
22. Family security: *safety for loved ones*
23. Social recognition: *respect, approval by others*
24. Unity with nature: *fitting into nature*
25. A varied life: *filled with challenge, novelty and change*
26. Wisdom: *a mature understanding in life*
27. Authority: *the right to lead or command*
28. True friendship: *close, supportive friends*
29. A world of beauty: *beauty of nature and the arts*
30. Social justice: *correcting injustice, care for the weak*

Instrumental values:

31. Independent: *self-reliant, self-sufficient*
32. Moderate: *avoiding extremes of feeling and action*
33. Loyal: *faithful to my friends, group*
34. Ambitious: *hardworking, aspiring*
35. Broad-minded: *tolerant of different ideas and beliefs*
36. Humble: *modest, self-effacing*
37. Daring: *seeking adventure, risk*
38. Protecting the environment: *preserving nature*
39. Influential: *having an impact on people and events*
40. Honouring of parents and elders: *showing respect*
41. Choosing own goals: *selecting own purposes*
42. Healthy: *not being sick physically or mentally*
43. Capable: *competent, effective, efficient*
44. Accepting my portion in life: *submitting to life's circumstances*
45. Honest: *genuine, sincere*
46. Preserving my public image: *protecting my 'face'*
47. Obedient: *dutiful, meeting obligations*
48. Intelligent: *logical, thinking*
49. Helpful: *working for the welfare of others*
50. Enjoying life: *enjoying food, sex, leisure, etc.*
51. Devout: *holding to religious faith and belief*
52. Responsible: *dependable, reliable*
53. Curious: *interested in everything, exploring*
54. Forgiving: *willing to pardon others*
55. Successful: *achieving goals*
56. Clean: *neat, tidy*

Reprinted from Schwartz SH (1992) Universals in the content and structure of values: theoretical advances and empirical tests in 20 countries. In MP Zanna (ed.) *Advances in Experimental Social Psychology*. San Diego: Academic Press, 1–65.

Values that are fairly universal like pleasure, true friendship and freedom – which were in a Scandinavian study targeting young women, found among the top five values (when the 56 Schwartz values were rated and ranked) – can easily be built into the brand and its communication. However this also suggests the tendency of organisations to build values around similar ideas. In 2004, the consulting firm Booz Allen Hamilton and the Aspen Institute conducted a study of 365 companies. The purpose of the survey was 'to examine the way companies define corporate values, to expand on research about the relationship of values to business performance, and to identify best practices for managing corporate values'. The core conclusions of the study were:

1. Ethical behaviour is a core component of companies' activities – 90% of those organisations that have written statements of values (89% of the total) include something on ethics.
2. Most companies believe values influence two important strategic areas – relationships and responsibility – but do not see the direct link to growth.
3. Most companies are not measuring their return on values.
4. Top performers consciously connect values and operations.
5. Value practices vary significantly by region.
6. The CEO tone really matters.

The choice of similar words to describe organisations does suggest a lack of variety of expression, yet if people find similar ideas appealing and managers recognise the common need to encourage high standards of ethical behaviour and customer orientation, this should not be so surprising. In any case we should consider that it is not the words themselves that create a point of difference, but rather the willingness and capability of the organisation to deliver on the values – that is the source of real differentiation. Rather than striving for pure but perhaps unsustainable differentiation in a brand definition, organisations should focus on action, for it is here that difference is achieved and that the nuances are conveyed. For example, if two airlines possess similar brand definitions based around such ideas as quality, innovation and service, will the customer experience be the same? Unlikely, because corporate cultures and the systems that maintain them are unique, so the interpretation of the words by leaders and employees will be different and the capabilities of the organisation will be dissimilar so that while one has the resources to innovate the other will not.

To carry this example through to the real world, compare something like the EasyJet brand with that of the short-lived SAS-owned airline, Snowflake. EasyJet is built on the idea of value, which means the airline has to be very tight on costs: customers book flights on online, there are no on-flight meals, many flights are to lower-cost, secondary airports and employee costs are minimised. To counteract the threat of companies like EasyJet, Ryanair and others, SAS decided to launch its own low-cost airline called Snowflake. The goal was also to communicate value, but the prevailing culture was that of SAS (historically the businessman's airline) and the resources were not in place: customers had to ring up and book their flights, flights were from existing primary airports and the large number of unions and existing contracts meant that employee costs were higher. A low-cost airline with higher costs than key competitors proved impossible to sustain. This example reminds us that the idea of marketing as the intersection of brand and customer cannot do without a third factor: capability or brand-building capacity. As Collins and Porras (1998) identified in their influential book, *Built to Last* (a study of 18 visionary and long-established companies (pre-1950) compared to 18 merely good organisations) it is not the adoption of ideology that matters, but rather the sincerity of, and commitment to, it:

> Throughout the history of most of the visionary companies we saw a core ideology that transcended purely economic

considerations. And – this is the key point – they have had core ideology to a greater degree than the comparison companies in our study.

In a study (2004) by Marshall Goldsmith and Howard Morgan, of the attitudes of 11,000 people in eight major corporations on leadership and corporate values, there was a clear finding that it is not corporate values per se that matter but the commitment of people to them: 'companies that do the best job of living up to their values and developing ethical employees, including managers, recognize that the real cause of success – or failure – is always the people not the words'. The implication is that values have to be translated into a language of actions, which then have to be implemented by managers and employees to make sense for those involved.

BEHAVIOURAL BRANDING

In the last chapter, we used de Chernatony and McDonald's definition of a successful brand as a working model to explore the market perspective to brand building. The definition also works from the insider perspective, but here we would change the interpretation to say that the brand elements of identifiability, augmentation, customer orientation and competitive sustainability should not be seen as abstractions that an organisational entity delivers, but rather as the result of the assumptions, beliefs and actions of the people within the organisation. It is about people, in the sense that the organisation delivers something of value to individual customers. Equally the delivery of the brand is down to leaders, managers and employees. This would seem obvious in the case of individuals with a public relations role and for customer-facing employees, as through direct interactions they have a strong influence on brand image. Yet all the abstract elements in fomenting a brand – naming, packaging, logistics, invoicing, advertising – are also defined by people. Relative to their competitors, part of the strength of the brand images of supermarket retailer, Tesco and homewares company, IKEA is due to the engagement of their people and the systems they have developed and manage – and the participation of their suppliers and partners in the process. We should recognise, therefore, that wherever we look in the organisation we will see brand deliverers.

However, in emphasising people in the branding process – in getting rid of abstraction – we create the potential problem of unfocused individuality. How do we ensure that employees deliver a consistent and appropriate service to customers? The reality is that brand delivery can never be absolutely consistent, but it can have a relative degree of consistency if people identify with and commit to the idea, not just the words, of the brand. When 'transmission'[5] takes place it creates a sense of unity brought about by people experiencing the organisational values through its frameworks, leadership, structures and common methods: 'by this means the corpus of knowledge, values, and know-how is brought out of yesterday into the present, stabilizing group identity via multiple two-way journeys' (Debray 2000: 6). This is when, as Blake Ashforth (1998) suggests, the individual becomes connected to the organisation, 'Identification, then, is the fusion of self and organization, thereby helping to address one's existential needs for meaning, belonging and even immortality' (Whetten and Godfrey 1998: 268).

The beneficiary of fusion of interest is not only the individual, but also the organisation. Research consistently shows that employee identification and commitment drives performance:

1. Simons, Walsh and Sturman (2001): employee study of 7409 hotel employees in the USA shows that employee commitment is a driver of customer satisfaction.

2. Maister (2001) 'Practice what you preach': study of 5500 people in 15 countries – raising employee satisfaction by 20% will increase financial performance by 42%. Maister argues that financial performance can be directly attributed to good client relationships based on a high quality of service, which in turn is determined by employee satisfaction.

3. Denison and Mishra (1995) demonstrate a correlation between involvement and consistency and employee satisfaction and they argue that 'culture may indeed have an impact on effectiveness'.

4. Rucci, Kirn and Quinn (1998) use causal pathway modelling to show the connections at Sears between 'a compelling place to work', 'a compelling place to shop' and 'a compelling place to invest'. The link they make (through Total Performance Indicators) is that in a cited 12-month period, a 4% improvement in employee satisfaction leads to a 4% increase in customer satisfaction, which equals, according to the predictive model, $200 million in additional revenues. The writers argue that the model says, 'it is our managers and employees, who, at the moment of truth in front of the customer, have achieved this prodigious feat of value creation'.

5. International Survey Research (2002) study of 362,950 employees from 40 companies between 1999 and 2001 showed that organisations with highly committed employees outperformed low commitment organisations in terms of operating margin by more than five percentage points.

6. Patterson et al. (1997) found that 12% of the variation between companies in their profitability can be explained by variations in the job satisfaction of their employees while 13% can be attributed to organisational commitment.

We could infer from this that encouraging identification is important to business success and that all organisations would encourage it. Yet the evidence is unclear. Several studies (Patterson et al.

1997, Gallup 2002, TEMO 2002) have demonstrated the lack of engagement among employees, and it seems that managers in stressing external brand building can perceive internal brand alignment as unimportant (Research International 2004). It may also be the case that some organisations prefer bland brands where a lack of distinctiveness neither attracts nor alienates people. Strong identities certainly seem to have a more polarising effect with the clear benefit that those who chose to work there have an increased potential for commitment. Ultimately the real problem may not be a lack of belief in the principle but the challenge of creating identification and commitment. In other words it is not for want of trying but more a problem of execution.

In our view there are two major (and connected) executional issues that tend to undermine the ability of organisations to be effective internal brand builders: participation and communication. As Debray (2000, 6) argues, 'communication needs only interest and curiosity. Proper transmission necessitates transformation if not conversion.' There is a view that the articulation of the brand needs to be a top management exercise and that wider employee engagement in the process leads to consensus-seeking blandness (Leoncini 2002, Burmann and Zeplin 2005). The top–down approach may be easier and quicker and more prevalent, but it probably reflects the preferences of CEOs and their advisors rather than the most effective method. Leoncini's belief that more participative approaches led to 'permission-to-play' values and that the best brand articulations are defined by small groups of senior people cannot be sustained by the widespread similarity of brand definitions that are largely created by exactly this process. In any case, if the cited evidence of Collins and Porras and Goldsmith and Morgan are to be believed, the words themselves matter less than the commitment to them. This indicates that brand definition exercises should concentrate on the process itself as a means of building employee identification rather than worrying overly about synonyms. More participative approaches have the advantage of (a) inclusivity: ensuring that all departments and divisions can use the brand; (b) credibility: that the brand reflects the reality of the organization; and (c) comprehension: that by the very process of discussion people come to understand and engage with the brand.

For example, when Baxter International defined its values the process took two years. The company adopted a bottom–up process that involved employees from all parts of the organisation in discussing and defining a set of values that were authentic and usable. The benefit of this participative approach was that it led to a very rapid buy-in from employees. Research a couple of years after launch found that over 90% of employees knew and understood the values. Gretchen Winter, VP Business Practices at Baxter says:

> The values were not a new thing. They reflected what people already believed. As a result they resonate with people. They are real; true. People see them reflected by management and in the decisions that are made. It goes beyond a theme. The two year period it took to define the values was critical to the process.

Similarly UNICEF UK, where the whole organisation took part in the process of brand definition, found that eighteen months after launch, 89% of employees understood how to incorporate the brand into their work. And some six years after the internal launch the brand was still alive and contributing actively to strategy formation. At outdoor clothing brand Patagonia more than two dozen people from every part of the company helped to draft the purpose and values statement. Every employee of the company then took part in group discussions of the draft, which led to some modifications before the agreement of the final articulation: our purpose – to use business to inspire and imple-ment solutions to the environmental crisis; our core values – quality, integrity, environmentalism, not bound by convention. Having agreed the definition, the company continued to support the brand by holding meetings with all employees in small groups three times a year. This process led to a shared understanding of the meaning behind the purpose and the values, such that the idea of 'quality', for example, changed from a focus on product quality to a more rounded appreciation of quality in all activities. This common perspective enables the organisation to operate a decentralised operation with a significant continuity of behaviour and communication.

The key to success in brand definition is to ensure that there is autonomy and diversity in the process. People have to bring different personal and organisational experiences, so that there is questioning. The principle of diversity is supported by a number of other key writers (Ford and Gioia 2000, Amabile 2001, Henry 2001, Thompson and Brajkovich 2003) who all argue that difference, in both skill and personality mix, are key factors in generating energy, interaction and a creative climate within organisations. Without differences of knowledge, styles and personalities, teams can quickly develop group-think (Janis 1982) where perspectives and debate become confined in a static framework of understanding. Without diversity and the resulting tension, the creative climate can become de-energised and demotivated (Ind and Watt 2006). To energise people from diverse backgrounds (in terms of position, function and geography) they need autonomy and the freedom to express their own ideas, but this needs to be accompanied by subtly supportive managers who set the boundaries for the group and help maintain motivation. Not surprisingly these principles marry well with the ideas of James Surowiecki in *The Wisdom of Crowds* (2005), who argues that smart crowds should be diverse, decentralised and independent and capable of developing ideas that can be synthesised.

Once a brand is defined, the temptation is to believe that communication to employees will generate 'transformation, if not conversion'. However, communication by itself is easily ignored.

As well as communication (it is a necessary part of the process), people need to engage with the brand and to explore its functional and emotional boundaries – much as we discussed in the previous chapter when we used Eco's idea of encyclopaedic definitions. This active use of the brand means that it can begin to permeate everyday action and to impact on the organisational culture. This participative approach to brand engagement is also recognised as valuable by Burmann and Zeplin (2005: 289) who state, 'the hypothesis of this paper is that employee participation will generate a stronger brand commitment based on identification and internalization, while imposed behaviour guidelines will only generate weak commitment based on compliance'.

CONNECTING EMPLOYEES AND CUSTOMERS

While the inside-out perspective tends to put emphasis on managers and employees, the rationale for so doing is not some altruistic desire to make people's lives better (although that may indeed be a benefit), but primarily because committed employees are more likely to deliver value to customers and other stakeholders. This suggests that people inside the organisation need to understand the brand and be capable of delivering it in a relevant way to customers. This idea leads us back to the concept of entrainment that we introduced in Chapter 1. Here we will explore the idea further and demonstrate how a strong brand can galvanise employees and lead to satisfied customers. This indicates the importance of customer-facing employees in particular, but it is the collective effort of the organisation that is important, for, as Chenet et al. (2000) suggest, service delivery is a combination of culture, leadership, commitment, systems, tools and technology. It also indicates the value of entrainment: the ability of the service provider to create a picture of the customers' situation and to be sufficiently flexible and creative to adjust to the individual customer's expectations and required solutions (Andreassen and Selnes 2001).

Probably the best examples of entrained organisations come from the world of sportswear: Quiksilver, Patagonia and the early Nike (Ind 2001, Ind and Watt 2004). Quiksilver achieves entrainment through several key mechanisms. It recruits people directly from the sports it serves (skateboarding, snowboarding, surfing), such that most people at Quiksilver, from the CEO and the key directors down are board riders and employees are encouraged to take an active part in their sports and at events. This helps to overcome the 'back to the floor' problem of remoteness and to ensure that managers and employees are taking an active part in an ongoing dialogue with customers. The directors of Quiksilver don't have to resort to dated or abstracted data to make informed decisions, they can work from current and direct experience. However, this is not just one way. Quiksilver encourage interested professionals, such as designers as well as board riders to contribute their ideas. The several hundred professional riders and an army of supported amateurs are an extension of the grassroots connection Quiksilver enjoyed in its early days when it was run as a hobbyist surf shorts business by two surfing fanatics.

Quiksilver knows creativity has to meet with the approval of the enthusiast audience both to ensure it is a trend leader and to maintain its authenticity. Some innovations are the direct result of input from riders, such as the development of surfing fiction books aimed at girls or the design of a wet-suit range and some ideas are the result of dialogue that provides inspiration for designers. Rapid feedback also tells the company when its products aren't working as they should or its communications aren't connecting. The important element of collaboration is the ability to listen. Quiksilver achieve this largely by treating the riders as insiders. The language of the company reflects this: riders are part of the organisational structure. They're welcomed at

Quiksilver offices and they meet with employees at sporting events. Their input is sought and their ideas acted upon. Marketing Director, Randy Hild, says, 'We believe in that collaborative process; in that input from our riders. If they're not connecting with it, then our consumers probably won't connect with it . . . It's our job to listen and to adjust.'

While having permeable borders is valuable in bringing the customer inside the organisation, as Hild says the ability to listen and adjust determines whether the input has value. This is about receptivity and Hild claims that Quiksilver is very good at it. This is largely a result of the company's heritage and corporate culture. The early days of grassroots marketing was about company employees (who were also sports participants themselves) and riders meeting at events and exchanging ideas. This practice still continues and Hild regards this as the company's large, continuous focus group programme. Within Quiksilver itself, the internal borders are played down and the importance of collaboration emphasised. Groups are formed from across departments to explore ideas in largely informal, intuitive ways. The sense of the brand, which is very strong, provides a template against which decisions are made, but there is also a strong belief in being open-minded so that good ideas – whether they come from inside or outside – are not missed. With such an emphasis on teamwork, and what the company calls a free-flowing culture, the one taboo is egotistical behaviour. If egos were allowed to dominate, it would have the potential to allow overly individualistic interests to disrupt people's sense of unity with the organisation and with the customer. Quiksilver's entrainment with its customers enables it to develop new ranges and communications without recourse to research. The company is able to set trends and to expand its range of brands. However, this doesn't mean that it always succeeds. There are products and ranges that fail: each year a third of the clothing range is given over to designers to experiment, which produces runaway success and failures. What entrainment does mean is that it gives the company the confidence to take risks and to innovate.

Up the Californian coastline from Quiksilver at Ventura is the outdoor clothing company, Patagonia. It also exhibits an entrained way of thinking and reflects many of the same traits as Quiksilver. It too grew out of a hobbyist business (making climbing equipment) and evolved through a close connection to its sports, such that the people who work there from the receptionist to the marketing director to the CEO are active sports enthusiasts. Also because the company has such a strong environmental ethos, alongside the sport orientation is a commitment to environmental activism: the company's purpose statement is 'to use business to inspire and implement solutions to the environmental crisis'. The company's core customers – the enthusiasts – represent a rich source of inspiration for the company and again via the dialogue between employees (especially in retail outlets) and customers there is an active listening process at work, which feeds through into product design and communications. The fostering of the dialogue seems to be related to the nature of the company's business and the nature of its foundation. Climbing, like many of the outdoor sports with which Patagonia is connected, involves much waiting – and then a burst of adrenalin-filled activity (which is when stories are told). Then, because of the blurring of the boundaries between Patagonia and its customers, the stories get retold in Patagonia shops, which tend to be populated by climbers and canoeists and surfers; they get retold in Ventura; they get retold in advertising; and they get retold in the form of field reports. People within Patagonia maintain a natural dialogue because their interests are entrained with customers'. Stories flow into the company anecdotally or in writing and then flow back out. Creative Director, Hal Arneson says:

> We have our songlines[6] – they're passed on and they're very seldom written down. They run through generations and they

extend out into the customer base. We definitely include our customers as part of that tribal culture.

We could argue that this is exactly the way authentic marketing should work, although interestingly, the marketing director, Chris van Dyke, who came from Nike, found that when he arrived at Patagonia no one knew what marketing was. It was only when he started talking about relationships and friendships that he was understood. We might add that Nike also exhibited this close connection with its customers in its early days when it was more clearly a sports enthusiast brand. Nelson Farris, one of its first employees and now corporate storyteller there, relates that when Nike was a young company, individuals spent their spare time at athletic events, taking part in track sports, talking to runners and listening to athletes' ideas about how to improve shoes. New products were developed by hand and given to people to test out. While Nike still tries to retain this entrainment through its sponsorships, it seems to have largely lost the close fit and mutual influence with the mass of its customers. Thus we might pose the question as to whether entrainment is viable when organisations become larger.

Scale does seem to represent a challenge to entrainment, but we would argue that there are mechanisms for extending the scope of the company's connectivity with customers. While scale might create complexity, the biggest challenge facing organisations in their goal of getting close to the customer is lack of commitment and passion among employees. This will be discussed in detail later, but for now we can observe that the key characteristics of Quiksilver, Patagonia and, to a certain extent, Nike are that managers and employees willingly and enthusiastically give their time to brand participation and because these businesses have membrane-like permeable borders, key customers are able to touch and participate in the organisation. This reciprocity creates the opportunity for entrainment.

The designer and innovator, Tom Kelley, argues in *The Art of Innovation* that passion tends to be strong in sports companies, because people 'live the lifestyle they're selling' (Kelley 2001: 74–5). However it can also be observed in the automotive industry and in software. This is how Sara Öhrvall describes the Volvo culture (Ind and Watt 2004):

> The culture is so passionate you become passionate. People read all the car magazines and there are opportunities to test drive Volvo cars and the competitors. People talk about cars all the time. The culture is also very friendly, so people socialise a lot after working hours. Mostly they spend their free time with other Volvo people.

Also to help the design process, the company structures teams that are closely connected to the customers they serve, such that when Volvo designed a car specifically aimed at women, the design and development team was all female. Similarly when Toyota developed the Lexus brand, they were aware the core market would be the USA and a certain type of affluent customer. To absorb the milieu the brand would have to operate in, the design team was moved to Newport Beach and asked to live there in a lifestyle akin to the potential customer and to drive the cars they would drive.

In software development there are many passionate people, but the best example of entrainment is Linux. This organisation was started in 1991 by a Finnish software engineer called Linus Thorvalds. He developed software based on a UNIX system, but realised that to fully develop the product he would need help. To do this he created a structure to ensure quality control was maintained, but he made the source code freely available, so that anyone who wanted to develop the software could do so. This meant that end customers and software engineers were able to participate actively in the product's evolution. The potential problem that someone might take the code and adapt it without sharing – known as the tragedy of the commons – was limited by peer pressure, but also through the creation of a licence system that ensures people share what they add to the software. This licensing approach stabilises a dynamic environment and has contributed to the development of the Open Source Movement which includes other software products, such as Apache, Perl and Mozilla. Raymond (1999) calls this the Bazaar model and contrasts it with the Cathedral model where the source code is a carefully guarded secret. He suggests that the Bazaar model is a more effective way of testing software code than the Cathedral model which has to second guess customer reactions. In reviewing the Bazaar and Cathedral model, brand identity expert, Andreas Mack writes:

> Looking at brands we discover cathedrals all around us. Polished up brands launching into stardom or disappearing into failure. Brands secretly pre-tested and pumped up with meaning, structure and visuals, creating identities to last a lifetime . . . A bazaar approach to branding lets consumers, retailers, press and public take a peak behind the scenes and have a say when decisions are made . . . Smart brands will welcome the consumer's role as a natural partner in a collective process of product and brand development. (Mack 2004)

Co-creation – the process of employees developing products and services together with customers – seems an obvious means of encouraging entrainment, but it does require, as the bazaar approach suggests, a certain humility; a willingness to accept ideas from outside the organisation. For many organisations, who view customers and partners as 'subordinates, rather than as equal partners' the attitude is more patronising: 'managers say they want to reap loyalty and respect, yet the opposite is sown' (Meyers 2003: 32).

CONCLUSION

These first two chapters have presented the two dominant schools of brand building. The first school represents the traditional and widely held view of branding that stresses marketing communication and a consumer orientation. The second school, deriving from organisational development, instead stresses the importance of engaging with the people in the organisation as a means of delivering value to customers. Inevitably these schools of thought are not neatly pigeon-holed as there are clear overlaps. Both are concerned with understanding the way people behave, both emphasise the potential unity created by the brand ideology and both face a challenge in overcoming internal barriers. Yet there is a clear difference in that the outside–in school (at least as an ideal) works from the market back into the organisation. This should stress the primacy of the customer. In contrast, the inside–out school works from the employee outwards (but ideally with one eye always on the needs of the customer). The two schools have their virtues, but as should be clear from these chapters they are also flawed. The outside–in school, while purporting to be customer focused, too often is oriented around what the organisation produces and relies on impersonal marketing based on abstracted thinking to move product. This encourages brand building to be seen as unstrategic and the preserve of marketing rather than an organisation-wide responsibility. Equally the inside–out school can easily lose sight of customers and become introverted. Internal branding/communication also lacks weight within the organisation and is sometimes seen as the preserve of human resources and therefore becomes too closely connected with the concept of the employer brand.

What we will develop in the following chapters is a synthesis of these two schools by suggesting that there needs to be a constant two-way flow between the inside and the outside, where the inside is not represented by a department, but by a joined up organisation with a common purpose. We suggest that organisations need to develop an effective balance between a market and organisation orientation. This dual orientation has the potential to strengthen the organisation's brand-building capacity. This branding philosophy is about connectivity: linking major dimensions or forces in the organisation with the needs and wants of customers to build brand equity.

NOTES

1. The adherence to militaristic metaphors is not surprising. Early examples of successful economic structures were staffed by and connected to the military. The huge Venice Arsenale (it employed around 5000 people in 1525) which built sailing ships from the fourteenth century onwards and sustained Venice's golden era was a sophisticated bureaucratic machine that was assiduous in its record keeping and its procedures for control. Later examples are the nineteenth-century American railroad system where military engineers developed the bureaucratic management systems and the new professionalism in US businesses led by West Point graduates after 1817, who adopted the West Point 'grammatocentric' approach (where everything was examined and written down) (Hoskin et al. 1997).
2. The shift from an industrial based structure occurred at different times, but services started to become dominant in Great Britain (1955), USA (1966) and Norway and Italy (1971).
3. Annual surveys in these categories are published in *Fortune* magazine.
4. Schein (1985: 193–4) argues that norms are due to a 'sense of groupness [that] arises though [*sic*] successive dealing with marker events, those that arouse strong feelings and then are dealt with effectively'.
5. Debray distinguishes between the personal nature of communication and the collegiality of transmission, which indicates transformation.
6. A songline is an Aboriginal concept, which was popularised by the writer Bruce Chatwin in his book *The Songlines*. It is an inner guide, which forms the basis of an Aborigine's spiritual life. An outsider cannot understand its truth. Interview with author, 2000.

PART II

PARTICIPATORY BRANDING AND THE ASSEMBLAGE

INTRODUCTION

In the first two chapters of this book we introduced the two core approaches to brand building (the market-led perspective and the inside–out perspective). It should have been obvious that these perspectives, while both offering benefits also have limitations. Our view is that there needs to be a synthesis of these ideas to deliver an approach that simultaneously delivers the opportunity for employee engagement and the production of customer value. The implications of this are significant, because it suggests that the organisation has to be focused, well wired and good at sense-making all at the same time. It also implies that past predilections that have led to organisational silos, short-termism and multiple expressions of ideology have to be discarded in favour of partici-pation and inspirational simplicity.

In the chapters that follow we will map out the participa-tive approach to brand building based on the concept of the assemblage and the impact of assemblage thinking on marketing, human resources, leadership, culture and evaluation. Inevitably for ease of explanation these ideas are divided into readable chunks, but we want to stress that all these areas are interlinked and we will attempt to ensure that connections are made. For example, leadership is not a separate element from people and culture, it both determines and is determined by them. Indeed, just as we will argue about the need to blur boundaries between the organisation and its customers and between organisational departments and divisions, so we should also recognise the fluidity of the terms we use. While it is always comforting to grasp the seeming fixedness of an idea, in reality there is always change. This requires a train of thought that (a) recognises that everything is part of an interconnected whole rather than a series of distinct fragments and (b) that everything is always becoming (Deleuze and Guattari 1980: 263) and eternally changing (Bohm 2004: 124). When we use a word such as branding we do not confuse it with painting, but there are many definitions of the term that stretch its boundaries and connect it to other ideas. This is not to suggest a world of chaos, where we cannot communicate, because we can apply a 'minimum of constant rules':

> All that the association of ideas has ever meant is providing us with these protective rules – resemblance, contiguity, causality – which enable us to put some order into ideas, preventing our 'fantasy' (delirium, madness) from crossing the universe in an instant, producing winged horses and dragons breathing fire. (Deleuze and Guattari 1991: 201)

Working within these rules, the concept of the assemblage only functions if people are sensitive to the movements in it and able to spot the important points of continuity and change that are relevant to their specific organisation. This is not about establishing a universal truth but recognising contingent movement and being continuously adaptive (Weick 2003: 96), such that the mind is free to pay 'attention to new differences and new similarities, allowing for the perception of a new structure of "things"' (Bohm 2004: 124).

The metaphor that Deleuze and Guattari use to convey this way of thinking is the rhizome which is a type of plant that can extend itself through its underground root system to establish new plants. In other words a rhizome creates connections and removes blockages and is susceptible to constant modification through interaction (Deleuze and Guattari 1980: 13): 'it creates and recreates the world through connections' (Parr 2005: 236). The rhizome is an open, fluid system that is composed of 'directions in motion'. Its opposite is the arborescent, which is seen as hierarchical and communication constrained. Most organisations are arborescent, because they are structured around command and control systems to a greater or lesser degree. However, some of the more citizen-based organisations we have discussed have moved to a more rhizomatic structure, where hierarchy is limited and connectivity is multiple. Here leadership is enabling, employees are empowered and dialogue with stakeholders continuous. The rhizome is an adaptive and creative system, because it thrives on change and to a large extent, is self-organising.

Hopefully the rhizome metaphor establishes some sort of mental picture of an assemblage. In Figure 1 we show the elements involved in the assemblage, but a flat illustration cannot do justice to the idea. A truer picture would be one that demonstrates all the connection points between the organisation and its environment and the changes in terms of speed and movement; the total flow of information internally and externally and a blurring and melding together of all the organisational boxes. The assemblage is more like a cubist film, where movement is looked at from many perspectives at the same time, rather than a graphic presentation. Equally in representing the assemblage as boxes and arrows we exclude something we are at pains to emphasise: that there are real people behind these abstractions of the customer and the employee and the brand. In the chapters to come, we will address these factors by stressing that brands are for and determined by people and by showing the multiple perspectives of the assemblage.

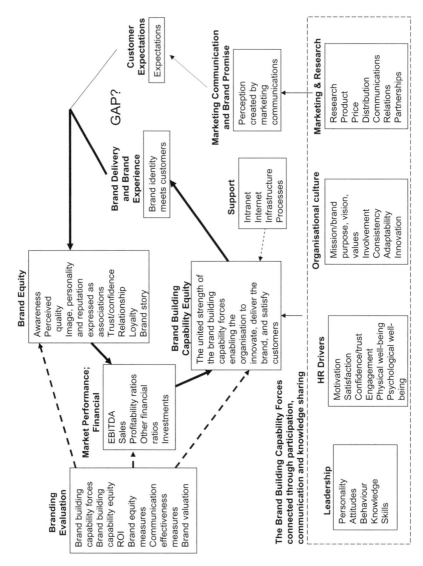

Figure 1 The assemblage

CHAPTER 3

A PARTICIPATIVE APPROACH
TO MARKETING

W
e start this marketing section of the book with a simple premise (which will be sustained by the arguments that follow): creating value for customers is an organisation-wide responsibility. This is the thinking behind the organisation-wide assemblage model in the introduction to this section of the book which communicates the idea that the brand-building capability of the organisation is determined by the combination of marketing, human resources, organisational culture, leadership and evaluation. This is a step removed from most approaches to the subject, which place great emphasis on marketing as the primary, if not the sole, driver in building a brand. In contrast, as we argue throughout this book, we see marketing as only an element (albeit an important one) in the creation of customer value. It is our contention that the role of marketing is about connecting with the other four forces in the assemblage to optimise the brand-building capability and brand potential. Consequently, in

the chapters that follow we do not intend to provide a comprehensive overview of marketing theory and practice, but rather (a) to suggest a different way of *seeing* marketing as a connecting mechanism and (b) to offer an alternative approach to the planning and executing of marketing activity.

FROM MARKETING TO MARKET ORIENTATION

E Jerome McCarthy's *4Ps* concept, which we introduced in Chapter 1, tends to be the default explanation on the nature of marketing: to manage price, product, place and promotion[1] in such a way as to create value for a customer. The essence of McCarthy's idea of marketing and many subsequent commentators who have developed his concept is valid as far as it goes, but it sustains the mistaken perspective of marketing as an instrumental and behaviouristic function or discipline. In this line of thinking, marketing is what marketers do to customers when they take what the company produces and re-present it. As should have become obvious by now, we challenge the traditional idea of marketing. First, in our view marketing is not a department but a process by which the organisation connects with the world around it. Secondly, marketing theory and practice should not only be concerned with the external but also with the difficult internal reality of aligning the 4Ps and the different parts of the organisation. As an illustration of this problem, take the instance of a market such as personal computing. In response to changes in customer behaviour in the use of digital equipment such as audio and video, it may make sense for an IT company to develop a range of software and hardware. Yet this will only be possible if the whole organisation supports the effort: finance need to provide the development funds, design needs to develop relevant products, supply needs to source material, engineering needs to innovate, sales need to open up the right channels, management needs to support the initiative and advertising needs to communicate the benefits of the products. The whole process needs to be planned and executed effectively in response to a clear customer insight.

When marketing only has a limited role; when it is disconnected from other activities within the organisation, the challenge of delivering a coherent offer is that much harder. Functional areas push in different directions and the appearance, functionality and presentation of the products begins to lack clarity. Alternatively if marketing is connected with the rest of the organisation; indeed if the whole organisation is involved in delivering the 4Ps, coherence is much easier to attain. If this sounds theoretical, this scenario applies to an actual case: the launch of Apple Computer's strategy based around the metaphor of a 'digital hub for a digital lifestyle' (Sjödin and Ind 2006). This metaphor, announced by Steve Jobs at Macworld 2001 in San Francisco, expressed a new vision for the brand and encompassed several new Apple products: new computers and integrated hardware for recording CDs and DVDs, iTunes and iMovie. Soon afterwards the metaphor heralded the launch of the iPod, Apple's expansion into audio products and services and the introduction of Apple's own retail stores. At the time, *Fortune* magazine (12 November 2001) was moved to compare Apple's success with Intel's problems:

> Why in the world would Apple want to jump from the frying pan of the virtually profitless PC industry into the roaring fire of the hypercompetitive consumer electronics business? After all, just a few days before Apple's splashy introduction of the iPod, Intel announced that it would close down its own disappointing consumer electronics division, which made, among other things, portable MP3 players, digital still cameras, kiddie videocameras, and a much ballyhooed digital microscope. For starters, the iPod fits right into Jobs' so-called Digital Hub strategy for the Macintosh.[2]

The vision encapsulated in the strategic metaphor not only was a driver for internal cohesion so that the organisation could focus on those areas that best delivered the idea, but also became a widely used phrase by the media between 2001 and 2005, such that each new service and product innovation launched by Apple was integrated into the metaphor not just by Apple spokespeople but also by journalists. The whole process thus became a self-reinforcing circular movement that has enabled Apple to be consistently interesting and interestingly consistent.

THE PRINCIPLES OF MARKET ORIENTATION

One of the developments within marketing thinking, that has tried to deal with the problem of marketing's overtly external emphasis which too often leads to disconnected thinking, has been the emergence of the concept of 'market orientation'. This approach extends the role of marketing by suggesting its role should be not only to sense movement in the environment but also to shape the organisational response by connecting with other business functions and departments. This indicates the role of marketers: to face simultaneously inwards and outwards and connect the organisation and its audiences.

Although the underlying ideas of market orientation have been around since the 1960s, it was two pairs of writers in 1990 who began to define and refine the concept: Narver and Slater and Kohli and Jaworski. Rather than simply focusing on the point of interaction with customers, they turned inward to explore how organisations could use customer knowledge to build organisation-wide responses. Kohli and Jaworski saw the concept as referring to 'the organisation-wide generation of market intelligence, dissemination of the intelligence across departments, and organisation wide responsiveness to it'. Narver and Slater (1990) featured some similar elements, seeing market orientation as: (1) customer orientation; (2) competitor orientation; and (3) interfunctional coordination. However, Narver and Slater's emphasis is on market orientation as organisational culture. This is a subject we will deal with in a later chapter, but the Narver and Slater viewpoint is that culture drives behaviour which means that market orientation can only exist if there is a culture that is oriented towards delivering customer value effectively and efficiently.

There is a small postscript we would add: while it is true that culture drives behaviour, behaviour also drives culture. If we accept the Narver Slater argument, we might come to the view that in a non-customer oriented culture, people cannot consistently be market oriented. This is a static view of culture, yet we argue that culture is dynamic. Leaders, of course, cannot simply tell people to be more customer oriented and expect a transformation to occur, but they can lead by example and committed groups of individuals can de-territorialise the organisational way of doing things by focusing on the delivery of customer value. These actions can lead to cultural change and enhanced market orientation. Jaworski and Kohli (1993) endorse the importance of leadership in their analysis of the antecedents of market orientation because of leaders' ability to stimulate an external focus 'through continual reminders to employees that it is critical for them to be sensitive and responsive to market developments'.

More recently Gainer and Padanyi (2005) have seen that market orientation is viewed among researchers either as a cultural construct or a behavioural construct (separate or connected/correlated), or even a hybrid incorporating both cultural and behavioural aspects. Their study of non-profit organisations showed that a positive relationship between market-oriented behaviours and organisational performance is mediated by market-orientation. Further, Kee-hung and Cheng (2005) used data from 304 organisations, which had operational quality management systems (quality orientation looks at the level of quality management implemented) to investigate the relationship between quality orientation, market orientation and organisational performance.

The study (based both on qualitative and quantitative data) revealed that quality orientation and market orientation are complementary and they authenticate the view that quality management and marketing reinforce each other in strengthening organisational performance.

Lastly, Matsunoa, Mentzer and Rentz (2005) think that although the topic of a market orientation is now much discussed, there is still no apparent consensus on its definition and on how to measure the construct. In the authors' endeavour to improve market orientation conceptualisation and measurement they compare three different scales (the scales of Kohli and Jaworski, Narver and Slater and EMO[3] – extended market orientation). Their conclusion: the Narver and Slater scale was found superior to the others in terms of predictive validity, but based on scale reliability, limited unidimensionality and construct domain, no single scale examined here was found satisfactory.

APPLYING MARKET-ORIENTED THINKING

The virtue of market orientation is that it stresses the importance of connecting the organisation together to deliver value to customers. It seeks to overcome the problem of siloisation that is prevalent in organisations and supports the concept of the organisational assemblage. Researchers may debate whether it is a cultural or a behavioural construct, but our view is that these two ideas are interlinked. We see market orientation as a way of facing the world – in that sense it is a cultural construct. However, culture is about the way of doing things. It determines and is determined by behaviours. Yet, the real challenge is that in spite of flatter, less bureaucratic structures, many organisations struggle with market orientation. Partly this is to do with the difficulty of changing culture in a managed way and partly to do with the problem of organisational fragmentation.

Yet there seem to be other factors at work. Jaworski and Kohli's 1993 paper addressed three specific questions: (1) Why are some organizations more market-oriented than others? (2) What effect does a market orientation have on employees and business performance? (3) Does the linkage between a market orientation and business performance depend on the environmental context? Based on two national samples the researchers came to the conclusion that market orientation is related to top management emphasis, the risk aversion of top managers, interdepartmental conflict and connectedness, centralisation and the reward system orientation. Moreover, a market orientation is related to overall business performance (but not market share), employees' organisational commitment, and esprit de corps. And even more important, the connection between market orientation and performance appears to be consistent across environmental contexts that suffer from varying degrees of market turbulence, competitive intensity and technological change. We might conclude from this that there are no environmental reasons to prevent market orientation and plenty of benefits. This is supported by other research:

- Slater and Narver (1994a) showed that the benefits of a market orientation are long-term even though environmental conditions are often transient. Becoming market oriented is cost-effective long-term in spite of any possible short-term moderating effects of the environment. 'A market orientation is a particular form of business culture', and 'becoming and remaining market oriented are essential to the continuous creation of superior value' (Slater and Narver 1994a: 53).
- Siguaw, Simpson and Baker (1998) discovered that a supplier's market-oriented behaviour directly or indirectly affects all the channel relationships examined from the distributor's perspective. In particular the distributor's market orientation, trust,

cooperative norms, commitment, and satisfaction have an impact on financial performance.

• Hampton and Hampton (2004) found that professionalism and rewards were positively correlated with market orientation. Further, the study revealed that market orientation was strongly and positively related to job satisfaction.

Of course, market orientation is not an absolute. It is something that organisations strive for over time. Yet the idea of market orientation has not been fully realised in organisations. There are a number of factors here. (1) Researchers, while connecting market orientation to business performance, have not explicitly linked it to brand building capability. (2) The measurement systems, as observed, have not been sufficiently deep. (3) Insufficient attention has been paid to the reality of how to engage the organisation to become market orientated. In particular, the whole area of implementation has been underplayed. A market-oriented culture is not only about interfunctional coordination (Slater and Narver 1994b), dissemination (Kohli and Jaworski 1990), or the type of organisational antecedents (factors) that enhance or impede the implementation of the business philosophy. Rather market orientation is a consequence of (although it in turn reinforces) a supportive organisational culture, HR drivers and leadership. To develop this line of thinking we have developed the concept of participatory market orientation: a fusion of internal and external market orientations with an emphasis on realising the potential of market orientation.

PARTICIPATORY MARKET ORIENTATION (PMO)

A participatory market oriented philosophy aims to build brand capability and brand equity. This suggests that the role of

Figure 3.1 Participatory market orientation as a value chain

marketing as one of the organisational driving forces is about helping the organisation to become participatory, such that all investments in external and internal marketing activities should maintain a high participatory market orientation and strengthen the brand. The PMO approach is depicted as a value chain (as shown in Figure 3.1), which indicates that PMO is an orientation that adheres to the idea of entrainment.

This belief in the value of participation steers the way investments are made in both internal and marketing activities and recognises their connectivity. It suggests as a principle that rather than an over-reliance on traditional marketing communications to build a brand that funds are allocated to become entrained with customers and to integrate a relevant organisational response encompassing communications and actions. An example of this entrainment process at work is the *grathak katha* (consumer's voice) events held by the Bangladeshi mobile operator, Grameen-Phone. Grameenphone is the leading mobile telecom company in Bangladesh with a 62% share of the market and 8.5 million customers (September 2006). This is a high growth market, but it is also extremely poor: the average GDP per head is $421 and GrameenPhone's business model is designed to work with customers whose average spend on mobile telephony is $2 per month.

To understand its customers better and develop innovative ways of selling its services, the company conducts regular market research studies into the performance of its brand and particularly the delivery of customer service. However, in addition to this research, GrameenPhone has initiated a process for removing the distance between the company and its customers. This participative approach involves regular meetings with customers in an environment that is both social and businesslike. The idea is to obtain direct interaction with customers both as a way of enhancing the reputation of the brand and as a means of learning about and learning with customers. At the event itself, GrameenPhone matches the attendees one to one with employees so that there is the opportunity for personal dialogue. On these occasions research is conducted and results presented, new products are discussed and customers provide ideas on new opportunities. The idea is to mix the formal and the informal and such has been the momentum behind the process that music performances at the events are by groups that combine employees and customers playing together.

GrameenPhone has discovered that the quality of the feedback is high and the comments are genuine. Customers are not concerned with trying to either attack or please GrameenPhone, they just try to offer input and to relate their experiences. In one year the company conducted more than 300 events with over 200,000 participants. The key to maintaining the interest in the process both within GrameenPhone and externally with customers is the rapid processing of information, the actions taken as a result of input and the feedback provided. Marketing Director, Rubaba Dowla Matin, argues that the success is due to the organisational capability to validate, categorise, analyse the data and to involve the relevant teams in the organisation. It is these cross-functional customer management teams that play the vital role in determining the nature of the insight and generating action and communication. This investment into deep and direct insight and the willingness to encourage organisation-wide participation have been the catalysts behind the success of the initiative and the company's burgeoning reputation as an innovator.

Overall, when such external/internal investments as that made by GrameenPhone are managed effectively it increases the brand-building capability of the organisation and its brand equity, which in turn enhances brand value. This final linkage is based on the premise that enhanced awareness and customer loyalty to the brand is the best indicator of the security of future cash flows. This way of thinking goes beyond market orientation because of its explicit link with brand value and because of the emphasis on engaging audiences to ensure that a market orientation leads to effective action.

Marketing's role then shifts subtlety in this scenario. When the overall organisational goal is to enhance customer value there is a requirement for an organisation-wide commitment to customers and a supportive culture, style of leadership, governance and human resources policies. Partly marketing must have an internal market orientation to help achieve this organisation-wide perspective and partly it must be a key element in building bonds with customers and sharing knowledge about them inside the organisation; externally sense-making and internally sense-sharing. This internal/external approach builds the brand.

The value of this twin perspective is endorsed by a study of Sweden's 500 largest companies[4] (2005) that shows that organisations with the highest brand orientation index (BOI), where branding is the hub of operations, are characterised by an ability to combine both an internal and external focus. Interestingly, the profile of high brand orientation companies is found in roughly the same frequency among business-to-business and business-to-consumer companies (50/50) and goods to services (57/43). This study reinforces the link between brand orientation and profitability suggested in the PMO value chain, by demonstrating the correlation between the two with the group of leaders in terms of orientation showing operating profits almost double the lowest brand orientation group: 'the most important outcome of this study is that we have been able to establish a clear link between brand orientation and profitability: the more brand-oriented a company is, the more profitable it is'. In spite of the BOI research, most operationalisations of marketing ideas are developed around products and external markets. Yet it should be clear that a focus on human capital and on enhancing brand delivery capacity is of vital importance in delivering customer value in both products and services.

In recognising the importance of human capital and internal market orientation, external market orientation must be kept in focus. It may be important to ensure that employees are truly engaged, but it must be remembered that the value of this engagement is in the delivery of value to customers. Therefore there needs to be a harmonic balance[5] between the internal/external orientations since they are dealing with two markets (employees and customers) that should be linked through a number of integration activities. Thus the marketing department should cooperate with the HR department in developing the brand, while it should also work at being finance orientated to improve understanding of the connection between investments in marketing activities and financial performance. Equally, responses to events, such as a change in competitor activity, a move in market share or new patterns of customer behaviour all require the organisation to work in an integrated way across internal boundaries. The ability to do this effectively requires a participatory market orientation (an outside–in, inside–out way of thinking). This is something that the organisational culture has to encourage and that leadership must demonstrate by its communications and actions – something the BOI study endorses with its (not surprising) discovery that in the most brand-oriented companies, the executive management group is very active in brand-related activity.

RECIPE FOR MOVING TO PMO

Market orientation suggests as its first principle that there is an organisation-wide responsibility to gather market intelligence.

We have already hinted in Chapter 1 that there are often problems in achieving this, especially if there is an over-reliance on
traditional marketing research. One of the challenges in conducting research is that the questions posed are never innocent and
the results must cope with organisational expectations. In con-
structing questions we must make assumptions. As Mary Douglas
writes (2004: 46),

> Uncomfortable facts which refuse to be fitted in, we find ourselves
> ignoring or distorting so that they do not disturb these established
> assumptions. By and large, anything we take note of is preselected
> and organized in the very act of perceiving.

Consequently, we tend to ask questions that fit in with an
established frame of reference (a zone of comfort) and seek
answers that integrate with the existing idea of the organisation.
The great temptation is to territorialise or to look for limited
de-territorialisation. Practising the art of living dangerously tends
to work against the desire for stability and homogeneity. To
overcome the research problem we have to question assumptions
and be willing to give up (for at least a while) the desire for the
concrete; to see that which our tendency to schematise hides
(Douglas 2004: 46).

In the course of the book we will develop this theme, but
the important action here is to use the principle of entrainment
to get genuinely close to customers, so that the interaction is
direct and unmediated. This is what Quiksilver do through their
free-flow connectivity and GrameenPhone achieve with their
grathak katha. These are markets of exchange, where organisations
seek to listen to and connect with customers. The challenge here
is not to organise the mechanisms of exchange but to approach
the customer with an open mind and a willingness to accept
ambiguity and uncertainty: 'any creative thinker who ventures
into new territory risks chaos and fragmentation' (Ehrenzweig
2000: 147). The implication is that not only does the manager
need to be willing to accept the possibility of chaos, they need

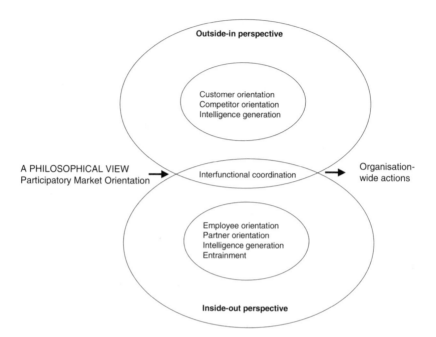

Figure 3.2   The merger between outside–in and inside–out

also to be confident they have the support of the organisation when it comes to action.

If the organisation has permeable boundaries, so that it can easily absorb knowledge, the next stage in participatory market orientation is the ability to connect people internally in developing a response. This requires a sense of organisational unity and a conducive communication climate. Referring to how organisations communicate internally, Van Riel (1999) writes that communications research 'stresses the importance of "soft" aspects in communication like openness, honesty and participation in decision-making, resulting in the necessity for managers to pay serious attention to communication climate, specifically their own role in improving the climate'. Making the climate effective will always be easier to achieve if there is a strong sense of unity built around the identification with and internalisation of the organisational vision and values and a connectivity with customers. If people have a common aim and a shared sense of accountability, it is easier to react to events. This is not to suggest that individuals simply operate on automatic based on the vision and values – rather it suggests that the implications of the vision and values are understood and help in decision-making both as a point of inspiration and as a guide to behaviour. In fact, the forward momentum in the process of discussion and debate needs to be contained within the vision and values themselves as this encourages the discovery of meaning through discourse. The vision and values should stimulates debate; the organisation needs the dirt that fuels creativity (Douglas 2004: 196).

This importance of a shared vision and values might suggest the denial of diversity. Yet we argue in favour of diversity provided there is a common understanding of the vision and values. An organisational acceptance of tension, a willingness to avoid too much control and an embracing of diversity creates the opportunity for innovation within the framework set by the vision and values: 'we are starting to think of heterogeneity as something valuable, not as an obstacle to unification' (De Landa 2003: 274). When there is a lack of connection with the vision and values or an attempt to force homogeneity, siloisation is more likely as people turn inwards to their own business unit agendas and away from the organisational whole. This fragmentation prevents the sharing of knowledge and inhibits the development of a unified approach to events. As Lou Gerstner observes

> one of the most surprising (and depressing) things I have learned about large organizations is the extent to which individual parts of an enterprise behave in an unsupportive and competitive way toward other parts of the organization. It is not isolated or aberrant behaviour. It exists everywhere. (Gerstner 2002: 249)

Although homogeneity may appear desirable it creates contradictions. If the organisation tries to prescribe employee behaviour in line with the vision and values, it is reducing the opportunity to discover the meaning of those same vision and values. It is trying to make static and unchanging, something that is inherently dynamic. It is far more productive to allow the meaning of the vision and values to emerge in response to events. This suggests that alongside the planned organisational systems, there has to be sufficient allowance for adaptive and emergent loops that can respond to events. We will come on to describe the human resources policies and organisational culture that facilitate the constraints and freedom of this approach, but we should note here that the element that separates the participatory approach is the idea of personal and direct engagement by managers and employees, who understand and are able to explore the framework of the brand. This approach runs counter to the management temptation to control. In that sense it is uncomfortable. It suggests an alternative of an ongoing dialogue with customers and with colleagues and relationships built on trust and openness.

As an example of these alternative management styles a study by Saxenian (1994) into the approaches of two regions – Route 128 around Boston and Silicon Valley – demonstrated the market orientation and adaptability of the latter region. Both regions developed as drivers of the IT industry in close connection with Massachusetts Institute of Technology and Stanford University respectively. And for a time both areas were highly successful, but following the recession of the early 1980s it was Silicon Valley that, now famously, regenerated itself and led the internet boom while Route 128 continued to stagnate. Saxenian's observation is that a decentralised system based on a network can draw on local knowledge and relationships. In Silicon Valley organisations may be highly competitive, but people are also willing to learn from each other. People know of each other, have often studied together and are networked through local groups, consequently, 'the boundaries within firms are porous, as are those between firms themselves and between firms and local institutions such as trade associations and universities'.

After the recession Silicon Valley as a region adapted to new circumstances, whereas the Route 128 region struggled to adapt. Saxenian argues that the reason was that new Silicon Valley start-ups adhered to the 'cooperation and collective innovation' which generated the region's success in the first place. The more open organisations of Northern California are closer to their customers and to each other. This regional entrainment can be compared to the closed boundaries of New England organisations where

> secrecy and corporate loyalty govern relations between firms and their customers, suppliers and competitors, reinforcing a regional culture of stability and self-reliance. Corporate hierarchies ensured that authority remains centralized and information flows vertically. The boundaries between and within firms and between firms and local institutions thus remain far more distinct.

CONCLUSION

The processes of marketing, market orientation and participatory market orientation all build on the traditional role of a free market in which most participants wish to optimise the process of exchange. In other words, parties involved in exchanges want to be as efficient and effective as possible: the organisation wants to acquire insight and deliver relevant products and services, and external audiences want to acquire resources and the accompanying rights of ownership or usage. In a market-oriented organisation the exchange is hindered potentially by several factors: (a) the ability to collect meaningful and usable insights; (b) the ability to share knowledge within the organisation; (c) the ability to unify organisational actions to deliver resources.

These challenges are not the result of a flawed concept, but more the lack of attention given to the operationalisation of the concept. This has been the motivation behind the development of the concept of participatory market orientation. This concept suggests a unity based on a closeness between employees and customers and between employees. It is only when employees are entrained with customers that they are able to acquire deep insight into behaviour and it is only when employees and managers are able and willing to work across organisational boundaries that value can be delivered consistently to the customer. Thus, the outside–in perspective is merged with the inside–out in that managers and leaders develop an appropriate balance between an internal and external orientation (Figure 3.3). This indicates the importance of such aspects as organisation culture and leadership

Figure 3.3 Steps in participatory market orientation – a circular process

that we will discuss in later chapters. It is only when the organisation is able to communicate effectively across boundaries that
closeness can be achieved. We believe that the more participatory
market orientation an organisation has, the more organisation-
wide listening, connecting, engaging, delivering and re-listening
will occur (Figure 3.3).

Such thinking is not far removed from Kohli and Jaworksi.
However, the whole process of market orientation can be more
or less participatory. The lower the involvement of customers in
the process, the more likely it is that the organisation will be
seller centric. The lower the involvement of employees the more
likely it is that the organisation will not meet expectations.
Therefore, the aim should be for high participation to become
entrained with customers and to delivering brand benefits, which
in turn leads to strengthened brand equity and financial value.

Finally, marketing is something other than a functional
department. This raises the issue of what marketing people should
do? The above idea of marketing suggests that many people in
the organisation are involved with the marketing process and
consequently with brand building. As an area of functionality,
people in marketing should be responsible for and focus on the
relationship with the customer: researching attitudes and behaviour, sharing knowledge internally, developing and executing
marketing communication plans (internal and external) and
stimulating collective thinking and actions. Within this range
of functions we would stress the need for genuine insight into
customers, the need to share knowledge internally and most
importantly, the ability to galvanise the organisation into action
to deliver the brand as a seamless entity.

NOTES

1. Promotion has largely been replaced by the term 'marketing communications' which encompasses advertising, sales promotion, graphic

design, PR and publicity, event marketing and sponsorship, and web/Internet.

2. The case demonstrates that while the metaphor seems to give a focus to innovation its power as an idea is sustained by its usage by media commentators.

3. Matsunoa, Mentzer and Rentz's extended market orientation model accommodates differences in the conceptualisations of Narver and Slater and Kohli and Jaworski by distinguishing market orientation as organisational culture (an antecedent) from market orientation as a set of behaviours (firm's conduct).

4. Brand Orientation Index: a research project on brand orientation and profitability in Sweden's 500 largest companies. Label AB in cooperation with Frans Melin, 2005.

5. This is what Macrae (2003) refers to as transparent trust flow mapping so that the creation of value for one stakeholder group does not destroy value for another (detecting win–lose conflicts and changing to win–win). Similarly Greenley, Hooley and Rudd (2005) question 'whether a market orientation approach focuses too heavily on customers at the expense of other stakeholders? Managers also need to address the interests of other stakeholders when making marketing decisions. This gives an orientation to each stakeholder group, which exist simultaneously, giving a multiple stakeholder orientation profile (MSOP).'

CHAPTER 4

PARTICIPATORY MARKETING

> *Mia*:   In conversation do you listen or wait to talk?
> *Vincent*: I have to admit that I wait to talk. (*Long pause*) But I'm
>   trying hard at this.
> Quentin Tarantino, *Pulp Fiction* (1994)[1]

The principle behind the idea of participatory marketing is a genuine ability to listen to customers and colleagues. Rather than first thinking about what we have to tell, either about ourselves or our brand, we should concentrate on openness and receptivity. This suggests that the first requirement is to orient the organisation towards the external market and the relevant stakeholder groups to identify needs and wants and to understand environmental forces. Then the organisation should use this external information to mobilise, organise and motivate people to deliver a united effort across departments to meet market demands and expectations. The step from phase one to phase two can be almost simultaneous but it requires the ability to listen properly, a positive communications culture and the systems to ensure knowledge is shared. When silos are strong, when the culture is unsupportive of communications, and/or when the knowledge sharing systems are weak, the process of internal engagement can be slow or flounder in a sea of politics. The ability to generate this participatory market orientation falls primarily on the marketing department and suggests that the same sort of energy and creativity expended on external engagement should also be used internally. Rather than relying simply on research data, the reality of customer lifestyles and behaviour should be brought to life through such techniques as observational video, lifestyle displays, informal meetings and participatory events.[2] The role of bringing the customer inside the organisation should be taken literally.

The final stage of delivering the product or service externally to the customer is an organisation-wide responsibility. Marketing can again take the lead here to unite the assemblage and to focus on the relevant methods of governance to ensure that the brand is delivered coherently. Senior and middle managers are vital to this process as they have the authority to lend weight to a participatory market orientation by becoming brand ambassadors themselves. The symbolic weight of leadership gives credibility to the concept and enables the key differentiating aspects of the PMO approach to be delivered. These can be defined as:

1. Traditional marketing thinking is typified by a uni-directional push; PMO argues instead for marketing that emphasises a two-way flow and constant interaction.
2. Customers are treated as an integral and active part of the marketing process, both as knowledge sharers and product developers; innovation is a shared process.
3. PMO argues for the active involvement of marketing people in sharing knowledge inside the organisation and the building of an organisation-wide response.

4. PMO suggests that internal systems need to be geared up to facilitate the effective sharing of knowledge.

5. In tandem with human resources, marketing should aim to build employee identification with the brand vision and values, thereby creating the basis for greater employee freedom and customer service enhancement.

6. PMO argues against the idea of finality. Constant movement typifies organisations and markets. Marketing strategies will always be emergent; unfolding as events change.

7. Marketing communications (the management of tangible brand elements) should focus on building genuine relationships with customers and thereby enhancing brand equity and the security of future cash flows.

8. PMO argues for the measurement of all key internal and external metrics and the active monitoring and usage of brand equity data through a narrative, interpretive approach.

9. PMO argues for a culture that is supportive of communications and that is open, transparent and authentic.

10. PMO is based on the principle of entrainment: the goal of achieving unity (but not uniformity) inside the organisation and between the organisation and the outside world.

Some of the above points are dealt with elsewhere in this book. This chapter will focus on: connecting and co-creating with customers; the role of marketing in building internal engagement; the integration of marketing activity and enhancing brand equity through the management of tangible brand elements.

CONNECTING AND CO-CREATING WITH CUSTOMERS

> *Lady Bracknell*: I have always been of the opinion that a man who desires to get married should know either everything or nothing. Which do you know?

> Jack (*after some*   I know nothing Lady Bracknell.
>   *hesitation*):
> Lady Bracknell: I am pleased to hear it. I do not approve of any-
>   thing that tampers with natural ignorance. Igno-
>   rance is like a delicate exotic fruit; touch it and
>   the bloom is gone.
>
> Oscar Wilde, The Importance of
Being Earnest, Act I

The idea of participatory market orientation relies on the ability to genuinely participate with customers, by reducing the distance between the organisation and the outside and to readjust the power balance. The scale of the organisation relative to the individual customer (except in areas of collective buying and powerful business to business clients) creates the tendency to believe in the myth that the organisation knows better than customers; that good ideas are best created internally and that customers can be manipulated into certain behaviours. This line of thinking provides security and comfort and maintains the status of organisational membership. It is clearly an arborescent state that does not encourage entrainment.

To become genuinely participative requires humility, a willingness to share power and to listen. As Oscar Soria, Communications Director of Greenpeace Argentina, argues, 'people outside the organisation have better ideas than we have'. As we saw in the cases of Quiksilver and GrameenPhone the ability to entrain with customers requires a more creative approach to connectivity. Soria believes that the formal processes are not enough if you want to share power and listen. You need informal environments where you can begin to create trust. He holds brainstorming sessions with communications professionals at home over dinner, idea generation meetings with university students in cafés and discussion groups that include tango dancing as a way of getting to know each other. Over one dinner session with teenagers at El Desnivel, the famous Buenos Aires steak restaurant, hundreds of ideas were generated, some of which were implemented including the development of a weekly television programme on the environment aimed at a youth audience. Soria adds that the idea generation process works when you are able to deliver on suggestions, which means that the organisation itself has to be receptive to outside views – something that Greenpeace in Argentina encourages by an integrated organisation based on a non-hierarchical, rhizomatic approach.

Pfeffer and Sutton (2006) endorse the importance of the value of ignorance, suggesting that too many organisations rely on received wisdom. Instead managers should look for patterns of change and experiment with ideas. They cite the case of the casino operator Harrah's, who in 1998 acquired a new Chief Operating Officer, Gary Loveman. Loveman was taking leave from his position as an associate professor at Harvard Business School and consequently knew little about casino operations. But he did have a professorial approach. He recognised that casinos produce lots of data that tends not to be analysed in a rigorous way. By using the data Loveman and his colleagues discovered that a lot of the myths about the way to run a casino were exactly that – myths. They challenged the accepted ways of doing things and conducted experiments to see if things could be done differently – they frequently could. They also demonstrated that it was worth investing in employee selection and retention. They discovered that: 'giving people realistic job previews, enhancing training, and bolstering the quality of front-line supervision, reduced turnover and produced more committed employees'.

This idea of the value of ignorance is also espoused at innovation consultancy, IDEO. Rather than assuming they know how to do things, they consciously seek stimulation from diverse areas. They look to employ individuals who have depth in their field, but also have breadth; people who are inquisitive about how different perspectives can create new solutions. They adopt a policy of co-creating with the buyers and users of products through 'unfocused' groups, involving outside people in idea creation and developing prototypes that can stimulate fresh insights. Lawer and Knox (2006: 121–9) see this form of engagement in terms of customer advocacy. They argue that there are four aspects to this: (a) building a brand advocacy network of partners with stake-holders; (b) co-creating a customer and partner brand commu-nity; (c) aligning brand values with empowered consumer value drivers; (d) focusing on customer transparency and trust. Citing such advocacy brands as Cisco, Harley-Davidson, Alaris, Progres-sive and E★TRADE, they suggest that brand managers 'must acknowledge the rising forces of consumer empowerment and then find new approaches to align the actions of the organisation with the needs of its customers' (2006: 127).

This line of thinking clearly chimes with the idea of entrain-ment and a participatory market orientation. Yet we would argue that PMO goes further in two core ways. While Lawer and Knox recognise partners and employees as co-creators, this element is underplayed. Secondly, achieving trust and transparency is not only an issue of management will, but is also culturally deter-mined. It is about whether organisational members have the confidence to accept that they may not have all the answers and are willing to challenge the conventional way of doing things by continuous experimentation; to de-territorialise the assemblage, so that the organisation is always developing and changing and reaching new levels of entrainment with its audiences.

BUILDING INTERNAL ENGAGEMENT

To create internal connectivity with the brand requires marketers to orient themselves towards employees as much as to customers. At a simple level this is concerned with the internal marketing of external communications: thinking about employees (and potential ones) as a primary audience of marketing communications. This helps to avoid the sort of problems that UK retailer, J Sainsbury encountered when using the comedian John Cleese in a television campaign in which he played his aggressive hotel owner character, Basil Fawlty. Part of the humour of this character is the way he berates his staff, especially his waiter, Manuel. In the Sainsbury campaign, Cleese would go round Sainsbury shops shouting at the staff – who acted as a proxy for Manuel. Not surprisingly the campaign played badly with employees and an internal rebellion led to the campaign being halted. It was also voted most irritating campaign of the year in a *Marketing* magazine poll. On a more positive footing, the rationale for the internal communication of external activity is to enable employees to reflect campaign messaging better through their behaviours and to enhance identification. As Dutton and Dukerich write (1991: 548), 'an organization's image matters greatly to its members because it represents members' best guesses as to what characteristics others are likely to ascribe to them because of their organizational affiliation'.

The potential for identification and then internalisation matters to individuals because it relates to their search for meaning in their working lives. For the organisation high levels of commitment are valuable because it helps to deliver greater productivity, as evidenced through the research studies mentioned in Chapter 2. In the move to a more rhizomatic way of thinking, high levels of control are not viable. The organisation has to accept the virtues of lower control in exchange for higher commitment. Pfeffer (1998) cites examples from semiconductors, oil refining, steel minimills, automotive, apparel production and consumer credit to demonstrate that commitment delivers economic benefits. To take just one of these case studies, an analysis of management approaches in steel minimills in the US characterised two styles: control and commitment. In the minimills with commitment management higher wages were paid, the workforce was more highly skilled, greater use was made of teams, decentralisation was encouraged and more training was undertaken. The result in terms of hours taken to produce a ton of steel and the scrap rate showed a 34% advantage over control management in productivity and a 63% advantage in scrap rate.

Yet it is not purely productivity that concerns us here. The requirement is to ensure that employee behaviours and processes align with customer needs and wants, and in turn that these help to deliver the overall organisational strategy. There is little value in building internal engagement with a brand idea that fails to connect with business strategy. One way to help achieve this alignment is by adapting the strategy maps of Kaplan and Norton (2000) to ensure that the linkage between internal activities, processes, customer strategies and overall business objectives is wired into the overall system. This delivers a balanced brand scorecard where for each key audience a set of objectives, strategies and measures are defined. This helps to ensure that actions designed to benefit shareholders, for example, do not undermine employees or customers, or that employee actions deliver value to customers and shareholders. To achieve this balance, organisations need to measure the relevant metrics and be adept at capturing and using information. Rather than adopting isolated measures of perfor-mance, it is important to inter-relate the metrics to see how the different elements in the assemblage, build brand equity.

Once we accept the benefits of organisationally aligned com-mitment, the marketing task inside the organisation has to focus on engagement. This cannot be achieved simply by exhorting people to live the brand. Rather managers and employees have to be willing participants. This suggests that the brand itself needs to be defined in a credible and appealing way. We have already suggested in earlier chapters the different ways of achieving a brand definition and the desirability of a highly participative approach as a way to achieving a balance between vision and reality, ethics and courage. Our focus here is to suggest how marketers can help achieve identification and alignment. The tendency in defining brands is to start with the brand articulation of the vision and values. Although this should be informed by external perceptions it should also clearly be about internal competencies. It is a requirement to have some tension in the values to encourage forward momentum, but too much aspiration will leave a discomforting gap between intention and reality.

When advertising is claiming a set of brand attributes, employees can be inspired by the claim to stretch themselves to meet the claim or they can feel inadequate if it is too far beyond current systems and competencies. From the customer viewpoint this will lead to a dissonance between perception and the reality of experience. This problem reinforces the need to avoid wishful thinking in brand definitions. A secondary aspect of the branding process is for marketers to define how the brand should seem to customers and other stakeholders – what Gad (2001) calls the 'brand mind-space' (Figure 4.1). This is the bundle of functional

FUNCTIONAL DIMENSION
Software, services and knowledge for automation and management of business processes. Flexible combination of software and services for small to large customers.

SOCIAL DIMENSION
Best at taking care of and developing customers. Supporting a knowledge based community of business managers interested in integrated business processes. Nordic & local.

BRAND MIND SPACE

MENTAL DIMENSION
Creating a new role for the business manager as an efficiency manager responsible for integrated business processes.

SPIRITUAL DIMENSION
Promoting Nordic competitiveness and growth by automation and integration of business processes.

Figure 4.1 Brand mind-space of Nordic software services company, Visma. (Reproduced with permission of Visma and with thanks to Thomas Gad.)

and emotional perceptions of the brand that exist in the mind of the customer – the perception of how the brand fits into a frame of alternative choices. In defining the brand mind-space, marketers determine how they would like the brand to be positioned in the minds of customers. Of course the reality may be different. There is no certainty that a desired positioning is matched by reality, especially if the competencies are lacking.

Our recommendation is to work backwards from the brand mind-space and to ensure that the linkages between the elements make sense. In other words, by using customer understanding (the stronger the degree of entrainment the more likely this is to contain genuine insight) a brand mind-space can be defined that positions an organisation as clearly distinct from competitors in a relevant way. We can then work backwards to think through the tangible brand elements that can create this perception to the more internally oriented brand definition that is more clearly linked to the organisational competencies. The process should then be gone through again from the brand definition to the brand mind-space to check the logic of the flow and to ensure that there are clear linkages between the different parts of the process. This two-way process helps to avoid the sort of situation where a brand value is not reflected in the desired brand mind-space or where the management of tangible brand elements such as advertising, packaging and point of sale loses its link to the brand definition and/or brand mind-space.

When the linkages in the brand process are strong, the potential for employee identification is heightened both because the external image seems achievable to people and because the brand

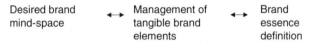

Desired brand   Management of   Brand
mind-space   tangible brand   essence
elements   definition

Figure 4.2   From brand mind-space to internal competencies (and back again)

definition is a true reflection of the current and potential competencies. Consequently employees are more likely to engage
with the values and to discover for themselves how they can
be used in their day-to-day work. The argument here is that
you cannot tell people to believe in something. The way to
achieve internal connectivity relies on developing a positive
organisational culture and the creation of the mechanisms such
as brand champions, education programmes, workshops, online
brand centres and brand guides.

INTEGRATED MARKETING

> There is only one thing in the world worse than being talked
> about, and that is not being talked about.
>
> Oscar Wilde, *The Picture of Dorian Gray*

To achieve a participatory market orientation requires an integrated approach to marketing. If the organisation is to deliver on
its desired brand mind-space it needs to be a consistent commu-
nicator. If messages are contradictory or the actions of individuals
do not marry with marketing communications the mind-space
of a customer is likely to be confused. It is never possible to be
absolutely consistent, but the more consistent the brand is, the
more likely clarity can be achieved. For a long time, integration
was talked about simply in terms of integrated communications,
such that advertising, direct marketing, public relations and design
should be cohesive (Hutton 1996), but as soon as we recognise
the impact of employees, partners and intermediaries on the
brand mind-space we have to recognise that integration is about
all the elements of the assemblage coming together to enhance
brand equity (Ind 1998: 323–9).

   This approach recognises that there are a multitude of potential brand contacts for both product and service brands where

brand representatives and customers connect. These brand meeting points need to be managed as effectively as possible if the organisation is to optimalise the contribution to increased brand equity at every brand meeting point. The challenge for companies is to identify these brand contact points, to focus on enhancing brand experience and to continuously measure brand performance at these points.

Using Keller's (2001) definition of marketer-controlled communication, we can see that marketing communications can be responsible for multiple brand contacts through brand meeting points such as (1) media advertising; (2) direct response and interactive advertising; (3) place advertising; (4) point-of-purchase-advertising; (5) trade promotion; (6) consumer promotion; (7) event marketing and sponsorship; (8) publicity and public relations; and (9) personal selling. All these communication elements, representing potential brand meeting points, are part of external communication and should contribute to brand equity, e.g. experience, perceived brand quality, brand image associations. Aligning them around the brand – using the brand definition as a point of inspiration and accountability – is the task of marketing.

Yet there are obvious flaws in this line of thinking. First, this view of marketing supports the myth of control. If the customer is an active participant in the brand, helping to develop it, providing feedback, and discussing it with friends and colleagues, then the organisation cannot control the brand. Indeed if we think about all the possible brand contact points, we come to recognise how little control over the brand the organisation really has.

Secondly, this approach to marketing communications sees it as primarily unidirectional with the organisation telling customers about features and benefits. Increasingly however, communications are interactive. Blogs, wikis and personal websites are multi-directional forms of communication that extend beyond organisational boundaries: 'with participatory media, the boundaries between audiences and creators becomes blurred and often invisible' (Kluth 2006: 4). These forms of exchange combine personal media experience with a social context, such that media is no longer the preserve of traditional media owners but an opportunity for everyone to share ideas and experiences.

Baya and du Pre Gauntt in their report on *The Rise of Lifestyle Media* argue that media market places will compete in their knowledge of consumers which they will use to interact more intimately with consumers and to better match advertising (Kluth 2006: 14). This process diminishes the weight of organisationally 'controlled' brand meeting points and instead emphasises customer to customer and networked communications. While organisations sometimes try to manipulate these meeting points and draw them back into their sphere of control, the scale of participation makes this an almost impossible task. An example of this was PR agency, Edelman and its attempt to create a blog for its client Wal-Mart about a couple travelling around the USA and sharing their experiences. A lack of transparency and an attempt to use methods of control that used to work led to much negative comment. Scott (2006) writes:

> Edelman wanted to make consumers think that Wal-Mart is a hip place that you'd want to use as the anchor point for a roadtrip. The problem is it's not. And because blogging is not a control-based medium, Edelman couldn't make Wal-Mart appear to be something it's not. It rang false, and they got caught.

The inference for brand thinking ought not to be how can we control participatory media, but rather how can we be authentic in our brand delivery, so that the conversations and dialogue about our brand are positive rather than negative. Inevitably managerial attempts to shape brand meaning merge together with input from critics, consumers, competitors, and others in the process of authentication (Brown et al. 2003, Muniz and O'Guinn 2005, Peterson 2005, Beverland 2006). Thirdly, as is clear from the range of brand meeting points, many of the key influencers on brand image, such as customer care employees, intermediaries and service and product quality lie outside the range of marketing communications.

This changing relationship between the organisation and its customers can either be ignored by managers or embraced. If it is embraced it has significant implications for the operationalisation of the brand. Clarity of brand image still remains desirable, but managers have to live with the fact that most of the brand meeting points are outside their control. What becomes of their role then? Our view is that authenticity and transparency have to become the guiding lights of marketing thinking. Rather than falling into the rhetorical desire to persuade customers of the benefits of a brand, marketers should be much more engaged with ensuring that the brand fills a real market need or want and that the quality of delivery in terms of product and service exceeds that of competitors and the expectations of customers. When this is effective customers can become advocates for the brand and the brand can be built in a genuine, largely unmediated, word-of-mouth way – witness Patagonia, Amazon, Wikipedia and Pret a Manger.

Without this sense of authenticity, the likelihood is greater that the buzz around the brand will be negative. People might be positive about the entertainment of the marketing communications but they are less likely to believe in brand itself. While everything should be focused on delivering value to the customer, this approach indicates that marketing must first pay attention to helping ensure that the organisation can deliver on its intended promises. This will of course be an ever-changing situation. Authenticity is not granted to a brand once and for all. Instead, we have to recognise that authenticity is always moving (Peterson 2005: 1094).

ENHANCING BRAND EQUITY

Before we can look at the nature of brand equity within the context of the assemblage model, we have to reach a workable definition of what it means. Brand equity and what we refer to as brand elements are much discussed in marketing literature. Kapferer's (1997) brand identity model suggests components or dimensions (brand elements) such as physique (a product's objective and tangible basis), personality (the character), culture ('set of values feeding the brand's inspiration'), relationship (love and friend), reflection ('the customer should be reflected as she/he wishes to be seen as a result of using the brand'), and self-image (one's own internal mirror stimulating an inner relationship with ourselves). Aaker and Joachimsthaler (2000) distinguish between product elements (scope, attributes, uses, quality/value, functional benefits) and brand elements (brand personality, symbols, brand/customer relationship, self-expressive benefits, emotional benefits, user imagery, country of origin and organisational associations).

These models represent just two of several ways to describe and enhance the understanding of the brand and its constituting elements. De Chernatony and Dall'Olmo Riley (1998a) presented an overview of various authors' opinions on what constitutes a brand. We have added a few authors' recent work to update the different views on what constitutes a brand. The elements could be of a concrete, physical character (tangible) or of a more abstract/immaterial (intangible) nature according to the authors. From Keller's (2005) point of view the intangible elements do not constitute brand elements as he believes a brand element is 'trademarkable' visual or verbal information that identifies and differentiates a product or service. He suggests that the most common ones are: names, logos, symbols, characters, slogans, and packaging, and that there are six criteria for choosing brand elements (memorability, meaningfulness, likeability, transferability, adaptability and ability to be protected).

However, these static models explain little about the roles of brand elements in building the brand as a dynamic process. The only model in the overview (Table 4.1) that aligns with our assemblage thinking is the 'Double Vortex Model' (de Chernatony and Dall'Olmo Riley (1998a) (see Figure 4.3). The starting point of the development of this vortex model was the 'atomic model' consisting of nine elements depicted as layers around the functional or core brand (de Chernatony 1993). However, based on research among British brand experts, new elements were added and the brand perspective was changed to inside out. In particular, it underscored the importance of the brand's vision, mission, organisational culture and values next to heritage and stakeholder value. This model implies that most of the value creation of the brand takes place inside the

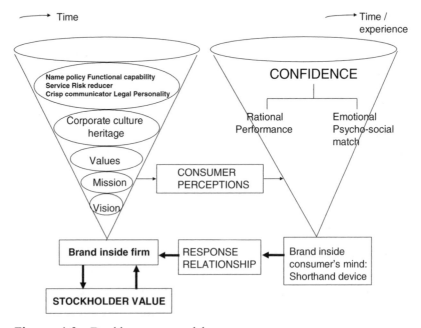

Figure 4.3 Double vortex model
Source: de Chernatony L, Dall'Olmo Riley F (1998a) Defining a 'brand': beyond the literature with experts' interpretations. *Journal of Marketing Management* 14: 417–43. Reproduced by permission of Emerald Group Publishing Ltd.

Table 4.1 An overview of brand elements by author

Authors	Tangible elements	Intangible elements
Keller (2005)	Names, Web URLs, logos, symbols, characters, slogans, jingles, packaging	Signage
de Chernatony and Dall'Olmo Riley (1998[a]) (the double vortex model)	Functional capability, naming policy, service	Risk reducer, crisp communicator, legal protection, personality, corporate culture, heritage, values, mission, vision, confidence
Dyson et al. (1996) (Millward-Brown)	Presence and performance	Relevance, advantage, bond
Bailey and Schechter (1994)	Name, logo, colours, brand-mark, plus advertising slogan	
Young and Rubicam (1994)	Differentiation	Relevance, esteem and familiarity
Grossman (1994)	Distinctive name, logotype, graphics and physical design	User identification; opportunity to share a dream
DMB & B (1993)	Product delivery	Symbolic value, service, sign of ownership, shorthand notation
de Chernatony (1993a and 1993b) (atomic model)	Functional capabilities, name, legal protection	Positioning, brand communications
Aaker (1992)	Symbols and slogans	Identity, corporate brand, integrated communications, customer relationships
Kapferer (1992)	Physique	Personality, relationship, culture, reflection, self-image
O'Malley (1991)	Functional values	Social and personal values

Source: Adapted/updated, based on de Chernatony and Dall'Olmo Riley (1998a).

organisation and that customer perceptions determine the fate of the brand.

The fundamental role of brand elements is to contribute to the formation and development of consumer confidence and trust. Yet, as observed earlier, brand elements by themselves do not create the condition of trust. If the story the brand elements convey is coherent, we are more likely to be receptive. We may then be willing to trust, but trust itself comes into being through experience (Williams 2005: 88). Incoherence and inconsistency seem to suggest the opposite – we might ask how can we trust this brand when it says it is one thing one minute and something else the next? When a person or a brand flits around we start to think that what they say is superficial, for how can there be authenticity without continuity? In this instance the idea of the brand as a promise becomes undermined for we can never know whether the promise will me met. For this reason we differentiate between brand elements and the driving forces inside the organisation that deliver the product and service and the combination of these two dimensions in the marketplace.

Thus vision, mission, values and cultural heritage should not be seen as brand elements. These should be categorised as driving forces from inside (defined by and defining the organisational culture) that guide the strategic directions of the brand. On the other hand, brand personality, defined by Kapferer (1992) as an intangible brand element, should be categorised neither as a driving force nor as a brand element, but rather as an important element of brand equity – the summarised image or a way to describe the image. Brand personality is a consequence of communications representing/containing types of associations.

To understand the role brand elements play in the brand-building process and where they are placed in a strategic brand-building process view, we need to define the overall organisational objective:

- *The overall objective for the brand owner is, through branding strategies and investments in brand building activities (inside the organisation and in the market place) and in brand elements, to strengthen the organisation's brand building capability, including innovation power to enhance brand equity, which will in turn enhance financial performance and brand value.*

The rationale behind this definition is that it indicates the linkage of everything inside the organisational assemblage together to deliver something of value to customers. It suggests that brand elements are only the concrete/tangible elements (e.g. functionality, service, names, Web URLs, logos, symbols, characters, slogans, jingles, packaging). All the other entities in the category of abstracts/intangibles contain a mix of terms and constructs that can either can be categorised as organisational elements, such as vision, mission, values, organisational culture, differentiation, positioning and HR drivers or as consequences of investments in brand elements and driving forces such as perceived personality, user identification, symbolic value, relationship/bond and perceived advantage/benefits. To facilitate understanding of the connections between these terms and the brand-building process, Figure 4.4 below depicts a dynamic framework that indicates the process of brand-building.

BRAND EQUITY AND FINANCIAL BRAND VALUE

The next stage in the brand-building process is to understand how the combination of organisation-wide forces and tangible brand elements delivers brand equity and financial value. For this we need to re-define what constitutes a successful brand and a brand supportive organisation:

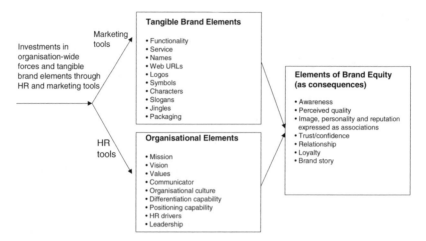

Figure 4.4 Building brand equity through investments in organisation-wide forces and tangible brand elements

- *A successful brand is a well-known representation of a person, product, service or organisation, identified by a logo, name, symbol, or other text described by target audiences and users in terms of favourable associations, which has been developed as a phenomenon by media, word-of-mouth, people constellations, and a brand-supportive organisation.*

- *A brand-supportive organisation is one that focuses on living out the business idea, vision, mission (brand purpose) and values by assembling, connecting and co-ordinating all brand driving forces to enhance and sustain the brand-building capability and brand equity.*

The financial aspects of brands are discussed by several writers such as Aaker (1991, 1996), Kapferer (1997), de Chernatony (1998), and Keller (2003), who differentiate between brand value, which has to do with the financial value of the brand, and brand equity which is about non-financial value based on consumers' perceptions (degree of awareness, liking, associations, preference, loyalty). These variables, which indicate the equity of the brand, can be referred to as intermediate variables and can be tracked on a continuous basis. Writers also use the term 'the health of the brand' when they discuss brand equity and intermediate variables, which indicates the relative strength and position of the brand compared with particular competitive brands. The measurement of the intermediate variables is part of the process of evaluation (see Chapter 8) as it correlates the relationship between investments in the driving forces and brand elements and the output in terms of brand equity and financial results.

It seems clear that Aaker (1996) and Keller (2003) have an external orientation to the brand- building process. They see the way to increase brand equity as investments in marketing efforts rather than in people. In contrast, de Chernatony and McDonald (1998) see equity as broader by including organisational dimensions as input variables in the brand building process. De Chernatony and McDonald (1998) describe brand equity as 'the differential attributes underpinning a brand which give increased value to the firm's balance sheet'. Their reasoning is more nuanced as the variables and links are easier to utilise for a whole range of organisations because the brand elements constituting brand equity vary in strength and importance and depend on brand elements. Figure 4.5 shows how we see brand equity in a market-orientated perspective. Increased financial brand value, a competitive edge and differentiation (which requires a clear market position) are developed through a market orientated organisation investing in HR and marketing strategies to strengthen brand elements and brand equity.

To assess an organisation's brand equity, each element and the relations between them should be evaluated and measured continuously and related to investment levels. However, the measurement activities will be more complex and extensive because of the outside–in/inside–out perspective of the organisation-wide branding philosophy. To understand the linkages between cause and effect, all key variables both inside and outside the

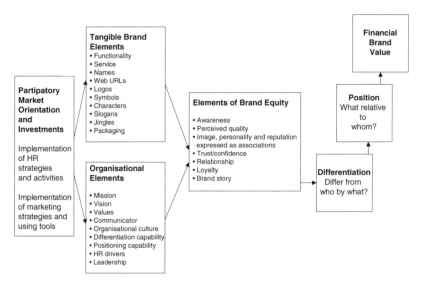

Figure 4.5 Developing financial brand value and brand equity through PMO

organisation should be measured (see Chapter 8) and movements in brand equity channelled back to the organisation to help build brand equity.

When it comes to linking brand equity to financial brand value, we can see there are clear linkages and that the same key parameters apply. Financial brand value is concerned primarily with the security of future cash flows. To measure brand value we need to understand three elements: (a) the anticipated cash flows into the organisation; (b) the contribution of the brand; (c) the risks to the brand. Future cash flows are based on projections into the future based on past experience and an understanding of the likely competitive situation going forward. The contribution of the brand is determined by an analysis of the demand drivers, which can be brand related such as customer service delivery, quality perceptions and product appearance or non-brand related such as location, logistical efficiency and price (although some of these non-brand elements can sometimes be brand elements depending on the brand). Finally, through competitive benchmarking of key measures, such as awareness, time in market, influence, customer share and loyalty, the risks to the future of the brand can be assessed. The important point to note in this process of evaluation is that the value of the brand is often determined not by the tangible brand elements which deliver primarily in terms of awareness and consideration, but rather experiential factors that derive more from organisation-wide forces (Figure 4.6).

It is the usage of the product, the interaction with organisational representatives and after sales service that encourage a bond between the customers and the organisation, which again indicates the importance and value of a highly participatory, entrained approach to brand building that brings the organisation and its customers close together. This participative approach is the real driver of potential loyalty and the determinant of the security of future cash flows.

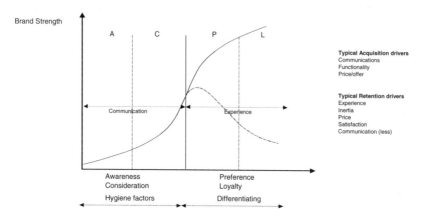

Figure 4.6 Brand strength model. (Previously published in Ind N (2003) Living the Brand: How To Transform Every Member of Your Organization into a Brand Champion (revised edition; first published 2001). London: Kogan Page. Copyright N. Ind.)

CONCLUSION

We believe that the only way of developing and governing brands is through a more inside–out perspective. The core challenge here is to focus on human resources to a much greater degree than previously. This suggests the importance of a specific management approach and leadership qualities and skills. The traditional way to think about brand building has been to emphasise the primacy of marketing communications as a rhetorical means of persuading customers about the efficiency and superiority of a product or service. This might have had greater credence in an era when organisations controlled to a more extensive degree the means of communication, when mass media was genuinely mass and when products were more dominant in industrial societies. But now, when services dominate both in their own right and in providing differentiation to products, media is highly fragmented and the control of communication has slipped away from organisations, a new way of thinking has to emerge that is more dynamic and people centred. It is the delivery of the product or service itself and the experience of ownership that matters most to brand equity and financial brand value. The implication of this is that if organisations want to cement relationships with customers and other stakeholder and build the value of their brands, investments generally should be reallocated from marketing communications spends to investments in leadership, talent and organisational culture – the antecedents of outstanding products and services.

NOTES

1. This scene between Mia (Uma Thurman) and Vincent (John Travolta) featured Mia making a video of Vincent. Tarantino cut the scene from the film because he felt the home movie idea was becoming clichéd.

2. Examples of these techniques include Doblin Group's use of video to record customer behaviour for such clients as McDonalds and SAS, the use of lifestyle displays by Volvo in formulating briefs and the German advertising agency Jung von Matt in creating the archetypal German living room in its offices, informal contexts as espoused by Greenpeace Argentina and high participation processes as used by innovation consultancy, IDEO.

CHAPTER 5

HUMAN RESOURCES

*B*randing is about people. It is about people in the sense
that in its combination of functional and emotional benefits,
branding creates something of value for those that use or consume
the brand. Branding may tend to abstract user groups and create
target segments, but behind these numbers and categorisations
are individuals with distinct preferences and behaviours. Equally
people inside the organisation, through their assumptions, communications and actions determine service delivery, product
innovation, communications and customer relationships. People
do not have to have face-to-face interactions with customers
to be representatives of the brand. Nor does brand building
simply apply to obvious business-to-consumer areas such as retail,
hotels and airlines. Every individual in every organisation is a
brand representative through the relationships they build with
other individuals in the organisation, the work they do that contributes to organisational culture and performance, the ideas they

generate and the communications they have with people outside the organisation.

A research chemist working on a cure for an illness must make decisions that involve colleagues and must make assumptions about the lives of potential patients; a financial administrator can help cement positive relationships with clients through accurate, clear and timely delivery of invoices and statements and can support the activities of colleagues through usable information; an A&R talent scout determines the quality of material that a record label produces and helps to build relationships with artists and buyers. Although an organisational structure may encourage fragmentation and introversion, the reality is that every individual has multiple connections with colleagues that give meaning to the very purpose of communication and directly or indirectly contribute towards the brand. Indeed, if we accept John Dunbar's view that each individual has the ability to make 150 relationships (Dunbar 1992), there is a huge potential for connectivity both inside and outside the organisation.

The implication of all this connectivity is that human resources management – the acquisition, retention, reward and development of people – is fundamental to the idea of brand building.

THE ROLE OF PEOPLE IN THE ORGANISATION

> The way we lead or manage, and the way we construct our institutions, depends on our theory of what it means to be human. (Koestenbaum and Block 2001: 100)

The traditional way of seeing people within the organisation was as machinic inputs; as a box on a chart that represented the power of collective bodies. This dehumanising perspective stressed the distance between managers and those over whom power was wielded and denied the independence of being of individuals.

The power relationship between manager and managed was also expressed by the use of working space as a sort of panopticon,[1] whereby the managed could be observed and controlled and performance corrected. The viewpoint signalled a fear of freedom and the anxiety of how freedom might be used, based on a strong sense of otherness predicated on the mistaken assumption among managers that employees are motivated by different factors to themselves. This belief in others as different encourages fragmentation and negative conflict and discourages participation. People become largely disconnected in an arborescent, bureaucratic structure that only stimulates connectivity based on physical and hierarchical proximity. Not surprisingly, it diminishes the opportunity for creativity by reducing information flows, imposing behavioural constraints and encouraging silo thinking.

As an example of the misunderstanding of extrinsic and intrinsic rewards and the power of participation, Chan Kim and Mauborgne (2003a) show that managers ignore these factors at their peril: their study compares the management of a VW plant with Siemens-Nixdorf. In the case of VW, the management of a plant in Puebla, Mexico offered a new labour agreement to its employees that provided a 20% pay rise. Although the sum was generous it led to a walkout and a prolonged industrial dispute. The offer itself was more than fair, but the lack of discussion and participation led to mistrust and disappointment.

Siemens-Nixdorf was the company formed as a result of the acquisition of Nixdorf by Siemens. From the beginning the company had problems and for four years it cut staff, failed to find a new corporate direction and lost money, accumulating losses of two billion DM. Not surprisingly morale was low. Then in 1994 a new CEO arrived. He decided to engage everyone in the company in a new turnaround programme. He provided people with an honest review of the business, stated clearly how

decisions in future would be made and then asked for employees
to come up with ideas to help transform the company. After three
months, 405 people had contributed their opinions and ideas.
Eventually 9000 people made suggestions. To ensure that good
ideas led to action, the suggestions were then auctioned to execu-
tives who took responsibility for implementation. Inevitably some
ideas were rejected, but importantly the process was seen as fair.
By 1995 employee satisfaction had nearly doubled and the
company was in the black.

We may judge that there are still plenty of non-participative,
arborescent organisations around, but increasingly there are
more rhizome-based structures where the attitude to people
is different and there is a greater recognition of the benefits
of participation. The transition has been driven largely by
the increased importance of intangibility to organisational value
to the extent that on average 78% of a company's value is
in intangible assets.[2] Inevitably the intangible stresses, not the
physical capital of the organisation, but the intellectual capital
which

> recognizes what counts in the modern economy of fast-moving,
> knowledge-intensive virtual corporations:
>
> - strong and enduring business relationships within networked
>   partnerships
> - the enduring loyalty of customers
> - the role of key employees, upon whose knowledge and com-
>   petencies the company's future rests
> - the commitment of the company and its employees to learn
>   and renew over time
> - and most of all, the *character* and *values* of a company, a crucial
>   tool for investors and executives when looking at mergers,
>   acquisitions, alliances, personnel hiring, and partnering.
>   (Edvinsson and Malone 1997: 19–20)

When it is clear that it is people's intellect that determines value, it is not viable to see an individual's role as purely machinic. Rather if the role of the individual is to contribute to the development of the overall culture, to build relationships, to work as part of a team and to bring their intellectual capability to solve problems and implement strategies, then the nature of the contract with the organisation is different. The psychological contract between the organisation and the employee binds 'the parties to some set of reciprocal obligations' (Rousseau 1990: 123) whereby in exchange for both intrinsic and extrinsic rewards the employee gives up some freedom, while the organisation for its part contracts to use the employee's abilities and knowledge for its own ends. It is partly for this reason that in most organisations the proprietary rights on original ideas pass from the individual to the employing organisation. Although there is often a written contract between the parties as well, the most important element here is the implicit contract based on trust. From the organisational side the expectation is that the employee will both fulfil the functional requirements of the job task and identify with the organisational purpose and values. The employee in turn, expects the organisation to deliver on its explicit terms and provide support in achieving fulfilment, which research shows is an important antecedent of affective commitment and job performance (Sturges et al. 2005).

Stated in the above terms the psychological contract might sound legalistic and arborescent, but there are a number of factors that make the rhizomatic version different. First, as we saw in Chapter 2, Frederik Herzberg demonstrated that satisfaction at work is largely intrinsic and resides in the ability to experience psychological growth through achievement, recognition, the work itself, responsibility and growth or advancement. Organisations that recognise this point work to create cultures and contracts that support the individual's desire for the fulfilment of their needs.

Secondly, while there is some reduction in freedom because of the requirements of organisational membership, a rhizomatic organisation only constrains freedom to the extent of setting boundaries within which freedom exists. This suggests that there is significant negative freedom, which can be defined as the degree to which individuals are free *from* man-made barriers. Equally in a rhizomatic organisation there can also be more positive freedom, which is concerned with the degree to which individuals are free *to* determine how they work and their ability to self-organise (Berlin 2005: 166–217). Some boundaries to negative freedom are necessary if there is to be focus to action in support of organisational goals, but they should not be so constraining as to inhibit creativity or reduce speed of action.[3] Indeed, the setting of boundaries should be a creative act in itself.

Thirdly, while the organisation uses the skills and knowledge of the individual for its own ends, we expect people to join organisations where there is the potential for alignment between individual and organisational values. As Steve Jobs observes, 'the only thing that works is management by values. Find people who are competent and really bright, but more importantly people who care exactly about the same things you care about'.

Lastly, the structures of rhizomatic organisations are non-bureaucratic and tend towards the networks or communities described in Morgan (1997), Fukuyama (2000) and Handy (2001), where social capital,[4] citizen behaviour and linked but loose networks facilitate constructive relationships and the ideals of positive freedom. For example in Morgan's 'spider plant' model the centre does not act as a control mechanism but rather nurtures often self-organising, autonomous teams that can respond dynamically to opportunities and challenges. In Deleuzian terms this approach tends towards nomadology (Deleuze and Guattari 1980) where groups form not because they are imposed by a hierarchy, but because they are responding to change, immanently. The conceptual space that groups occupy is not pre-determined but is a result of sense-making and the movement of the group in response to inputs. This approach helps ensure that changes in the internal or external environment are sensed quickly and that reactions are fast and creative.

A nomadological approach also suggests that creative acts are less likely to be 'royal' (from senior figures in the organisation) and more likely to be nomadic[5] (from within the organisation), (Deleuze and Guattari 1980: 405–6). This may seem to be idealistic, for as Philip Herbst (1976) argues alternative hierarchies are still hierarchies and Dirk Baecker (2003: 188) claims: 'since organizations have existed, management can claim to have made use of the autonomy of the part and the domination or hegemony of the whole'. Yet we are not arguing here against structure as such, nor the need of management to set boundaries, but rather for the benefits of participation and connectivity in the organisational culture – something that can benefit the organisation and the individual. This does not deny the potential for manipulation. Managers can use identification as a means to deny freedom and to try and mould behaviour. But they can also accept freedom and what it confers in terms of individual creativity. This suggests the importance of participative thinking that encourages rather than suppresses fluidity and freedom of action.

We might conclude that people (or talent) in modern organisations contribute more than pure productive power. Rather it is their ability to add value to customers and other stakeholders and contribute towards the intellectual capital of the organisation that matters. An interesting example of this is the Apple Genius Bar. In Apple retail outlets there is a section of the store where customers can go and get free advice from 'geniuses' on getting the most out of their hardware and software and technical support for their Macs or iPods. This creates an excellent opportunity for Apple to build strong relationships between the organisation and its customers. It also generates huge amounts of employee pride.

Geniuses are specially trained at Apple's head office in Cupertino, California and wear special and highly sought after t-shirts. To be known as a genius creates a powerful status, but also one that has to be lived up to.

THE RIGHT PEOPLE

Enhancing intellectual capital implies a need to attract the most appropriate individuals to the organisation. This sounds simple but if we question the meaning of 'attract' and 'appropriate' then the thought becomes more complex. To attract people to an organisation suggests that it must have an appealing profile. For that to occur there has to be a consistent and public expression of what the organisation believes in and how it operates. This has generated a concept that is popular in human resource circles: the employer brand (Ambler and Barrow 1996). The idea behind the employer brand is that the organisation should take an active role in promoting its image as a desirable employer. As a principle we concur with the idea, but we also have some reservations. In corporate branding theory, organisations seek to determine a unifying idea of their brand that can act as a template for decision-making and communications. It recognises that although the tone and content of messages to different audiences may vary depending on need, that there is always accountability back to the overall brand.

Part of the rationale for this way of thinking is that it is impossible to pigeon-hole audiences or ring-fence communications. Investors will see consumer advertising and potential employees can also be suppliers. If messages lack cohesion there is the potential for disunity and confusion. For this reason we would argue that from the organisational perspective the brand is the brand and that the creation of a separate entity (whether it is a media brand, an investor brand or an employer brand) can confuse both internal and external audiences. There is also an implicit danger in the active (or over-active) promotion of the organisation as an employer: its ability to match word and deed. Research studies suggest employees try to select organisations based on the perceptions of fit between individual and organisational values (Chatman 1989, 1991). The ability to do this depends on the transparency of the organisation's values (are they explicit, well-communicated and true to reality?) and authentic (are they genuine?). If the promotion of the employer brand makes claims that do not meet these requirements, then the likelihood of fit is reduced.

This also indicates the importance of transparency and authenticity in approaches to corporate social responsibility (CSR). Turban and Greening (1996) point out that companies with high corporate social performance ratings have more positive reputations and are more attractive as potential employers than firms with lower ratings. This is partly an issue of communication but it is more about the commitment to and delivery of socially responsible action. When CSR is integrated into the brand value system such elements as diversity, environmentalism and social engagement become part of the fabric of decision-making. Equally when companies fail to act in a socially responsible way there is an impact on current and potential employees, because of the dangers of association.

When Nike was being lambasted in the media for its labour policies in Asia, the impact on employees was profound. Nike's chief storyteller, Nelson Farris, says that Nike employees were appalled to discover that instead of working for the Robin Hood of corporate America, they were working for the Sheriff of Nottingham: 'employees were embarrassed and disenchanted and confused' (Ind 2001: 148).

'Appropriate' individuals are those that match the functional requirements of a job, but also have the potential for identification with the organisation's values – that is, their self-concept 'fits' in some way with the nature of the organisation. This may often be an intuitive decision on the part of the individual and the organisation. The individual must possess sufficient self-knowledge to recognise and understand the nature of their own values and have sufficient information to judge the implications of the organisational values. Equally, while the organisation can undertake personality and psychometric testing, those people responsible for recruitment will still have to make a judgement as to the likelihood of a match (always assuming that they know and understand the organisation's values themselves).

While the techniques for determining fit have become more sophisticated the ability both to define and judge fit represents a challenge (O'Reilly, Chatman and Caldwell 1991). This again stresses the importance of having a clearly defined set of values that can be used to steer the tone and language of communications and the methods of recruitment to generate interest from high potential fit candidates. When the fit between the organisation and individual is good then the outcomes tend to long-term and positive (Boxx, Odom and Dunn 1991; Chatman 1991).

However, the lack of distinctiveness in communication approaches and the challenge of matching based on values leads to a tendency to default to recruiting against functional requirements. It's easier to recruit someone based on a specification that they have a degree, five years' experience and have had managerial responsibility than trying to establish whether they are creative, empathetic, good at working in teams and self-motivated. This hints at the importance of emotional intelligence (EI) as a key requirement of people in business life.

This area has become mainstream in business since the publication of Daniel Goleman's book *Emotional Intelligence* (1995).

Goleman and others (Mayer and Salovey 1997, Bar-On 2000) argue that a person's emotional intelligence and cognitive intelligence are interwoven rather than independent. In a business context this is important, because if an organisation assesses individuals solely on their cognitive intelligence, it will ignore attributes that are important to effective performance, especially in the area of communication skills that contribute to the effectiveness of the assemblage model. When it comes to overseeing participative processes, the ability to recognise emotions in oneself and in others, and to manage those emotions so that growth and learning are stimulated, is vital.

The implication of this is that people should be recruited who have the emotional intelligence to work with people of diverse backgrounds, to communicate effectively and to make the most of their knowledge. These are the people who have the ability to challenge internal silos and to build good bonds with customers. Testing procedures designed to uncover emotional intelligence have been developed, but we might also be wary of this. Some have criticised the concept of emotional intelligence, arguing that it is just another form of management coercion. This view is substantiated by the focus of much emotional intelligence literature on controlling emotion and using an understanding of the emotional needs of others to influence and focus action. This is the potential danger of over-emphasising the concept, but it is an important reminder that employing people solely for their cognitive intelligence does not lead to a successful organisation. Empathy with others is a key element in creating effective participation.

The tendency to rationality and the lack of attention paid to emotional connectivity can also be seen in the approach to recruitment advertising, which tends to emphasise the factual aspects of the organisation (size, success, global reach) rather than what interests potential candidates (supportive work environments, challenging and interesting work and advancement opportunities) (Backhaus 2004). In many ways what seems to occur in recruitment is an extension of the challenges we have pinpointed in branding: internal fragmentation; a lack of engagement with the brand; lack of connectivity with external audiences; a lack of strategic orientation; and a production mentality (selling what the organisation produces). We also believe the remedies are similar:

- the brand needs to become an *integral* part of the recruitment process
- recruiters need to become *entrained* with their audiences
- recruiters need to understand organisational *strategy* and recruit people that can help meet organisational goals
- the importance attached to recruiting for values and *attitude* needs to be heightened
- communications should emphasise what matters to employees in an *effective* tone and language

Integral indicates that human resources managers need to engage with the brand. This is important not only for recruitment, but also for the ongoing reward, retention and development of individuals. If HR managers understand and engage with the brand they are able to devise recruitment procedures and tests that can unearth the potential values match. This seems to be rare, as the brand still seems to be seen as the preserve of the marketing department and internal barriers seem to inhibit the engagement of HR. As Kristin Backhaus observes with reference to recruitment (Backhaus 2004: 131): 'most organizations fail to differentiate themselves in any material way from their competitors, indicating that in most firms the employer branding strategy has not successfully taken hold'.

Entrainment is a concept we introduced in Chapter 1 and refers to the ideal of generating a close connectivity between the organisation and individuals. In recruitment terms this implies an attitudinal shift and a certain systems approach. In terms of attitude it suggests human resources managers need to actively engage through networks with potential recruits and demonstrate a willingness to encourage potential recruits to become involved with the organisation. This process is facilitated by seeing recruitment as an ongoing relationship, which implies software systems that are capable of helping to match people based on values and also to maintain dialogues in an appropriate way. For example, if an organisation receives 500 applications for a job, that represents 500 opportunities to engage with an individual and either enhance the brand or undermine it. It also creates a talent pool of potentially 499 people (although some will be inappropriate values matches) to continue a dialogue with and to re-contact when the next job becomes available. Of course, many organisations already have systems in place to do this, but the point we would stress here is the focus on values matching as an indicator of the opportunity for identification.

Strategic is a word much used both by marketers and HR professionals, yet both lack a strategic orientation in that they tend to focus on their own operative areas rather than the larger concerns and direction of the organisation. Recruitment in particular is a strategic issue, because it is future oriented – concerned with identifying the people who will join the organisation and sustain its direction. For example, Amazon which is a strongly customer-centric organisation is very rigorous in its recruitment procedures, seeking out not only technical excellence, but also searching for individuals that have an orientation towards customers and a willingness to 'raise the bar' as they describe it, in terms of delivering value.

Recruiting for attitude requires that the organisation knows the attitude it wants, otherwise it becomes a rather hollow expression.

The desired attitude must relate back to the brand and also the strategic intent of the organisation. For example at the Ice Hotel in Jukkasjärvi in the Arctic Circle in Sweden, the important attributes of the brand are connected to listening and excellence in customer service and people are recruited for their propensity to deliver this, rather than for their technical skills. Equally the sports company, Quiksilver, has a brand that stands for sporting excellence and it believes in humility, active listening and creativity. The recruitment of creative director, Natas Kaupas, a former skateboard icon, typifies this (Ind and Watt 2004). Although Kaupas had no formal training in design, he had a passion for the art used in the decoration of skateboards and a fascination with the way images are built in people's minds. Largely self-taught, he became a magazine art director and then developed advertising for the brands he was involved with. Quiksilver recognised his talent and the value of his understanding of the sport. As Marketing Director Hild says, 'we so respect his understanding of the culture and the history (of skateboarding) . . . we really rely on him to tell us where we should go'. Kaupas is in tune with the motivations of his audience, not because he has read about them in a research report, but because as he says, 'where I grew up [in Dogtown, South Santa Monica] everybody boarded and surfed. I was four or five years old when I started.' Other organisations might feel uncomfortable about putting an untrained person in such a position, but for Quiksilver, attitude is more important than proven technical skills. To help support the latter, the company provides a supportive structure where there is regular input from experienced professional mentors.

Effective communications suggests that the brand adopts the right language and tone in its communications, consistently. This is far more likely if some of the above are delivered – in particular when the brand is integrated into the decision-making of the organisation and when there is a strong sense of entrainment. Thus, we are not arguing for more visually striking or distinctive communications (although that is valuable) but rather communications that are candidate oriented and true to the overall brand. When this way of thinking exists all the small details that add up to the brand experience for the candidate align to create a powerful image. For example, if you apply for a job with Nike, you receive the typical thank you for your application. However, they add this powerful credo: 'Use your imagination. If you are sure about what you want to do, you're halfway there. There are no limits. Everyone at Nike has a dream. We use our life skills and professional talents to work towards it every day of our lives.' The statement integrates with what we see of Nike from its other communications, so it feels credible, but importantly it is also inspirational. This sort of thing only happens, however, if the brand is deeply ingrained in the organisation.

BUILDING IDENTIFICATION, INTERNALISATION AND COMMITMENT

In Jane Austen's novels, economic necessity and reputation loom large. Social contacts are developed and maintained because of the advantage they offer and marriages are encouraged for social standing and money. Austen's heroines, however, stand against these mores by seeking out relationships that are socially engaging and fulfilling and by marrying for love. In *Pride and Prejudice* the heroine, Elizabeth Bennet reflects on her friend Charlotte's marriage to the priggish Mr Collins, 'she had always felt that Charlotte's opinion of matrimony was not exactly like her own, but she could not have supposed it possible that, when called into action, she would have sacrificed every better feeling to worldly advantage'. Elizabeth is of course in an advantageous position in that she does not have to marry to survive, but the principle she adopts is that she will not give up her higher needs of self-esteem, socialisation and self-actualisation.[6]

When it comes to careers these needs are also dominant.[7] Our willingness to identify with the organisation we choose to join is determined by our perception as to whether we believe the organisation will enhance our sense of feeling good about ourselves by offering a rewarding job in a positive culture; whether it will create the opportunity for us to engage with interesting and stimulating people; and whether we will realise our potential to be what we can be (Gagliardi 2002) (or as Maslow says, 'to become everything that one is capable of becoming') (Maslow 1998: 3).

At the point of joining the organisation, the perception of oneness is based largely on the quality of interactions through marketing communication and meetings in interviews. The picture of the organisation is therefore likely to be imperfect and imagined. However, the degree of identification, even at this stage will be enhanced if the organisation has a unique set of values and behaviours that separate it from others (Ashforth and Mael 1989: 24, Ind 2003: 3–15). Organisations with strong identities attract potentially committed people because the opportunity for self-realisation is enhanced, whereas undifferentiated organisations may be safe choices, but they are also likely to be less engaging (Whetten and Godfrey 1998: 270).

For example, the outdoor clothing company Patagonia has a very distinctive purpose statement ('To use business to inspire and implement solutions to the environmental crisis') and clear values ('quality, integrity, environmentalism, not bound by convention') that permeate all its decisions and attract employees who share its sporting enthusiasm and commitment to the environment. The perception of Patagonia as an outdoor, environmentally conscious organisation is driven not primarily by marketing communication, but through a close connection with customers (entrainment) and consistency of behaviour that heightens the potential for identification at an early stage and also subsequent internalisation and commitment. As creative director, Hal Arneson says, 'most of the people here are risk athletes. They're outdoor people working in an indoor environment that allows them to work here because it respects that about them. People are passionate about their sports and they bring that into the workplace. People spend time here agonising over whether what they do has meaning.'

The transition from potential identification to actualised identification and then internalisation and commitment, is determined by whether expectations of the organisational fit are delivered. Effective induction programmes, supportive management, the power of symbolic behaviour and the reality of the organisational identity will define the speed and intensity of the transition. Ideally organisations would like to achieve this transition as quickly and as powerfully as possible, but there are two dangers in this.

First, in actualising identification there is the opportunity for abuse. Generally we do not think this is such a danger with commercial organisations because manipulation can be resisted and individuals are able to leave the organisation, but if we think of dominant organisations in a community where there is little in the way of alternative employment prospects or even neo-religious cults and criminal groups, we can see the destructive potential. Thus we might question where the moral boundary is when organisational leaders try to 'encourage' employees to adopt certain values and behaviours.

Secondly, if the organisation becomes too successful in recruiting like-minded people and achieving identification, there is a danger of group think – the phenomenon observed by Irving Janis (1982) where the cohesion of the group discourages questioning and creative thinking. To counter these challenges is difficult because group cohesion thrives on shared identification and the reduction of self in favour of collectivity. But we might argue that in the organisational quest for identification there needs to be an allowance for freedom and diversity (Ford and Gioia 2000, Amabile 2001, Henry 2001, Thompson and Brajkovich 2003, Ind and Watt 2006) for mavericks as well as acolytes; for the expression of unpopular views. This may be uncomfortable for the organisation because of the desire for normalcy and rationality, but there need to be people who stimulate de-territorialisation as well as those who territorialise.

Researchers argue that social identification (I am) – the perception of oneness with or belongingness to some human aggregate – can be distinguished from internalisation (I believe) on the basis that the former is a categorisation of which groups one is part of, while the latter is about the ability to incorporate into selfhood the values and attitudes of the group (Ashforth and Mael 1989). One of the challenges of 'I am' is that although we would like to think of ourselves as having a single unified identity, we can also sense that we have multiple selves that vary with context (Guignon 2005). It is through our socialisation with others that we find our identities such that we may identify within the organisation with a creative team, a business unit and the corporate entity.

However, we would only identify with all of these if the social category is rich enough 'to permeate and affect many of the most important aspects of life.' (Williams 2005: 202). In other words we only to choose to identify with and then internalise the values of a group if what it represents matters enough. This indicates that the deeper purpose of the organisation and the specific groups within it need to link to people's needs and also align with each other. The tendency will be for the individual to identify with their most immediate group. If this group has a strong identity that resonates with its members, while other groups and the corporate entity have weak or very different identities, it creates a recipe for siloisation and behaviours that work against the assemblage model which aims to encourage connectivity. Groups will compare themselves and members will seek to raise their self-esteem by uncovering their points of difference – their sense of uniqueness. This encourages the establishment of strong internal barriers and introverted thinking. To achieve the inter-connectedness that facilitates an assemblage where the work of individuals and groups can be challenging, critical and vibrant yet can still coalesce around the organisational brand, each level of identification has to be meaningful, relevant and inspirational. When there is a clear link between the group and a strong organisational identity, people are less likely to be negative about other groups (Brown and Williams 1994) and more willing to work across organisational boundaries.

In trying to make sense of their work environment employees may initially identify with their group and the organisation. By then participating in decision-making and through actions the individual may come to internalise the relevant values and subsequently demonstrate passion or commitment. In some organisations where there is a strong sense of identity born out of a long shared-experience the main means of transmission is through direct contact and observation. Peer groups in organisations such as Quiksilver and Patagonia demonstrably live the brand in their day-to-day lives and use it as a template for decision-making. Not surprisingly the commitment of existing employees transfers to new ones. Partly this takes place through informal dialogue within the organisation, but it may also involve the use of organisational stories, myths and metaphors as a means of conveying the organisational uniqueness. In the context of building an effective assemblage with strong connections, one of the core attributes of a story is the ability to unite people around an engaging idea, which is why storytelling is so prevalent in Quiksilver and Patagonia.

RETENTION AND DEVELOPMENT

> The longer employees stay with the company, the more familiar they become with the business, the more they learn and the more valuable they can be . . . It is with employees that the customer builds a bond of trust and expectations and when those people leave the bond is broken. (Reichheld 1996: 63)

Having recruited someone into the organisation, the big challenge is as to whether the individual stays and develops their skills and contributes to the organisational cause. It could of course be argued that it is not always desirable for people to stay. An organisation without new blood can atrophy and lack dynamism. The need for creative questioning and the avoidance of group think suggest that there needs to be an ongoing transfer of some people out of the organisation and the introduction of new faces with distinct competencies and approaches. Indeed the writer Jim Collins argues that before you decide where you want the organisation to go, you have to 'first get the right people on the bus (and the wrong people off the bus)' (Collins 2001). The need for greater employee mobility can be challenging for businesses in some communities, but the opposite problem of too much mobility is more common. High staff turnover rates generally suggests that either the organisation has been insufficiently transparent and efficient in its recruitment and selection processes or that it has failed to deliver on employee expectations and the individual desire for self-actualisation.

To take these problems in turn: a lack of transparency in presenting the organisation to new people leads to misjudgments about corporate culture that are only uncovered when employees encounter the organisational reality; poor efficiency in the recruitment process delivers employees with inappropriate skills or incongruent attitudes which reduces the likelihood of identification and internalisation; a failure to invest in the development of people denies people the opportunity to realise their life and career goals – what the US project 'Meaning at Work' identifies as the crucial factors in our working lives: sense of purpose, oneness, ownership, fit and relationship building. The disappointing reality of corporate life is that organisations recruit generally enthusiastic people and manage to metamorphose most of them into disgruntled and disappointed individuals. To some extent this is a result of growth – the individual and the organisation will both change and can fall out of love with each other, but there are certainly more fundamental causes.

The international research company, Gallup, has explored the challenge of employee engagement and found that, for example 31% of US employees (2005) felt strongly connected to their jobs. But the downside is more notable: some 69% are not engaged and not psychologically committed to their jobs. Less than a quarter of the US sample of actively disengaged employees (representing 17% of the total) plan to stay in their jobs for more than 12 months. Gallup estimates that the cost of active disengagement in terms of lower productivity is $370 billion annually. The comparable figures for Germany (2003) shows only 12% of employees are engaged and that the estimated annual cost is €260 billion.

Gallup's definition of employee types

1. *Engaged* employees work with passion and feel a profound connection to their company. They drive innovation and move the organisation forward.
2. *Not-engaged* employees are essentially 'checked out'. They're sleepwalking through their workday, putting time – but not energy or passion – into their work.
3. *Actively disengaged* employees aren't just unhappy at work; they're busy acting out their unhappiness. Every day these workers undermine what their coworkers accomplish.

It should not be surprising that actively disengaged employees cost organisations money both directly in terms of lower productivity and tangentially in terms of disruptive behaviour and negative impacts on colleagues. Equally, as Reichheld (1996: 100–1) argues there are a series of benefits to the retention of engaged employees:

1. *Recruiting investment*: the cost of recruiting
2. *Training*: the cost of training new hires; the free training benefit of knowledge transfer from long-term employees
3. *Efficiency*: generally people who stay with the company because they're proud of the value they create are more motivated and work harder.
4. *Customer selection*: experienced people are better at finding the best customers.
5. *Customer retention*: long-term employees produce better products, better customer values and better customer retention
6. *Customer referral*: sometimes employees are a major source of customer referrals
7. *Employee referral*: long-term employees often generate the best flow of high-quality job applicants.

The business benefits of engagement and commitment have been explored in a number of studies. For example the research organisation, ISR conducted a study on employee commitment (2002) among 362,950 employees in 40 countries and found a difference in the operating margins of organisations with high commitment employees against low commitment ones of 5 percentage points. Equally some of the studies cited in Chapter 2 provide substantive evidence of business benefits: Denison and Mishra (1995), Rucci, Kirn and Quinn (1998), Maister (2001), Simons, Walsh and Sturman (2001).

Accepting these connections between employee commitment and organisational performance we are still left with the challenge of how to retain and develop employees. There are several factors that seem to be important here. Partly retention is determined by the organisation's willingness and capability to deliver on the psychological contract; that promises made or inferred are actually delivered on. Partly it is to do with the organisational climate which is the collective strength of individual identifications. Partly it is to do with creating a strong communication culture because, as Smidts, Pruyn and van Riel (2001) observe, a positive culture where there is a willingness to communicate regularly and to stimulate dialogue encourages identification – this links to the theory of conversational spaces (Baker, Jensen and Kolb 2002) that sees conversation as a creative process of understanding, determined by the needs and emotions of human interaction and communication. In other words a culture that encourages conversation creates a greater opportunity for individual self-discovery and emotional engagement.

These retention drivers take us back to the concept of the citizen company and also the idea of nomadology, where employees are active participants in the evolution of the organisation and are given sufficient latitude to be self-organising in response to threats and opportunities. This enhances the sense-making capability of the organisation, because individuals are not waiting on the authority of managers and hierarchical decision-making, but are rather taking responsibility within agreed boundaries for action, which should be determined by the organisation's vision and values. In this context, individuals then are more likely to feel the potential to self-actualise and to develop in line with their own expectations. However, we should note that while citizenship may confer certain freedoms it also requires heightened accountability. Lars Nittve, the Director of Moderna Museet in Stockholm says,

> I can't think of any areas where there is a need for creativity where it can work without a high level of trust. Trust in the sense that

if someone is given responsibility, they're trusted to take that and run with it. But also you need to create a climate that is a safe place for ideas and where you can say stupid things, but you're not made to look stupid. It's about trying to create a non-blame culture . . . on the other hand people need to be responsible. That's a difficult balance.[8]

As Nittve indicates, the role of the manager here is to help create the right climate through a willingness to empower people while also supporting them. This helps to create a basis of trust. Managers need to be good mentors, to be capable of setting clear goals, of coaching and developing individual and team needs and delivering on promises made. For their part, employees need to engage with the organisational brand, to align their behaviours with corporate goals and to assume responsibility for their actions. This interactionist perspective (Schneider and Reichers 1983) suggests that the organisational climate is a result of the interactions between the organisation and the individual. It is a social process defined by the nature of the organisation and an individual's attempts to understand their role within it. Therefore structure does not determine climate directly but rather affects the interactions between individual and organisation that define the climate:

> processes are then more relevant than structures, and (management) design could be more appropriately be seen as a social process and as a dialogic exploration during which differing views of the world, cognitive maps, strategies and interests are set against each other and mediated. (Gagliardi 2002)

Similarly Ashforth (1985: 838) notes that meaning does not arise out of things but out of the interactions attempting to understand those things or episodes: 'meaning is inherent in the episode or play, that subsequently unfolds, not in the setting or the actors'. The advantage of the rhizomatic structure discussed here is then not that the structure is somehow inherently superior, but rather because it helps to create an open and social organisation that stimulates participation and encourages the building of long-term relationships with customers, collaborating partners and employees by creating trust, commitment, satisfaction, and collaboration – something that is seen as valuable by several writers (Grönroos 1994, Morgan and Hunt 1994, Chenet et al. 2000). When people feel less constrained by rules and procedures they are better able to network with others inside the organisation. Indeed we might also argue that in an entrained culture, such as Quiksilver, it is not only internal social interaction that determines climate, but also the contribution of customers and external mentors. This interplay of employees and external audience is what helps to create a participatory brand.[9]

There is no better example of participatory engagement than Chip Bell, the positive and enthusiastic head office receptionist of outdoor clothing company, Patagonia (Ind 2001: 10–11). In a one-to-one interview, the question asked of him was whether he had been told to behave in a certain way? Were there rules or did he just do as he thought appropriate? This is part of his reply:

> I'm genuinely feeling groovy. It's seamless for me to give customer service and interact with people and to give them a feeling that it is a different place; that it is a business where you can be yourself – caring and giving top-notch customer service. It's easy for me . . . My reactions come naturally from absorbing all our values – environment, integrity, quality – all of that is relayed back out when I'm on the phone . . . The best bit is working with our customers and working with our vendors; being the image and the voice of Patagonia. I think my job is one of the most important in the company and I'm well respected within our community of employees.

The clear inference of this quote is that there aren't defined rules. Indeed, as Bell notes his reactions 'come naturally from *absorbing* all our values'. This emphasised word makes clear a point of distinction, because most managers would think that values are learned through communication, whereas Chip Bell says elsewhere in the interview that he sees the values being used, and feels involved with the way they are applied. When values are absorbed, employees can and should have the freedom to explore their meaning. The Bell interview also serves as an example to contradict the belief that managers' role is to motivate employees. Chip Bell doesn't need to be motivated, but he does need a supportive climate.

Of course, not everyone is like Bell and there are always disengaged people. Surely motivation is key in those cases? Perhaps, but our argument is that the most important thing is that managers need to be emotionally intelligent; to be capable of adapting to the differences in individuals, but their role is not primarily to motivate (Koestenbaum and Block 2001: 104). People are motivated by the quality and engagement of the work they do and the psychological climate. Managers need to focus therefore on appropriate job design and building a culture of trust that is based on openness, transparency and the delivery of promises. In this type of environment individual development is possible (remember again the NUMMI Director of Welding Improvement in Chapter 2).

People can train and enhance their knowledge and skills and apply that knowledge within the organisation, thus avoiding the frustration that people experience when new skills encounter rigid cultures that prevent their application. The classic case that exemplifies this was the failure of an International Harvester intensive class-room programme to effect permanent change. Interestingly there were significant changes in attitude from the attendees between the first and last days of the programme, but later measures when people returned to regular work were not sustained, because the working practices and culture of the organisation remained the same and impervious to change (Mann 1957).

The International Harvester case suggests two important elements in the area of development. First, while people might have expectations that the organisation will develop their skills and knowledge, it is the responsibility of individuals to determine what they learn and how. The organisation may place limits on what it is willing to fund but ambitious people recognise that there needs to be a certain congruence between individual and organisational goals. The managerial view that treats employees as children or pupils will tend to look to prescriptive learning, while a view of employees as free thinking and responsible adults will encourage participative learning where people become engaged in defining their goals, defining their learning pro-grammes and monitoring the results.

Secondly, arborescent structures tend to be rigid and non-adaptive, which means that individuals who develop become frustrated with the immobility of the organisation. The rhizom-atic organisation instead encourages change, so that there is a greater chance of the individual having the opportunity to de-territorialise it. The challenge here is that leaders need to have the confidence to promote change and encourage the individual freedom that employees need to be able to execute tasks without role conflicts and to correct mistakes quickly and effectively.

This refuting of the idea of the managerial duty to motivate may seem contentious, but if what managers have been trying to do in the past has been about motivation, it would seem from Gallup's research that it has failed in no small measure. If, instead of thinking about motivation, managers concentrated on creating a culture of participation and engagement based around the organisational brand, it would create the opportunity for the alignment of individual growth *and* organisational development. This perspective also refutes the idea that businesses are created around a few key individuals, whom need to be retained and developed. An organisation may have its stars, but today's stars may not be so tomorrow. The hierarchic and static view of people fails to recognise that there is often huge untapped potential that can be nurtured in the right culture and that intellectual capital is a result of all the interactions of an organisation. Development implies movement; the individual and the organisation are always in a state of becoming.

CONCLUSION

It might appear that our advocacy of individual freedom might create happy and satisfied employees who do little to benefit the organisation. However, our argument is not about pure freedom. In an organisation, freedom must be bounded by frameworks that ensure a good degree of alignment between the individual and the organisation.

If the things that make employees enthusiastic are also fundamental to business success they will remain through both good and bad times and become central to the organisational culture. Here it is valuable to evaluate the overall performance of the brand. Of course, organisations can and do measure the specifics of employee satisfaction, commitment and motivation. This knowledge can be of value in determining engagement strategies, but often managers are unclear as to how this knowledge should be used. It is important that the knowledge is fed back to employees without overly sanitising it and that employees are encouraged to participate in defining and implementing improvements. This process of internal brand building adds value to the brand and increases employee satisfaction. This is necessary to build profitable relationships with external customers and fulfil the organisation's brand promise (Booth 2003).

Thomson et al. (1999) suggest that a good understanding of brand strategy and values enables employees' to understand how their actions can enhance the brand, particularly though the delivery of good customer service. This indicates that the real validity of employee measurement metrics is how they connect, what we term as HR drivers (employee-based variables such as satisfaction, identity, creativity, mood and motivation, that seem to have direct influence on individual and company performance) with the likely long-term loyalty of customers.

NOTES

1. The Panopticon was an institutional building, described by Jeremy Bentham, that was designed to ensure that its inhabitants could be continually observed. Michel Foucault describes how the principle of panopticism (supervision, control, correction) is carried through into society as a whole, as a way of supervising the control of individuals and ensuring they adhere to rules (Foucault 2000, 57–59, 70).
2. Average across Fortune 500 companies.
3. In 'On Liberty', John Stuart Mill argues that individual liberty is vital, for without it civilisation cannot advance; the truth will not, for a lack of a free market in ideas, come to light; there will be no scope for spontaneity, originality, genius, for mental energy, for moral courage. Society will be crushed by the weight of 'collective mediocrity'. Cited in Berlin (2005: 174).
4. Fukuyama (2005) describes social capital as 'an instantiated set of informal values or norms shared among members of a group that permits them to cooperate with one another'.
5. Dr John Warnock of Adobe Software talk about this in terms of success being when 'good ideas come from everywhere in the company'.
6. These needs relate to the higher elements in Maslow's hierarchy of needs, although Maslow talks about esteem which he relates to the idea of dignity and the esteem of others. However, Elizabeth Bennet is more concerned with her self-esteem; about feeling comfortable with her own choices.
7. Over 25 years the National Opinion Research Center at the University of Chicago has conducted the General Social Survey, which shows that in attitudes to work, the most important attribute is important work that gives a feeling of accomplishment.
8. Interview with author, 13 November 2003.

CHAPTER 6

CULTURE

Whereas the previous chapter on human resources focused on the individual and the changing relationship to the organisation, this chapter will concentrate on the context that individuals operate within: in other words, the organisational culture. However, before we analyse the role of organisational culture in participatory branding it is important to understand what is meant by the terms 'organisational' and 'culture'. The term 'organisational' though seemingly simple is complex. When we talk of an 'organisation' we are referring to a structured entity but the use of a noun creates a sense of something static that has a fixed identity. If we look at an organisation, or indeed write about it, we are forced into a judgement at a fixed point in time, yet the reality of organisational experience is one of constant movement. Change goes on all the time.

In contrast if we use the verb 'to organise', we create a sense of movement which is more in tune with the idea of the organisation as an assemblage that is ever-changing, ever-becoming. We also convey the sense of trying to fix and contain the process of change. Yet this use of the verb 'to organise' hardly works when we attach it to the concept of culture, because culture will not be organised. Consequently we should retain organisational as a descriptive device, but keep reminding ourselves that the organisation itself is becoming: 'everything is in the absolute restlessness of becoming. But becoming is not a process that leads to another thing, because it is the condition of every thing' (Nancy 1997: 12).

The second complexity of 'organisation' is the inter-relationship of the abstract entity, the organisation, and the people that form it. When we refer to an organisation such as Quiksilver or Greenpeace, we are talking about an entity that has some form of collectivity. Yet these organisations do not possess collective thought. The organisation itself does not think, rather it is the individuals in the organisation through their actions that define the organisational entity: 'the sharing of singularities in movement, becoming, desire and decision' (Nancy 1997: 78). This does not mean that the organisation is a unified whole for that would require a group of automatons. Although public pronouncements might suggest univocity, the organisation is inevitably polyphonic. What 'organising' does is to give some shape to polyphony:

> Organization is an attempt to order the intrinsic flux of human action, to channel it towards certain ends, to give it a particular shape, through generalizing and institutionalizing particular meaning and rules. At the same time, organization is a pattern that is constituted, shaped, *emerging* from change. (Tsoukas and Chia, 2002, 570)

We can observe here that an organisation is being (or becoming) in common. There is something shared, to whatever degree, between individuals in an organisation: a common purpose or need. Without this sense of community there is nothing to determine the organisation from the unstructured world outside. Although we have stressed in this book the idea of permeable boundaries between the organisation and its customers, there is still a boundary that determines those who are non-organisation. Some aspects of commonality determine who is part of and who is not part of the organisation. Indeed in many cases it is an external threat or danger that galvanises the organisation:

> the group constitutes itself on the basis of a need or common danger and defines itself by the common objective which determines its common *praxis* . . . it makes itself a community by feeling individual need as common need, and by projecting itself, in the internal unification of a common integration, towards objectives which it produces in common. (Sartre 1960: 350)

Sartre draws a distinction between groupings, different types of groups, organisations and institutions, but what he reinforces through the example of a bus queue is the importance of communication in the process of organising (1960: 256–69). He observes that a morning bus queue in Place Saint-Germain is a grouping of people – we cannot judge its nature more explicitly, although it is likely to be a grouping of regular commuters waiting for the bus who are united in an abstract generality: going to work. Sartre notes that we may objectivise the grouping by referring to it as an entity – the queue – but it is comprised of individuals. What denies any sense of organisation in the bus queue (apart from the adherence to the rules of the queue itself) is the isolation of the individuals, who typify urban living by turning their back on their neighbour: 'isolation is a project' which social forces encourage. There is no dialogue between the individuals and any memory of events about late buses, cancellations or diversions is interiorised. It would be difficult therefore to think of the bus queue as an organisation because it lacks real order. However, it could become an organisation if change is forced on the inertia of the individuals in the queue. Perhaps if the bus company (RATP[1]) decided to double the fares it would provoke dialogue, the sharing of stories about buses being late and the formation of an action group to challenge RATP. Through exteriority, the grouping would acquire a deeper unifying purpose and a structure. It would acquire the capacity to make decisions and to communicate those decisions, which Luhmann sees as the vital element of organised social systems (Luhmann 2003: 32). The group might also acquire some visible manifestation of protest such as pamphlets and button badges that declare 'Non á la hausse des prix!'

When we come to the word 'culture' we find more complexity. We may observe an organisation's symbols, hear its stories and encounter its representatives, but we cannot touch culture as such. Culture shows itself in results. It is hidden within the assumptions of the individuals in the organisation who only acquire a degree of unity as they begin to absorb the way things are done. As an observer it is possible to make judgements about a culture based on the actions of individuals, but individuals are not always conscious of culture. Everyday life is a continuous series of singular events not a theorising about the core assumptions that drive us. Thus it is the way we act in the organisation that is determined by, and also determines, culture.

Writers see the term 'culture' in an organisational context in different ways, although there is some common agreement about the main content. Most definitions see it as reflecting the history of the organization and that it is related to rituals and symbols and shaped and maintained by a group of people that together form the organisation. Culture is also characterised as difficult to change (Hofstede 1991, Schein 1985, Wilson 2001, McMurray 2003), which may be true if we see culture as something to be managed. Schein (1985: 7) defines organisational culture as

> the pattern of basic assumptions that a given group has invented, discovered, or developed in learning to cope with its problems of

external adaptation and internal integration, and that have worked
well enough to be considered valid, and, therefore, to be taught
to new members as the correct way to perceive, think, and feel
in relation to those problems.

Schein (1985) argues that organisational culture can be analysed
from three different levels or dimensions: artefacts, values and
norms and basic assumptions. Other researchers claim that organisational culture consists of two levels: the visible and the invisible
expression of culture. Visible elements are characterised as artefacts while the non-visual elements are defined as values and
norms and fundamental assumptions (Van Maanen 1977, Manning
1979, Barley 1983, Wilson 2001, Brønn 2003). Underlying these
different ideas is the sense that culture may affect and be affected
by individuals, but it is a social construct. It is a shared memory
formed through past experience that determines future actions.
It is carried in dialogue and conversation and narrative. In
Deleuzian terms, it becomes embedded through territorialisation.
Thus culture can only exist when an organisation has some
shared sense of identity; when the way of doing things is observable, understandable and sustainable.

The challenge here, as we have noted throughout this book,
is that cultures often encourage isolation between departments
and from customers. A culture that is responsive – in the sense
that all the elements of the assemblage model fuse well together
– must have high levels of participation. The idea of isolation
either from the outside or between people on the inside encourages siloisation. It is only when people are communicating effectively with each other that the way of doing things becomes
shared. Internally this suggests that the right people are employed
(see Chapter 5, 'Human resources') who have emotional intelligence and are willing to communicate across boundaries. Externally it suggests that there is an ongoing interaction – the idea
of entrainment – between employees and other audiences. In this
chapter we will be suggesting strategies to enhance the overall

organisational culture and to improve its sense-making ability through participation.

UNDERSTANDING CULTURE

Organisational culture is difficult to evaluate. As noted, participants inside the organisation tend not to dwell on it overtly and outsiders tend only to see a point in time. The visible aspects of culture (artefacts), such as office buildings and offices, art works, locality, language, dress code, histories, ceremonies, rituals and behaviour (Schein 1985, de Chernatony 2001, Gagliardi 2006) can be read but there is no certainty of a common reading and even if cultural behaviours are measured, that measurement must be converted into a language that can never do justice to the subtlety of culture.

For example we might say that the culture of the NGO, Greenpeace, is confrontational. People inside and outside the organisation might affirm that the cultural description is broadly true, but what does confrontational mean exactly? We could observe it in the desire for argument in meetings, in the imagery the organisation uses and the stories it narrates, but when we come to describe confrontational we revert back to narrative as a means of explanation: 'we are beasts condemned to language'.[2] This is not to argue that we should not try to measure culture, or observe it but rather that we need to dig deep to understand the intensities of what we observe and that ongoing observation/participation in an organisation is a better way to understand those intensities.

If a researcher joins an organisation and attends its meetings and observes decisions being made at first hand over a period of time there will tend to be a deeper insight. The researcher can observe behaviours and ask people why they are doing things in a certain way and thus observe both the behaviour and the explanation of it – through laddering techniques, actions can be probed. Conclusions can be drawn. But, of course there are still limitations: the presence of the observer affects behaviour, the sharing of the observation with others has to battle with the challenge of subjectivity and language and the description is already of a past event. More quantitative approaches can be used such as Cameron and Quinn's Organizational Culture Assessment Instrument (OCAI), which looks at such factors as dominant characteristics, leadership style, treatment of employees, organisational glue, strategic emphases and the criteria for success or Denison's model which combines adaptability, mission ('perhaps the most important cultural trait of all is a sense of mission'), involvement and consistency.

The value of Denison's model is that it recognises the dynamic contradictions at the heart of management which we also see in the assemblage model, such as the need for both stability (territorialisation) *and* flexibility (de-territorialisation), for an internal *and* external focus and for top–down mission *and* bottom–up involvement (Denison 2000). In our view the best way to evaluate culture is to combine qualitative approaches that allow the researcher to dig underneath the organisational surface to expose intensities with quantitative approaches that provide comparative and trend data. The latter is important because, as observed, culture is difficult to change in a managed way, but cultures do change all the time. Actions (provided they are shared) impinge on a culture continuously.

Take as an example of the interplay between action and culture, the Museum of Modern Art in Stockholm – Moderna Museet.[3] The culture of Moderna Museet in the early 2000s was perhaps typical of a national museum. It had to deal with conflicting audience pressures – a government that was keen to ensure that its subsidy was well spent, a critical media, a demanding Stockholm public and a more remote public in the rest of Sweden. Within the museum itself there was also a tendency to focus on the art itself, which encouraged an inward-lookingness. This was typified by some of the language used in external communications, which was too esoteric to be understood by everyone, but was comfortable and familiar to those involved with modern art. The pressure to be accessible to as wide a public as possible and be relevant to the art world created a sense of embattlement. Within this culture, actions were constrained by concern over the impact of decisions particularly on the media and government.

Then in 2002 there was change: a new director called Lars Nittve arrived from Tate Modern in London and a problem of mould in the building was discovered which required the closure of the museum building for two years while remedial work was carried out. These events combined to challenge the existing culture. Nittve brought his experience as director of Tate Modern in London and the Louisiana Museum of Modern Art in Denmark to his role. At Tate Modern there had been a balance between contemporary and modern art and also the needs of the local community and a larger national audience, while at Louisiana as much emphasis had been placed on the visitor as the art.

The closure of the museum site itself in central Stockholm meant taking temporary premises and having to think of new ways to exhibit the works of art. Part of the solution was to have art travel to people around Sweden in a mobile exhibition and to have shows in buildings in Stockholm and to hold art in public spaces such as city squares. As a consequence of taking these actions the museum had to become more accessible and the people who worked at the museum began to encounter its audience more directly. By the time the museum moved back into its premises the culture had evolved away from being inward-looking towards a more outwardly focused organisation. In fact there was a realisation as people talked about what had gone on, that the building itself mattered less than they thought and that the meeting of the art with the public mattered more. Lars Nittve says about the managers and employees:

I think they're passionate about the museum and the art. And I think they're growing more passionate about the audience . . . So here we've had a very clear process of defining the vision and leading through the vision also. The vision is in a sense a short story. It's about three things: it's about a paradox between the museum and the contemporary role; second, you're not only here for the art, you're also here to create this meeting place (the mantra is excellence and access); third is to develop an understanding that we need to change all the time, because art in so many ways is changing and ever expanding.

With the culture evolving towards becoming more audience-oriented, ideas that would have seemed inconceivable in the previous culture were adopted. The museum decided to adopt a free entrance policy, to work harder at making the museum a genuine meeting place for a wider audience and to make the art experience itself as engaging as possible. In the case of the last, one of the interesting introductions was the use of hosts. Rather than having someone sit statically in front of artworks watching people, hosts (*vårds*) were recruited to protect the art and engage visitors in discussion and explain the paintings, sculptures and installations. The hosts, many of whom have art history backgrounds, are informally dressed and rotate their jobs. During a day this means they will spend time on the reception desk, checking coats and talking about art in the galleries. While they are briefed by the curators on the art works, the hosts develop their own expertise through self-study and share their knowledge with each other. The customers who engage with hosts (about one-third) are very positive about the experience with 98% rating it as very good.

Importantly from a cultural standpoint the re-categorising of the museum as a meeting place proved to be highly successful with visitor numbers going up from 250,000 a year to 680,000 in the first ten months after reopening. The success not only changed the attitudes of visitors, but it also created a more positive climate among the media and with government. What we can observe overall about culture in this case, is that prior to the closure of the museum, decision-making was constrained. Undoubtedly the culture itself was slowly evolving as decisions were taken, but the core attributes of the culture were not changing. There was little de-territorialisation taking place, because there was an absence of trust and confidence. The major challenges of closure and a new director could have led to a greater focus on territorialising the assemblage, but in fact the opposite occurred.

Actions taken by Nittve and his managers were designed to cope with the challenges in a relevant and consistent way – because those actions deliberately involved many people, the dialogue that took place began to change perceptions about the museum and its meaning. This de-territorialisation was forced on the assemblage, but it had the impact of shifting the organisational culture. It's impossible to tell whether the closure by itself would have led to change or the introduction of Nittve by himself would have changed the culture, but we might imagine here that the closure of the building and the arrival of Nittve together had an impact that led to a sustained change.

If we were to map the nature of organisational culture and its evolution, we can see the changes in the culture of Moderna Museet in the context of the model depicted in Figure 6.1. When events are everyday they have little impact on the organisational culture: the culture itself determines how people respond as orders are fulfilled, invoices sent, meetings attended. However, more significant events generated either in the external environment or internally can create a sense of movement. Luhmann (2002: 40) observes in his description of autopoietic organisations that noise or disturbance in the environment only becomes meaningful when it impacts on the decision-making of the organisational system. Through research and feedback the organisation

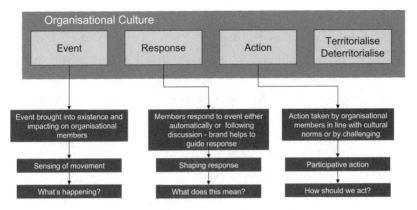

Figure 6.1 Mapping cultural reinforcement and change

actively seeks noise, but as we observed in our critique of research in Chapter 1 much research fails to permeate strategic decision-making. Equally there may be relevant noise in the organisational environment, which organisational members ignore because culture constrains what is sensed (Gagliardi 2006: 566): 'one may imagine organizations as continuously oscillating between acceptance and rejection of noise' (Luhmann 2002: 43).

If the movement or change is sensed as significant; if it touches a member or members of an organisation, then people start to ask 'what's happening?' In a rhizomatic organisation with high levels of self-organisation the response might lead to a nomadic team or an individual taking action. In a more structured organisation there may be meetings, discussions and reference to higher levels of authority. There will be formal discussions in meetings and workshops and informal talks among colleagues. The result will be a response that is culturally influenced, either by accepting the constraints that the culture imposes or by challenging it − in the case of the latter the spectre of culture is still in evidence because it is the departure point for new thinking. In the instance of Moderna Museet, the event of the closure of the museum led to a sort of existential crisis because the initial reaction was that the museum was the building itself. Like Tate Modern in London or the Guggenheim in Bilbao, the Moderna Museet was a distinctive building which people were proud of and which attracted visitors through its location and architectural appeal. It was only through discussion that organisational members realised that the museum was more than the building; that it was the art collection and its meeting with the public that mattered.

Once a response has been considered, then an action may take place. The action (and the preceding and perhaps subsequent discussion) will impact on the culture – this suggests why culture is difficult to change in a managed way, because it is actions and what they communicate that in large part defines culture. Even when inertia or internal barriers dictate that nothing happens in response to a sensed movement – the process of discussion and non-action influences the culture. However, if the people within the organisation have sufficient will and cohesion to address the movement, an action may occur. It may involve only a few people or the whole organisation, but usually the action will be to some degree participative, because there will be dialogue. The action itself can either territorialise (confirm the beliefs of the existing culture) or de-territorialise (challenge the beliefs of the culture).

In the case of Moderna Museet the action was a de-territorialising one that impacted the whole organisational assemblage. The interesting thing in the Moderna Museet example is that when the organisation moved back into the museum building it maintained much of its newly discovered ways of working rather than reverting back to previous cultural norms. These significant transitions in culture can only occur if the experience of action is shared. Although Luhmann argues that 'decisions are communications',[4] we could imagine a sole individual or small group acting without communicating about their decision – something that creates the experience of surprise among organisational members when they hear belatedly an organisational story. When there is no sharing of the narrative about events and actions the impact on the assemblage remains limited and it can neither reinforce nor challenge the organisational culture. As Jean-François Lyotard (1984) writes:

> Narratives, as we have seen, determine criteria of competence and/or illustrate how they are to be applied. They thus define what has the right to be said and done in the culture in question, and since they are themselves a part of that culture, they are legitimated by the simple fact that they do what they do.

THE USE OF NARRATIVE

In the early 1990s, Wolfgang Lohbeck, head of Forests at Green-peace Germany commissioned two researchers from the Munich Society of Environmental Research (Gesellschaft für ökologische forschung), Wolfgang Zängl and Sylvia Hamberger to photo-document the decline of Alpine forests. In documenting the decline of forests the potential for long-term photo documentation of glaciers was seen. The solution to providing a long-term perspective was to acquire historic Alpine postcards. The researchers, scoured antique shops and antiquarian booksellers for the cards and managed to amass a collection of more than 5000 dating as far back as 1893. The Greenpeace Germany board was persuaded to fund a further stage of the documentation project and Zängl and Hamberger were asked to photograph a selection of the exact views in the postcards. They spent six summers in the Alps taking several hundred photos of twenty glaciers in five countries. The collection of powerful new images was produced alongside the original postcards to demonstrate the extent of global warming on the glaciers, which was produced as a book and a traveling exhibition. The impact was profound. Not only were individuals persuaded to lend their support and commitment to tackling global warming, but a number of local conservation organisations gave support.

This is a story from a workshop undertaken with Greenpeace. It narrates a past event that is known by some people in the organisation who use it to explain the environmental impact of global warming. They could of course, cite statistics (they do that as well), but the story gives us something more. It suggests the accidental nature of discovery, the importance of documenting environmental problems and bringing them to the attention of a wider audience, the cooperative process of working to stop environmental degradation and a sense of movement from an initial challenge to an action. As Schein argues (1985: 81):

> stories and myths about how the organization dealt with key competitors in the past, how it survived a downturn in the economy, how it developed a new and exciting product, how it dealt with a valued employee, and so on, not only spell out the basic mission and specific goals (and thereby reaffirm them) but also reaffirm the organization's picture of itself, its own theory of how to get things done and how to handle internal relationships.

In other words, Schein is referring to the organisational culture. In an organisation, stories will be told all the time to define challenges and to share successes. Even though people when they tell anecdotes or just spread gossip through the internal grapevine won't necessarily think of what they do in terms of storytelling that is exactly what they're doing. It is a function of internalisation that people share in, believe in and proselytise a set of values. It is a result of the need to communicate that we narrate stories rather than just list things.

Some organisations also use narrative as an explicit method to define the uniqueness of the organisation and as a means of engendering identification and internalisation. This moves the storytelling process away from a naturally occurring phenomenon into a managed process. There is far greater clarity in a story that illustrates a way of doing things than suggesting that a list of values should determine behaviour. A story sets an example; something to emulate. Of course, stories should flow naturally, but if siloisation is strong and/or communication is poor, then stories may get stuck in pockets of the organisation.

To encourage flow it is also possible to manage the storytelling process to a certain extent – the limitation being that there cannot be control. A story that may look appealing to management may simply be of no interest to employees. Also, what is intended as the point of communication by the writer of the story will not necessarily be the reader's take-out. The subjective nature of reading and interpretation will lead to different meanings and the story itself will evolve, as in Chinese whispers. Indeed, the Russian philosopher, Bakhtin argues that both the speaker and the listener are active participants in the dynamic development of meaning: 'according to this view, the listener instead of being a powerless observer actively processed information and prepared a reply, further developing the meaning of the message' (Belova 2006).

Nonetheless, what a programmed approach can do is to formalise or structure the informal; it is about capturing, evaluating and disseminating the stories that seem to best communicate the mission, vision and values and that convey a point of difference about the organisation to internal and also external audiences. A story can be used in many different ways: to communicate strategy to a financial audience, to generate more committed and more energised employees delivering more aligned communication and to generate a clear personality in the minds of customers. It can be of particular value when organisations are going through change in helping to accelerate the adoption of a culture aligned with the desired brand positioning. In this instance new stories need to be found and given momentum that reflect the desired values and norms of the new brand positioning. These stories might celebrate success, and talk about how people have overcome internal, competitive, marketing or technological challenges in ways that show the power of the brand, while helping to create a shared vision of the organisational future.

An example of a story that is designed to communicate the brand is one told inside the Norwegian mobile operator, Telenor. The story is that Norway is sparsely populated (population 4.5 million) and that especially in the north of the country where the Sami (Lapps) live, extending mobile coverage does not always make economic sense. However there are other issues such as reputation and social responsibility that are important for Telenor. In the Sami community of Hellemobotn a single phone box served 150 inhabitants. When the phone rang (there was an external bell) two boys had the job of running to answer it and then running from house to house or searching the woods to find the person. Telenor's Head of Coverage was invited to meet the community and when he saw their needs to decided to prioritise them. The agreement for mobile coverage was signed with the President of the Sami government (Ting) in the phone box.

This small story not only distinguishes Telenor from its competitors, but it also supports the big brand story that is expressed in the vision statement of 'we're here to help' (the idea that Telenor help customers get the best out of communications in their daily lives) with its accompanging narrative and a set of values: make it easy, keep promises, be inspiring and be respectful. These small stories which are summarised in the one big brand story provide the source of differentiation and positioning (Figure 6.2).

To encourage the flow of stories within the organisation requires a process that enables stories that best reflect the culture (and its underlying mission, vision and values) to be selected and communicated. In broad terms there are five elements in the process: connecting; collection; compilation; communication; co-evaluation.

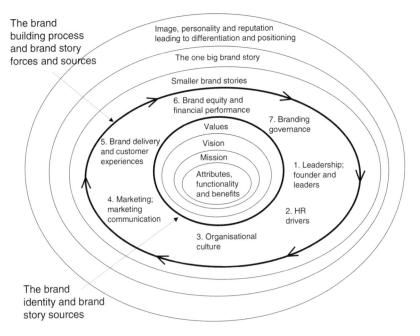

The brand building process and brand story forces and sources

Image, personality and reputation leading to differentiation and positioning

The one big brand story

Smaller brand stories

6. Brand equity and financial performance

7. Branding governance

Values

Vision

5. Brand delivery and customer experiences

Mission

Attributes, functionality and benefits

1. Leadership; founder and leaders

4. Marketing; marketing communication

2. HR drivers

3. Organisational culture

The brand identity and brand story sources

Figure 6.2   Brand story forces and sources

- *Connecting*: for a storytelling programme to have organisational credibility it needs to engage with the dominant culture(s) of the organisation. If it is seen as the province solely of the marketing or communication department, it is likely to be seen as corporate propaganda. Therefore the project leader needs to engage with key people in other departments both to ensure that stories connect with the rest of the organisation and to make the linkage between brand and business performance. This process of involving people from different parts of the organisation is important, because when at a later stage stories are communicated to a broader audience it helps to ensure the message of the story and its tone and language are appropriate.

- *Collection*: the requirement here is to capture the stories that swirl around the organisation. These stories can come from a variety of sources: from informal conversations, presentations, speeches, customer feedback, printed material and through direct involvement.

• *Compilation*: once stories have been collected they need to be evaluated and structured. The evaluation criteria need to be firmly established, but the key is that the story should be aligned with the organisational values and supportive of business strategy. For stories in general to travel through an organisation they also need to be memorable, credible, reasonably succinct, interesting, and salient to the audience. Other criteria that can be applied include: degree of relevance to business; credibility of narrative hero; novelty of story; interest of storyline; challenge of adversity overcome; business impact and potential for differentiation. It is important to recognise that some stories might appear to be perfect business stories in terms of what managers would like them to say about the business, but if they contain insufficient drama/elements of adversity they will not get re-told. A story does not necessarily need to have the scale of Homer's *The Odyssey*, but there does need to be a significant challenge to overcome; as the literary critic Harold Bloom writes, value 'has much to do with the idiosyncratic, with the excess by which meaning gets started' (Bloom 2001). However there does need to be a balance here, for as the Russian writer and critic, Viktor Shklovsky, suggests there needs to be both believability and novelty (Barry and Elmes 1997: 434).

• *Communication*: stories can be seeded into the organisation in a variety of ways: direct dialogue, presentations, speeches, films, publications, intranet and internet (including blogs), induction and training programmes. They can be used externally as well as internally. Again credibility will be enhanced the more natural the process is. For example, Nike employ someone to tell stories whose prime role is to enhance the Nike culture. He does presentations externally, talks to the media, takes part in induction programmes and does workshops as part of the corporate education programme. And because he has a long history as a Nike employee he is believable as a presenter of corporate stories.

- *Co-evaluation*: how valuable is storytelling? Often it is hard to judge, because paradoxically the more successful it is, the less noticeable it is. This should be a subtle process. However, individual stories can be qualitatively tested and evaluated for impact by seeing how far they spread and how they are received, and the overall impact of storytelling (in terms of increasing identification with and commitment to, the brand) should be tested through employee research into the culture. This can be qualitative but it can also be tracked through regular employee studies.

When storytelling is successful it reinforces the sense of why someone works for a particular organisation. These stories may contain adversity or elements of negativity, but they are selected to affirm the overall values of the organisation. When a story is strong it may not only have currency inside the organisation, it may get presented and retold externally, which reinforces its credibility for employees and helps to generate pride. However, the opposite is also true: employees can also feel undermined by negative stories. Thus the narrative process, whether natural or to some extent managed, is part of the process of cultural formation. When events impact on the organisation, the resulting discussion and agreement to act will involve narrative. There will be a sense of temporality as the story unfolds with each point reached both seeming to reveal and conceal something; offering something to the reader, but also holding something back. The uncanniness of narrative, its revealing and concealing, is always evident – from the Gospels to Dickens to Hitchcock. The difference is that in the Greenpeace story in this section, the story was structured with a beginning and an end (although the story of melting glaciers goes on), whereas in our lived lives and in our dealing with events we are taking part in a story that is unfolding. We never know whether the story will have the end we hope for. We will tend to see these lived stories through the lens of the organisational culture we are part of, especially when the story comes to some sort of resolution and becomes part of the evolving culture.

ORGANISATIONAL SENSE-MAKING

Sense is a word with a double meaning. It identifies the process by which we sense something through our faculties and it is also 'the sense, the thought, the universal underlying the thing' (Hegel 1975). Yet as Nancy (1997: 46) points out, these two meanings have the same sense, because the meaning of the word is derived from the passage of one into the other:[5] 'sensibility is becoming; passage from a simple determinateness to a property'. This understanding of sense raises two questions. First, how is that organisations sense what is going on? Secondly, how is sensory experience translated into something that makes sense?

We have discussed some of the issues connected to the first meaning of sense, in the section on research in Chapter 1. Organisations attempt to stay close to their customers through the mechanisms of research and direct observation/contact. In large organisations there is a tendency to rely on the former, which often creates a problem of a surfeit of data (Bakken and Hernes 2003: 65, Weick, Sutcliffe and Obstfeld 2005: 415). The challenge for decision-making therefore is to make sense of the noise in the environment; to be capable of giving form to sense so that it makes sense. This requires organisational members to be able to understand the movements of data and then have the ability to share that knowledge with others in the organisation so that it has the potential to impact on the corporate culture. This will only happen if the knowledge is encoded: 'actions, like thoughts and speeches, are contingent signs, destined to vanish if they are not reified' (Gagliardi 2006: 570).

We have also suggested that another way organisations sense is through direct contact and by achieving entrainment with customers. Employees in organisations with permeable boundaries are in constant contact with customers and are therefore able to achieve a deeper insight into their needs and wants. For this to occur in practice, organisations need to be genuinely customer centric and have the humility to accept that good ideas are not necessarily the preserve of a few people inside the organisation, but can come from anywhere.[6] Sensing indicates that people have to allow themselves to be touched by what goes on around them. This suggests that we need to be open to the world, but it is inevitable that we are also culturally constrained. The culture of the organisation and the focus created by the sense of the organisational vision and values, cuts out some areas of sensing (this is the flow of thought affecting sense), which is why one organisation will see something of relevance in a market movement and another will not. This is an inevitable process that reflects our individual methods of sense-making. We cannot encode everything that goes on around us in our world, so therefore we have to make selections based on what we perceive to be important and we switch off to the rest (Schacter 2001).[7]

For example, an organisation that places little emphasis on customer knowledge is far less likely to notice a change in buyer behaviour than one that emphasises it. Receptivity is thus to do with conditioning. We see and hear what we choose to be receptive to. The recipe for changing cultural receptivity in a planned way is to address both actions and measurement. The actions, especially of leaders who are important for their actual and symbolic power, demonstrate to the organisation what is seen to be valuable while measurement systems also indicate to members what the criteria for success are. When Lou Gerstner, the former head of IBM (Gerstner 2002) was confronted by the inward-lookingness of the company in the early 1990s, he found a culture focused on tribes and politics. His focus was to try and build, through highly symbolic actions and an emphasis on different measurements that placed external performance at the core, a culture that was less interested in internal status and was more interested in customers. The change of culture described by Gerstner was a lengthy and painful process, but it reiterates the point that cultures cannot simply be willed into existence. It is consistent actions that lead to change.

The second question posed here was about how the sensory experience – the hearing and the seeing – is translated into something that makes sense. This is about the movement of the sensory into a thought for an individual and then in the context of the organisation how the thought is communicated to others; it is the movement of the external to the internal. Weick, Sutcliffe and Obstfeld (2005: 409) note that sense-making occurs when a flow of circumstances is turned into 'words and salient categories'. They go on to argue that 'reading, writing, conversing and editing are crucial actions that serve as the media through which the invisible hand of institutions shapes conduct'. In commenting on Weick's earlier thinking, Bakken and Hernes (2003: 60–1) observe, in contrast to Luhmann's autopoietic (self-reproducing) systems approach, that it is the individuals within the organisation that sense and that the systemic effect lies at the level of actions. The transition into words and the resulting actions are based on the individual's ability to contextualise the sensory. The observation of a movement in a tracking study of customer preference or the experience of meeting with a highly valued customer has to be committed to language either through formal reporting or in dialogue and anecdote.

This emphasis on rhetoric indicates the potential displacement that can occur when an observation or experience has to be retold: sense is both given and lost in translation. As Ricoeur suggests (2003: 80) 'discourse always occurs as an event, but it is to be understood as meaning'. This is about the relationship between the sign and the things denoted; the relationship between language and the world. This is fraught, for while we are trying to relate things to the world, we have to confront the problem of constancy of meaning: 'constancy of meaning is never anything but the constancy of contexts. And this constancy is not a self-evident phenomenon' (2003: 89). The likelihood of effective translation is heightened if the culture itself is cohesive and there is a common understanding of language. Interestingly in organisations where teams are seen to be important there is a better ability to adapt to change and for learning to be shared. As Rezania, Lingham and Dolan (2006) suggest 'cognition at the team level is dependent on sharing of mental frames, knowledge and on interaction among team members'.

PARTICIPATIVE CULTURES: PARTICIPATING AND NETWORKING

> The real voyage of discovery lies not in seeking new landscapes, but in having new eyes. (Marcel Proust)

There tends to be a viewpoint expressed in conversations about culture that strong is good and weak is bad. Yet strong can also be myopic, unquestioning and arrogant while weak can offer freedom, diversity and humility. This might suggest that strong and weak are the wrong words to describe a successful culture or cultures.[8] Rather perhaps we should think about descriptions of culture as fulfilling or not, where the idea of fulfilment relates to the interlocking needs of different audiences. Does the culture meet the existential needs of employees, the experiential needs of customers and the monetary needs of investors? Fulfilment requires participation – as the concept of social intelligence suggests, our brains have evolved not to cope with the environment, but with the world of the social; we are *mitsein* (being with) above all else:[9] 'we are always already involved, and can never wholly extract ourselves from our living involvements with the others and the otherness around us' (Shotter 2005: 118).

Therefore trust among organizational members (both internal and external) becomes a key antecedent. The importance of trust should not be surprising, both within the organisation and outside in relationships with internal and external clients. Yet trust is often taken as a given. In reality it needs to be earned over time, if the tendency to expediency and tribalism in organisations is to be mitigated (Ind and Watt 2006). This view is endorsed by a quote from an individual cited in Shotter and Cunliffe (2002) who is vice president of a health care company:

> I think the essential management skills – as I use the term, the management of people – reside on this continuum that has things about communication, your ability to communicate your ideas, to empathize with other people . . . you make meaning with them jointly . . . you present ideas that are powerful – but you can't do that unless people have faith in you.

The participative approach is designed to build trust, by encouraging dialogue and openness – as Bakhtin argues, thought itself 'is born and shaped in the process of interaction and struggle with others' thought' (Morris 2003: 86). When people are open with each other and receptive to different viewpoints the process of discourse enables meaning to emerge through 'the ceaseless flow of living language-interwoven relations between ourselves and others' (Shotter 2005: 130). In describing the architect Frank Gehry's method of design, Weick (2003: 94) argues that the architect and the client (in this case the Weatherhead School) act their 'way into deeper understanding'. Weick goes on to argue that there needs to be a tolerance of the ambiguity in the unfolding of the relationship as the process of design flows towards some sort of conclusion. He suggests we need to stay in motion not in a negative sense, but such that each new phase 'breathes new life into the dream'. The challenge of this idea of staying in motion is to keep discovering something new and revealing at each stage. As designers of buildings or organisations we need to keep challenging our ideas[10] so that we develop a rhizomatic approach to management. The Deleuzian writer, Bernard Cache, suggests that we need this rhizomatic approach because 'the whole is not given but (is) always open to variation, as new things are added or new relations made, creating new continuities out of such intervals or disparities' (Harris 2005: 39).

Openness also makes it more difficult to hide personal or silo agendas. Providing the larger goals of the organisation and the mission, vision and values are clearly communicated and internalised, there is the opportunity to create significant degrees of freedom and connectivity within the assemblage. This is not to suggest that the assemblage is a unified whole. It is still polyphonic, but it is united around a common (though ever evolving) sense of purpose. When there is a lack of common purpose or a narrow agenda there is fragmentation. An example of this is well told by Daniel Ellsberg (2002: 53) in his story of the Pentagon papers and the Vietnam war. Talking of his time as an advisor to the Lyndon Johnson government he writes that the prevailing philosophy was do what's good for your boss, the man who hired you; put that above what you think is best for the country, above giving the president or the secretary of defense your best advice if that would embarrass your boss.[11]

The appropriate degree of freedom in an assemblage will vary. In an organisation that is strongly systems based, such as a courier or logistics company, the need for freedom may be limited, whereas in a design or film company where creativity is more important there may be more significant degrees of freedom encouraged. Even within one organisation, there may be higher levels of freedom say for a product development team as opposed to the finance department. As discussed with reference to Berlin's notions of freedom from and freedom to, there may also be variable approaches to negative and positive freedom, such that there could be a low level of constraint, but a tighter control on 'freedom to'. These degrees of freedom must be decided on and lived up to – especially as one of the key elements in the creation of trust between leaders and employees is delivering on promises (much as it is also between organisational members and external audiences such as customers and investors).

If we adhere to the principle about cultures being about ful-filment, it is not necessarily the case that individuals in organisations want total freedom: 'Does my life achieve fulfilment? That is the only ethical question. Freedom is a secondary concern, for I must first find out how my life is to achieve fulfilment' (Schirmacher 2005: 92). There needs to be a balance between order and self-expression. If there is total freedom and a lack of structure, people can feel vulnerable and isolated, while too much structure can reduce trust and risk taking. In connecting the parts of the assemblage, there needs to be territorialisation and also de-territorialisation; to meet changing needs and opportunities, requires not only a receptivity to the outside, but a willingness to communicate and respond effectively inside the organisation based on the right degree of freedom to create a culture of fulfilment.

The assemblage connects well when organisations have the systems, the will and the culture to communicate and act across internal boundaries. This requires networks of relations that are constructed to go beyond the specified structure and to connect people (either in a managed or in a nomadic way) based on relations determined by shared passions and interests as well as the pragmatic interest of power – the need to make sure that the network has the authority and influence to get things done. This encouragement of diversity in response to events also helps to avoid the challenge of group think.

An example of the connectivity of people in a network is that of the process of managing the development of the Volvo Cross Country. Prior to the launch of this vehicle, the typical Volvo way of developing a new vehicle was sequential. In other words, it was passed from department to department and then offered to marketing at the end. With the Cross Country, the team brought together to develop the vehicle was from different parts of the organisation. From the outset the engineers, designers, marketers and even the advertising agency worked collectively together to a brief based on a clear definition of the Volvo brand values and a deep insight into the behaviour of the target audience. This way of working was seen to be stimulating for all concerned, but especially for the engineers who welcomed the experience of developing ideas based on an understanding of people's lifestyles. This diversity was not without conflict, but that was seen as valuable as things got worked out in the tension of different viewpoints and encouraged team members to settle their arguments with reference back to the needs of the target audience they were designing the car for (Ind and Watt 2004).

The Volvo experience required of the team a high degree of receptivity. Team members had to understand the events taking place in the outside world, which were changing people's attitudes to vehicles and they had to be receptive to the idea of working across organisational boundaries. Through this open way of working within the Volvo culture, fulfilment was achieved for all audiences. This openness is what Shotter and Cunlife (2002) call 'relational-responsive understanding' where the dialogue with the environment is an exploration of meanings based on a receptiveness to things rather than an *a priori* sense of fixed meaning. It is also akin to what Schirmacher (2005) calls 'homo generator' where individuals create their own authentic worlds through an openness to their environment – something he labels as artificial which he sees as a positive concept based on self-conception.

The underlying theme of this method of cultural engagement is that it opens up the possibilities of the assemblage. In the introduction to the assemblage model in this book, we noted that we can never be sure of what an organisation is capable of. This means individuals need to be capable of seeing movement and the intensities beneath the observable. Then by rethinking and rewiring, new possibilities open up, encouraging us to think and act in new ways (Lorraine 2005: 172). These acts of *poiesis* actualise the virtuality contained within the assemblage and enable actions that impact on organisational culture. Referring to Wittgenstein, John Shotter says of *poiesis* that it is

> of making, of creating, of bringing something new into existence, rather than merely discovering already existing things. So that with this capacity to see previously unseen possibilities, to create livable links and relations between previously unconnected aspects of our surroundings, we can move around within them . . . (Shotter 2005: 129)

CONCLUSION

This chapter has tried to show that for an organisation to create value for stakeholders there needs to be a supportive and fulfilling culture: one that stresses the importance of engaging customers and employees. Yet these types of culture cannot simply be wished into existence. The major challenge of cultural change is that culture is transformed through actions. That is a double loop process: actions determine the nature of the culture and the culture determines the ability to notice movements in the environment; to observe events and to understand them. To change culture requires that the process of dialogue within the organisation and the actions that result are transformed in a consistent way. Here is a primary role for leaders: to deliver effective change, leaders have a significant symbolic role. They can demonstrate through their actions the organisational priorities. Once change begins to take place, the key factor in enduring cultural change is the organisation's ability to learn. This does not just occur but rather it evolves out of the history of the organisation (Argyris and Schön 1978) and the organisational communication environment. Key to this process of learning is the role of narrative, which is a naturally occurring phenomenon in the organisation, but which can be harnessed to reinforce particular aspects of the organisation's culture.

The organisational culture also plays a fundamental role in sense-making. The more emphasis given to the importance of understanding the external environment and particularly the attitudes and behaviour of customers, the greater the opportunity for entrainment to occur. However, this requires that the organisation can fuse itself together internally and to overcome the tendency towards tribalism. This bringing together of the assemblage means that sense can make sense. The key antecedent here is trust, built on genuine participation. As Lars Nittve says:

> You work with proper delegation. Not say that you delegate and then look over the shoulder and then take things back as soon as you get a bit worried. You do proper delegation which means more staff have a fuller responsibility for what they do and the consequences of what they do . . . Some of it is structural and a

big part of it is a matter of style. And I think it is believing in people and taking less control.

NOTES

1. Régie autonome des transports parisiens.
2. Lyotard, Jean-Francois, 1984.
3. Having made the previous comments about observation of culture, the story here of Moderna Museet is based on working with the organisation as a consultant under its previous director and then a number of interviews (2003–05 with the current director, Lars Nittve and several members of staff who work as hosts at the museum.
4. Luhmann also goes on to point out that this does not preclude the fact that one can communicate about decisions (Luhmann 2003: 32).
5. According to Merleau-Ponty, Cézanne also sees sense in essentially this way: Cézanne did not think he had to choose between feeling and thought, as if he were deciding between chaos and order. He did not want to separate the stable things which we see and the shifting way in which they appear; he wanted to depict matter as it takes on form, the birth of order through spontaneous organisation. He makes a basic distinction not between 'the senses' and 'the understanding' but rather between the spontaneous organisation of the things we perceive and the human organisation of ideas and sciences (Merleau-Ponty 1993: 63–4).
6. An interesting example of this was the development of the electronic calculating machine known as Colossus that was used to decipher German High Command codes during the Second World War. The deduction of how the code worked was achieved by a team led by a Cambridge mathematician, but the actual engineering was done by a non-academic outsider from the Post Office, called Tommy Flowers. After the war, Flowers was ordered to destroy his notes and the report on the machine was only declassified by the government in 2000, but it can make a serious claim to be the prototype of the modern computer.
7. It is one of the roles of art to make us see the things we stop encoding, such as how Van Gogh gets us to think again about what a poplar or olive tree looks like or how Cézanne makes us see the solidity of an apple or the substance of a building.

8. This hints at a polyphonic rather than a homophonic conception of organisation (Andersen 2003: 166).

9. 'If there is indeed something which constitutes this 'being' or this 'existence' in which, or according to which, we are . . . it is that we are with one another. We are *with* (someone, others and the rest of the world) just as much and exactly as we are *tout court*' (Nancy 2005: 440).

10. Nietzsche wrote in his notebooks: 'A Very popular error: having the courage of one's convictions; rather it is having the courage for an attack on one's convictions!!!' (Nietzsche 1974: 152n).

11. In an echo of the past, Bob Woodward in *State of Denial* (2006) relates that David Kay who was given responsibility within the CIA for finding Weapons of Mass Destruction in Iraq was critical of George W Bush's national security adviser, Condoleezza Rice for her lack of candour: 'she could have stopped trying to be the best friend of the President and be the best adviser and realize that she's got this screening function'.

CHAPTER 7

PARTICIPATORY LEADERSHIP

*I*n this chapter on participatory leadership we look at the role leaders can play in helping the assemblage to focus outwards on delivering value to customers and inwards on giving direction to employees and in breaking down silos so that entrainment is possible and brand-building capability can be enhanced. The chapter is clearly linked to the previous one because, as Bass and Avolio (1993) argue, organisational culture is created and shaped through leadership. We would also argue that leadership is defined by culture. The cultural milieu determines how leaders see their role and what they are capable of doing. Leaders are influenced in the same way as other employees by the flow of event-response-action-(de)territorialisation. Yet leaders also carry greater influence in influencing culture and de-territorialising the assemblage.

Here we focus on the way leadership should function in setting and delivering a vision for the organisation and its component parts. However two points should be noted immediately. Leaders are many. The overall leader (the CEO or executive director) is of vital importance, but so are the leaders of divisions, business units and teams throughout the organisation, all of whom have a role in vision delivery (and sometimes setting). Secondly, the word vision indicates something that is future oriented. Organisations often have vision statements, but these can tend towards bland descriptions of the future. In the way we describe vision here we are using it more broadly to encompass not only a sense of the future but also the strategy for achieving it. This concept of vision can be related directly to the brand because it encompasses the way in which the organisation will connect internally and externally with customers. It provides direction to managers and employees as to how best to deliver value to customers and other stakeholders.

The nature of the leadership role is described in the model below (Figure 7.1), which is circular to indicate the continuous basis of vision setting, delivery and reinforcement.

In the initial phase of defining a direction there needs to be dialogue. Leaders need to be adept at asking questions, probing beneath the surface of individual viewpoints, understanding the needs and wants of external stakeholders and building consensus. This dialogic approach to participation in itself helps to create thought. As Bakhtin writes, 'our thought itself . . . is born and shaped in the process of interaction and struggle with others' thought' (Morris 2003: 86).

In the second phase, dialogue leads to the emergence of a vision. Ideally this is not just the vision of strategic planners removed from the reality of delivery, but rather the envisioning of a future and a strategy to achieve it by those who will be actively involved in the process of delivery. When you have remote planners you end up with disasters such as von Schlieffen's misguided plan for the German invasion of France that was used in the First World War and President Kennedy's and Johnson's

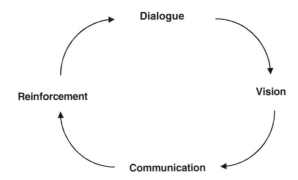

Figure 7.1 A participative approach to leadership

Vietnam policy (Ind 2001: 50–1). Importantly the vision should contain the potential to transform the organisation from what it is to what it needs to become.

In the third phase there is an emphasis on communication. However, this is not just the sending out of statements or producing press releases or making speeches. Rather it is communicative actions. It is actions by leaders that signal to the organisation the importance of the vision and its implications for the way people think and behave. Here leaders have an important symbolic role to indicate to the organisation that the vision does matter.

Finally there is a reinforcement role. It is a not uncommon experience as a consultant when asking leaders whether they are good communicators to receive a positive answer and then to find in employee workshops that people know nothing of the organisation's vision. Employees have busy working lives and are often too busy to pay too much attention to the latest management initiative. The value of a vision can be put across through communications and symbolic actions, but for it to be interesting and credible to employees, there needs to be the evidence of an ongoing commitment and the potential for the active involvement of employees in the process so that they can absorb the vision into their day-to-day behaviour, thus bringing about the possibility of genuine cultural change.

The loop is not quite complete without the final section. There needs to be ongoing feedback from both internal and external audiences and the adjustment of the vision. There will always be organisational tensions that need to be worked through to uncover meaning and a requirement to balance consistency and adaptability (Denison 2000).

FROM ARBORESENCE TO ASSEMBLAGES

> In the years ahead, we believe the new terrain for business will introduce an additional imperative for continued success, namely *adaptive advantage*, which is rooted in understanding the world. Adaptive change will come to those best able to adapt swiftly and wisely to the changing external environment. (Kelly, Leyden and GBN 2002)

In traditional arborescent organisations, the nature of leadership is primarily concerned with control. A direction is determined and then systems are designed to implement it. The emphasis is on efficiency. Not surprisingly the approach tends to favour more rigid hierarchies that tend to build a distance between leaders and employees and structures that maintain order and facilitate the flow of commands.[1] Arborescence can work well in mechanistic businesses, but as Japanese manufacturers such as Toyota have proven in outperforming their US counterparts, even in industrialised areas, a more participative and adaptive style can be more effective. Certainly in more knowledge-based and creatively led businesses, arborescence works against the principle of building intellectual capital and the importance of adaptability.

The management writer, Stephen Bungay, in his book on the battles in North Africa during the Second World War – *Alamein* – provides an interesting historical example of these different approaches. He contrasts the performance of the German Afrika Korps with that of the British Army and its allies. Although the perception of the British was that the Germans were teutonically rigid, in fact they 'had greater intellectual freedom, which they turned into greater effectiveness on the battlefield'. In reality it was the British who suffered from rigidity and a silo mentality, while the Germans operated an adaptive system known as mission command, which had been developed during the nineteenth century:

> the idea of mission command is that officers should understand their mission, but be left free to decide for themselves how best to accomplish it . . . this enabled them to adapt to changing circumstances as the chaos of battle took hold and exploit unpredictable opportunities. They were under an obligation to show initiative. (Bungay 2003: 31–2)

As intellectual capital has become more important to success, dominantly arborescent organisations have been replaced by more loosely connected assemblages that are better able to adapt to changing circumstances. In the assemblage there is less control and more trust.[2] Rather there is a collection of adaptive, heterogeneous elements which are constantly changing as they territorialise and de-territorialise the assemblage. The rapid change in environments, the reduction of hierarchy and the emphasis on loose, self-forming teams all indicate a more rhizomatic structure. Here the role of leaders is fundamentally different. There is far less emphasis on directing and monitoring – the core elements of what is known as transactional leadership and a far greater emphasis on engagement around the organisational vision, values and strategy – what is known as transformational leadership. We might judge this is about the ability to motivate individuals, but in many rhizomatic organisations, motivation is not the issue. There is already passion and commitment.

At the software company, SAS Institute, there are high expectations for performance and trust which becomes self-fulfilling and provide people with the freedom to meet those expectations. David Russo, former head of HR at SAS Institute says,

> I don't think you can really manage someone's performance. I think you can observe the results . . . I think you can set short- and long-term goals. And you can sit back and see if it happens or it doesn't happen. (Pfeffer 2002: 98)

Instead we argue that leadership is about giving focus to people's commitment, so that they fulfil their potential and their efforts align with organisational goals. It is about creating a realisable and persuasive vision of the future and the role of the organisation and the individual in attaining it.

The idea of developing and implementing a vision, becomes all the more important in a rhizomatic structure. To allow people within the organisation sufficient freedom to adapt to changing circumstances and to deliver exceptional service to customers, there needs to be a framework. Here the vision should suggest to people a picture of the future, while the values and strategy should suggest the way of working towards it. Therefore the quality and relevance of the overall vision itself is important if it is to have the potential to provide meaning. Yet potential is not enough. As Warren Bennis (1997: 156) writes, 'What effective leaders are going to have to do is create not just a vision, but a vision with meaning . . . the vision has to be shared.'

The meaning behind the vision will only come to have power for organisational members if it is communicated in a persuasive manner and it affects people's performance. Senge (1998: 198–202) argues that this is only possible when managers are capable of both inquiry (asking questions) and advocacy (promoting a point of view). His view is that managers tend to be better at the latter, although there may be cultural variations in this. Scandinavian management practice tends to emphasise its social democratic milieu and encourages consultation more than Anglo-American organisations. Certainly the ability to define and deliver a vision requires a certain set of attributes: the ability to link the past to the future and to marry effectively internal competencies to external needs and wants; the humility to listen to others and to absorb the implications of different viewpoints; the ability to share an idea consistently through communication and action over time; the ability to trust others.

All of this would be easier in a static environment, but the reality of organisational life that is reflected in the concept of the assemblage model is one of movement. This fluidity is difficult to describe but obvious if we stop to consider for a moment our own organisations. We are always reacting to events and trying to build understanding and meaning. We have to cope with decisions made in one part of the organisation that undermine our plans or a legislative *volte face* that reduces a programme to irrelevance or a competitor action that derails our brand's positioning. This means we have to accept that while me make plans they are always emergent. As the historian John Lewis Gaddis writes in *Foreign Affairs* (2005): 'Setting a course, however, is only a starting point for strategies: experience always reshapes them as they evolve.' The core leadership challenge here is to cope with this uncertainty and to ensure that the vision retains its relevance and meaning so that employees can align with the organisational strategy and help to enhance performance.

The ability to imagine a future and to see the role of the organisation within it is inevitably an imprecise process. It requires an understanding of the important drivers in the external environment and an appreciation of internal capabilities. The ability to imagine what a future might be like requires both analysis and creativity. Of course this should not be a solitary process – the more people that participate, the greater the potential for new ways of perceiving the world; the better entrained leaders are with employees and customers, the more likely the relevance of the vision.

The challenge here is to move beyond the obvious and mechanical. In defining the important aspects of leadership, the philosopher Peter Koestenbaum argues that there needs to be a balance between vision, reality, ethics and courage. His view is that leaders operate on two dimensions at most, with 'reality' being the most commonly adhered to and 'courage' the least prevalent. 'Vision' is much talked about, but rarely practiced. The difficulty is that in imagining a future we work from the past and therefore we become constrained by memory. When we try to work through the challenge of a problem we tend to resort to existing ideas or adaptations of those ideas that integrate with existing patterns (Bohm 2004: 50–75).

The appeal of writers such as Edward de Bono and Tudor Rickards who have focused on individual training and development techniques such as brainstorming, mind-mapping and lateral thinking, aimed at promoting creativity, is due to the desire to unlock the potential of thinking beyond the constraints of memory. Although this training can be valuable it tends to encourage the idea that creativity happens in a vacuum. Instead we should remember that the organisational culture impacts on the vision and that the development of the vision itself will be a social process. To try to overcome the constraints, vision makers need to be aware of the problems of memory and culture and be willing to challenge them. Leaders need to question existing directions and to be sensitive to the implications of movement – to the shifts in the intensities underneath visible change. As Bohm writes:

> one has to be sensitive to the eternally changing differences that are actually to be observed within each thing, and to the unceasing emergence of new similarities and relationships across the boundaries of the various things. (Bohm 2004: 124)

The rationality of business planning tends to obscure this connectivity and to reduce receptivity. There are no easy ways to overcome this, just a willingness to challenge ways of thinking by adopting different modes. For example, one of the ways the

Dutch bank, ABN AMRO does this is through the provocation
of art – the bank owns some 16,000 modern art works – which
are designed to question and challenge. The art historian, Henk
van Os, tells of a trip to Siena with senior managers of the bank
to look at paintings and frescoes that generated an opening of
minds and a telling of stories. He relates that art is too often at
the margin or our lives, where it is 'no more than a pleasant,
nice little something to be glanced at', but the Siena trip did
something else:

> it appeared that the outer crust of our conditioned behaviour could
> spontaneously disappear during interaction with art, because you
> allow yourself to be caught off guard and ravished by what you
> see. (van Os 2002: 7)

Of course, it is still possible to be ravished by what we see and
then close our minds when we reflect on the experience. Equally,
we can, if we work hard, maintain openness and move beyond
conditioned behaviour. It is then that we have the potential to
see new patterns and possibilities. This is akin to the connection
that John Kao (1996) makes of jazz improvisation and innovation
in 'Jamming'. His argument is that jazz is a good example of
fluidity. Business is not like an orchestra (although that analogy
is also made) because there is not the degree of control suggested
by conductor and musician performing a pre-arranged musical
piece. Rather jazz with its mixture of knowledge and naivety
mixes high skill levels without preconceptions. It aims to create
an environment where it is possible to experiment.

Not surprisingly, given its slogan of 'think different', Apple
Computer is deft at generating vision and courage. If we
recall Steve Jobs' strategic metaphor – a digital hub for a digital
lifestyle – we can see a good balance between the vision of the
idea when it was first launched in 2001 and the reality of its
delivery over time through ongoing product innovation (in particular the iPod); between the integrity of delivery and the

courage to position Apple in this way when the personal computing business was suffering and Apple itself had just seen a 57%
drop in sales and a 74% fall in its share price. While the media
was pronouncing the death of the personal computer, Jobs was
proclaiming a new golden age with the personal computer as a
hub linking together consumer devices such as MP3 players, cell
phones, PDAs and digital cameras. While most pundits couldn't
see the future because of the difficult situation in early 2001, Jobs
and Apple foresaw the rapid take-up of the devices and the likely
need for a central resource to enable people's desire for self-
expression through developing their own music and film libraries
and the opportunity to share that expressiveness with others.

STORYTELLING AND TRANSFORMATIONAL LEADERSHIP

> One reason why we live in a soup of narratives, why narratives
> permeate our lives and understanding, is that resorting to narra-
> tives is the way in which we have learned to cope with our world
> of enormously complex phenomena. (Denning 2001: 112)

One of the inspirational qualities of Jobs as a leader is his ability
as a storyteller – the ability to contextualise vision and strategy
as narrative. Too often management rhetoric is dry and perme-
ated by the rationality of facts and figures. Yet if a vision is to
be valuable it has to be engaging. It has to move beyond inquiry
into rhetoric. For Aristotle, rhetoric was a distinct sphere of philosophy that concerned itself with the art of persuasion. Now
often we equate rhetoric with simply style, but Aristotelian rhetoric was also based on argumentation and composition. It was
seen as a technique of proof (Ricoeur 1975: 31–3). It is stories
that persuade us through their re-presentation of facts, because
we are able to achieve a closer identification with the ideas presented. We might try to persuade someone to deliver exceptional

performance through a listing of elements required or alternatively through a story that illustrates the principle. In the former all the recipient can do is process the facts and engage intellectually with the idea. In the latter, potentially the recipient is inspired through emotional engagement. With leaders who adhere to the rational we tend to get transactional leadership. With a narrative approach there is the greater possibility of transformational leadership in which leaders articulate a vision of the future that both challenges followers' thinking and supports their individual needs. Writers on the subject of leadership note that leaders tend to be a mixture of the transformational and transactional and indeed non-transactional (hands off management style), but that effective leaders more often display transformational behaviour. More transformational leaders seem to be characterised by four components (Bass):

1. *idealised influence*: where genuine trust exists between leaders and followers based on strong moral and ethical standards
2. *inspirational motivation*: the ability to motivate followers to engage in shared goals
3. *intellectual stimulation*: the ability to encourage followers to question assumptions and generate creative solutions
4. *individualised considerations*: the ability to treat each follower as an individual and to provide coaching and mentoring.

Transformational leaders integrate creative insight, perseverance/persistence and energy, intuition and sensitivity in relation to other's needs. In contrast to transactional leaders, transformational leaders encourage 'management by expectations'. In innovative and positive organisations there are more likely to be transformational leaders who develop a culture based on such principles as: people can be trusted; everybody can contribute with something unique; problems ought to be solved at as low a level as possible in the organisation. These principles are designed to stimulate mutual trust, whereby leaders create a set of expectations through their communications and actions and then deliver on those expectations, while employees also make commitments and deliver on them. This helps to generate a willingness to work together to deliver the vision. Compared to the distance that exists in arborescent structures, the transactional approach brings leaders and employees closer together and helps to generate social capital in the organisation, which Fukuyama (2000) defines as the values and norms shared among a group of people that enables them to cooperate. He argues that

> If members of the group come to expect that others will behave reliably and honestly, then they will come to *trust* one another. Trust acts like a lubricant that makes any group or organization run more efficiently . . . The norms that produce social capital, must substantively include virtues like truth telling, meeting obligations, and reciprocity.

Such ideas are not only discussed as a part of organisational culture by Schein (1985), but also by recognised marketing/brand building researchers such as de Chernatony (2001), who claims that developing an appropriate organisational culture is a part of the brand-building process. Transformational leaders not only try to affect people's attitudes through the organisational vision but also by impacting on behaviour by encouraging employees to take responsibility to reach it. This suggests a culture with a greater focus on creative change and de-territorialisation.

To become transformational, leaders need to pay attention to the dominant elements of the organisational culture; to observe the rituals, language and actions that define the way people really behave rather than the documents and espoused processes that suggest the way they ought to behave – 'otherwise they will miss the tacit knowledge produced in improvisation, shared through story-telling, and embedded in the activities that form around these activities' (Brown and Duguid 2000: 79). This suggests both the importance of close observation of organisational reality and the development of visions and symbolic acts that use the language and imagery of the dominant culture. For example, if the dominant language of a shipping company is that of logistics and branding is seen as not particularly relevant to performance, it makes little sense to frame a vision in the language of brand building as this will create barriers to acceptance. This is not to argue that leaders should always pander to the prejudices of organisational members, but they should at least be aware of the impact of language use and understand different speech genres as part of rhetoric.[3]

SYMBOLIC ACTS

> Leaders must make clear, to themselves as well as those they lead that everyone has the responsibility to choose a commitment to values. To live is to have such a commitment ... And in choosing the values we chose also the consequences of our choices. (Koestenbaum and Block 2001: 100)

If the process of vision setting has been a participatory act, the communication of the vision by leaders will be less of a surprise. Indeed, people may already have begun to absorb the implications of the vision for the way they think and behave. However, at some point leaders have to communicate visions through both what they say and what they do. The receptivity to the vision will depend on three core perceptual factors: (a) credibility, (b) charisma, and (c) commitment. Credibility, for example, is in large part determined by past events: have previous visions been adhered to? Has management put the resources to deliver the vision before? Have leaders kept earlier promises? Leaders can make a vision more credible through charisma and seeming commitment, but it may be the case that the vision is launched into a sea of indifference, or worse, cynicism. It is not normally possible to transform cynics suddenly into evangelists but people can be taken on a journey that takes them step-by-step to engagement. Again transactional leadership is important here because it is concerned with delivering change, which makes it more credible for employees when claims are made. Bono and Judge (2004) found that there was a good correlation between transactional leadership and attitudes such as trust, confidence, job satisfaction, commitment, engagement, and work performance at individual, group and organisational level. Also they suggest that there are links between transformational leadership, job satisfaction, and work output.

Charisma is difficult to describe and is shrouded in mystery. We know charisma when we see it and also when it seems to be missing. As Rubin, Munz and Bommer (2005) observe most of the research on transformational leadership has been on outcomes rather than the underlying basis of the behaviour itself. Yet they note that extraversion and agreeableness are key traits in producing engagement and Bass (1985) clearly sees charisma as a part of transformational leadership. What we can observe is that charisma is closely linked to emotional intelligence. Indeed Ashkanasy and Tse (2000) describe transformational leadership behaviour as the management of leader and follower emotion. This indicates the importance of leaders to be able to understand the perspectives of others and to frame their communications and actions in a dialogic way – clearly imagining the antecedents to a statement or action and anticipating the possible responses. This is not a planned process but an intuitive empathetic manner. Yet we might also be wary about charisma. A charismatic individual can be inspiring, but they can also become too much the focus. Jim Collins argues (2001: 72) that less charismatic leaders often produce better long-term results than their more charismatic counterparts.

Leadership cannot be a remote exercise. There must be involvement and commitment. The passion with which a strategy is pursued says a lot about leadership belief. It is the willingness to confront difficult issues and make hard choices that defines personal leadership. Lou Gerstner (2002: 236) argues that commitment – or rather passion as he calls it – is the single most important characteristic of leadership:

> most of all, personal leadership is about passion. When I think about all the great CEOs I have known – among them Sam Walton of Wal-Mart, Jack Welch of General Electric, Juergen Schrempp of DaimlerChrysler, and Andy Grove of Intel – I know that the same common thread among them is that they were or are all passionate about winning.

However, it is difficult to manage passion if a leader doesn't believe in the organisation or the vision. Again this reminds us of the importance of the ability of individuals to align with organisational values and also for leaders to absorb uncertainty by a rigorous approach to defining a vision before undertaking symbolic actions.

Symbolic actions are powerful communicators that indicate something deeper. Take, for example, the introduction of new visual identity and brand essence by BP in 2001. BP defined its beliefs in terms of four values: green, progressive, innovative and performance driven. To ensure that the organisation engaged with the implications of the values an award scheme called Helios (the same name as BP's visual symbol and the Greek god of the sun) was instituted. The concept behind the awards was that employees could enter ideas and programmes against the individual values. Thus for example the 2005 award for the value 'green' was the In Salah Gas Project in Algeria. This plant produces CO_2 rich gas, which is removed before sale. Re-injection of the extracted CO_2 has reduced the project's projected CO_2 emissions by over 60% and makes this one of the world's largest

CO_2 capture projects. The CO_2 emissions saving is estimated to be equivalent to taking 200,000 cars off the road.[4] In 2004 the number of entries for the awards was 1651 and approximately 10,000 employees were involved in the different projects. The team that run the awards argue that one of the keys to success is the very visible commitment of CEO, John Browne. He promotes the awards within the company, is involved in the judging of the finalists and attends the awards ceremony. This demonstration of involvement signals the importance of the values to the organisation and the benefit of integrating them into day-to-day work.

In terms of leaders' actions symbolic acts are the indication of commitment and caring. These instances are made all the more powerful if they seem consistent. For example, Ingvar Kamprad, founder of IKEA, the world's largest furniture retailer, stresses the importance of cost consciousness in the running of the business. This is reinforced by stories of corporate thriftiness, but also in the way he lives his personal life. In spite of his multi-billionaire status Kamprad drives a twelve-year-old Volvo car, uses public transport to go to work with his pensioner card and flies economy class. Similarly, when Design Director of BMW, Chris Bangle wanted to stress the importance of design and engineering working cohesively together to develop the BMW X3, he took the designers and engineers out of the corporate constraints and siloisation of the company's research and innovation centre, known as FIZ (Forschungs und Ingenieurzentrum) and let them work together in a secret location of their own choosing (Elizabeth Taylor's former house in Malibu, California) and away from his prying eyes. He says:

> Both the designers and the engineers learned that the key to a passionate BMW is a synthesis of engineering passion and design passion. They saw that engineers do a better job when they work with designers, and designers do a better job when they work with

engineers. You can't teach that. They had to learn it for themselves. (Breen 2002)

The purpose of symbolic acts is to create stories that demonstrate the potential for identification and internalisation. It is not always the case that the acts themselves need to be developed anew as a result of thinking through a vision. Sometimes it is rather the re-framing of current or ongoing initiatives in the language of the vision. The acts and the communication of those acts create points of inspiration which determine the reception of the longer-term delivery of the vision for employees and customers. The degree of change (and therefore potential discomfort) suggested in the vision can vary from the slight to the significant. Debray (2000: 12–13) points out that generally the more radical the nature of a symbolic message, the sturdier the means of transmission must be: 'because an excess of originality affects reception adversely, one must know how to use signs that are dispensable – or already familiar to the ambient milieu – to be understood'. In other words the more nonconformist the message the greater the need to shroud it in a reassuring language and means of delivery.

The other major challenge here, as depicted in Figure 7.2 is that because the vision needs forward momentum there is the potential for a gap to open up between what a story intends to communicate and the reality of its reception by internal and external audiences. If the gap is bridgeable then it will create momentum, but if there is too much space between what the story seems to say and the reality of delivery there will be a problem of credibility. Again past performance is often taken as a guide to future behaviour. Employees, for example, will be more willing to accept aspirational communications from a leader whom has proved reliable in the past than one who has failed to deliver on promises.

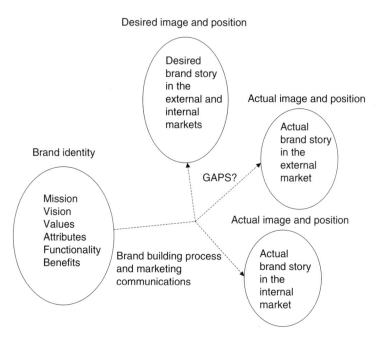

Desired image and position

Desired brand story in the external and internal markets

Actual image and position

Actual brand story in the external market

Brand identity

GAPS?

Mission
Vision
Values
Attributes
Functionality
Benefits

Actual image and position

Brand building process and marketing communications

Actual brand story in the internal market

Figure 7.2 Communicating a vision

REINFORCING THE VISION

George Orwell (1981: 100) in an essay about Charles Dickens wrote, 'you can only create, if you can care'. We might argue that the same can be applied to the idea of leadership. Leaders have to be capable of listening to others, of determining a vision, of making choices and then acting out the implications of those choices, consistently. If the commitment to the vision is only superficial, then actions are likely to be inconsistent. If an organisation espouses its commitment to innovation, a willingness to challenge accepted ways of doing things and a belief in customer orientation, it will be hard to achieve if the leader does not commit to the same principles. If a leader only pays lip service to the vision it becomes clear to audiences quickly. Relevant language, attention to detail and consistency of action all become hard to sustain when someone is merely acting out a role.

In the context of an assemblage the role of leaders is to bring cohesion to the organisation by stressing the linkage of the different elements and reinforcing this by their actions. For example, the leaders of the engineering and construction services company, Aker Kværner, take responsibility for integrating the organisation. The CEO, Inge Hansen and CFO Bjørn Erik Naess try to exemplify the organisational idea – Powered to Perform™ – which is designed to communicate and emphasise an inside–out business philosophy. The emphasis on the 20,000 employees who work for the organisation and the potential new employees (3000 new people were employed in 2006) indicates the importance of intellectual capital to the organisation and the way organisational values are seen. As the company itself states: 'values become concrete and visible when people take decisions'. Of course this could be empty rhetoric but the leaders of the organisation do work to integrate marketing, organisational culture, HR drivers, and branding governance to enhance brand equity[5] and brand value and take an active role in the Business Leadership Programme (a part of the Aker Kvaerner Academy). In this way senior managers function as champions as they exemplify and demonstrate the essence of the vision.

Whereas in the communication phase, pronouncements and symbolic acts can suggest a leader's intent, in the reinforcement phase new ways of doing things have to be developed based around the vision. For leadership teams this is about becoming the embodiment of the vision and incorporating the thinking into new processes and avoiding the temptation to drift back into old ways. This is challenging, because although it can seem exciting, it also heightens anxiety as new experiments are attempted.

For example, prior to joining Moderna Museet in Stockholm, Lars Nittve was Director of Tate Modern in London (Ind and Watt 2006). To reflect the vision of the art gallery as a place which connected the diversity of art and audiences, a new way of curating was developed, which bucked the norm of chronological presentation, opting instead for a thematic approach based around history/memory/society, landscape/matter/environment, nude/action/body, and still life/object/real life. Within each theme there are also sub-themes and interesting, thought-provoking juxtapositions, such as Matisse's paper cut-out swirl from 1953, known as *The Snail*, next to Ellsworth Kelly's 1974 *White Curve* which uses shape and colour to suggest landscape, next to a Calder mobile with its treelike movement.

What is of particular interest here is the way teams were used to explore the meaning of the brand. The definition of the thematic approach emerged from a small and cohesive core team of Lars Nittve, two curators, and an education curator, who worked to the key principles they had defined. However to avoid groupthink, the group was then expanded into a diverse think-tank with artists, philosophers, and art historians. Nittve says about this diversity:

> I think we valued different voices, and we also knew that we all came from the same direction. And it's not given that that is the only direction. At certain moments in processes it's good to have some friction, because it breaks up patterns and models of thinking. Sometimes you're moving too automatically ... Also, we wanted to move towards having different voices in how we displayed and talked about the collection – to move away from this institutional voice to a more multiple voice.

At this stage the process was defined by the vision, but within boundaries there was considerable latitude. Once the four themes had been realised through this interaction, the requirements changed. The goal now was to flesh out the basic themes and to test the viability of ideas. Whereas the first work group required diversity of background, the new groups, which would explore the themes, needed to have diversity of knowledge but within a cohesive field. A series of bigger think-tanks was formed with curators from the Tate's central collection. These people used their specific expertise to define how the four themes could be realised. Finally, once the bigger think-tanks had reached agreement, a small group was formed to fine-tune and detail each individual room within the themes. This accordion-like process was designed to provide different levels of diversity and homogeneity at different times. At the earlier stage, when the boundaries were at their broadest, diversity was encouraged to help create connections that might not have been seen by a narrowly defined group. However, when the level of creativity in the later stages became more detailed and the boundaries narrower, homogeneity was more valuable. At this point, the requirement was not to question the fundamental approach to curating the museum, but rather to provide creativity in the specifics of installation.

The success of this approach not only can be seen in the critical plaudits the gallery received when it opened in 2000, but also in visitor numbers: During its first year the gallery received 5.25 million visitors, making it the most popular modern art gallery in the world.

What becomes clear during this phase is that the leader's role is to provide direction and support without becoming overly proscriptive as to how things should be done. This is not the same as laissez-faire management. It is transformational leadership. This is a mentoring role rather than a controlling one where leaders encourage self-discovery and learning. The vision should give people sufficient focus to know where the boundaries of decision-making lie. If leaders live out the vision they help to set the example for organisational behaviour. Of course this does require trust on the part of leaders and the imparting of a sense of confidence and it equally requires honesty and responsibility from employees. As Nittve argues, the hard part is to avoid the temptation to seize back power when a leader gets nervous where things are going. There may need to be adjustments, but trust is easily lost when leaders show their nervousness or demonstrate fear of change.

One way to encourage this trust is by helping to reduce uncertainty. People are always troubled by the anxiety of choice. Overall we should recognise that anxiety is good for us. It pushes us to do things: 'anxiety is thus essential to growth. In fact, the experience of anxiety *is* the experience of growth' (Koestenbaum and Block 2001: 139). Yet if we experience too much uncertainty then we can get overwhelmed. We should also recognise that people's propensity for dealing with anxiety varies. By providing clear direction and determining parameters, leaders can produce an appropriate degree of anxiety – one that is inspirational not crippling.

The final element of the leadership cycle is feedback. Some leaders are so seemingly impressive and powerful that people are too intimidated to give their honest feedback. Those loops that are built back into processes then become counter-productive. The bigger the distance between leaders and employees the harder it is to generate an open dialogue. This is another reason why arborescent structures should be attacked and a free flow of information encouraged. The feedback process should be both formal so that employees evaluate leaders on a regular basis and the impact of leadership monitored, and informal so that the dialogue between leaders and employees provides genuine insight into the way an organisation works, rather than simply how it is perceived to work from planning charts and reporting processes. This openness also facilitates the appropriate evolution of the vision, so that it is a dynamic element guiding the organisation to better value delivery.

CONCLUSION

When it comes to searching for the formula that creates the perfect leader, we are sadly disappointed. Leadership has to be adapted to the circumstances. A successful leader in one organisation may not find the same success in another one or indeed the leader who is working wonders one minute may be demonised the next. As Figure 7.3 suggests, sources of a leadership success may be attributed to personality, attitudes, behaviour, knowledge and skill (leadership qualities). However there are some things that seem to be more consistently important – although it is always possible to think of successful leaders who don't fit even into these generalisations. Effective leaders have the ability to listen to others and to hear advice and then to make decisions. Leaders tend to have good emotional intelligence so that they can empathise with other points of view and form valuable relationships with people inside the organisation and outside. Leaders need to able to advocate a clear direction and demonstrate their commitment to it by their communications and actions. Leaders

Figure 7.3 Requirements of assemblage leadership

need to have confidence in themselves and be able to trust others and to give them sufficient support and direction without wanting to control. Leaders need to be open to feedback and to negative opinions.

As we can see in Figure 7.3 there are so many demands on leaders that it is impossible for one person to be good in all spheres, which makes the last important point about leadership: self-knowledge. Good leaders (although probably not autocratic ones) know themselves and their own strengths and weaknesses and try to improve themselves and use the skills of others to overcome deficiencies.

NOTES

1. Mintzberg et al. (1998) argue that a lot of what is called strategic planning actually amounts to strategic control.
2. Hugo Lettiche (2004: 69) points out that control and trust are not pure opposites for without a concept of trust there cannot be control and that trust is a form of control because it is 'grounded in one's trust in the predictability of demands and behaviour'.
3. Mikhail Bakhtin argues that the choice of speech genre is determined by 'the specific nature of the given sphere of speech communication, semantic (thematic) considerations, the concrete situation of the speech communication, the personal composition of its participants, and so on' (Morris 2003: 83).
4. From www.bp.com (downloaded 19 October 2006).
5. Aker Kværner was rated the third most admired brand in Norway (2006).

CHAPTER 8

EVALUATION

*T*his chapter brings the elements of the assemblage together. By adopting an organisation-wide view of brand building we need evaluation mechanisms that provide a broad perspective on the impact of the assemblage. Our argument has been that it is misleading to adopt a narrow perspective because it is possible to destroy value by only looking at the performance of a part of the assemblage. For example, brand awareness could be improved by investing heavily in advertising, but if there is a lack of investment in brand delivery (systems, product, customer support) then awareness is not likely to convert into sustainable sales. Equally, a significant increase on spending to support employee skills might enhance individuals' potential to deliver the brand, but if there is a lack of attention paid to product and pricing, there may be a shortage of customers to deliver good service to. This indicates that the impact on brand equity of different brand investments needs to be understood and aligned with the overall organisational objectives. In simple terms this means that each element of the assemblage needs to be wired to the other. We need to assess how an investment in leadership impacts on human resources and organisational culture and how it affects the overall brand building capability of the organisation. We need to be able to monitor the result of specific initiatives and to connect the specifics together in an overall perspective.

The challenges here are threefold. First measurement by itself is only of value if it is translated into a narrative that impacts on decision-making. This means that the information generated needs to be used in a relevant way throughout the organisation. Secondly, data collection becomes a major under-taking because the assemblage itself is an organic, ever-changing set of relationships that needs to be constantly monitored and the movements of relevant change observed. Thirdly, measurement by itself does not guarantee effective branding governance. That is determined by how well leadership, culture, people and systems are integrated.

THE IDEA OF BRANDING GOVERNANCE

The core concern of branding governance (the management or control of organisational brand policy) is the fusing together the elements of the assemblage to deliver value to customers and other stakeholders. This is about understanding the perspectives of stakeholders and the nature of the operating environment and defining and implementing a vision. It is concerned with making investments in activities that strengthen brand equity and brand value. As Lou Gerstner argues, (2002: 223–4) citing the example of IBM, effective strategies are about rigorous analysis of appropriate and reliable data and the incorporation of that data, combined with 'wisdom, insight and risk-taking', into tactical and strategic plans.[1]

To implement a successful brand building strategy requires the development and use of information systems that can organise brand information both to improve the brand owner's knowledge and to enhance intellectual capital. One of the important aspects here is to build up a repository of brand data that can compensate for the departure of employees who may hold specific information and also to give changes context. Effective brand management based on an organisation-wide perspective demands a comprehensive approach to realise the effect of brand investments, rather than isolated marketing information and data such as awareness and preference. It requires the evaluation of key economic measures, including market share, average prices, price premiums, gross margins, profitability and other financial variables. The full potential of brands can be fully understood only when marketing information and data are linked to organisational and financial figures in a brand governance system. This enables managers to understand the relationships between (a) investments (costs) in assemblage or participatory brand building activities, (b) brand building capability, (c) brand equity, and (d) financial performance.

Effective branding governance therefore requires the ability to structure data, to recognise movement in it and to be able to explore the underlying intensities that stimulate change. The information that is generated, while primarily numerical, however requires narrative interpretation if the abstract is to be given meaning. The ability to interpret and use data is determined by the elements we have been talking about throughout this book. A rhizomatic organisation that is highly adaptive is more likely to be willing and able to respond quickly to movements than an arborescent one for the simple reason that there is greater fluidity inside the organisation. People are able to self-organise and respond to events better than a structure that has a more formalised approach that necessitates a bottom–up/top–down discussion followed by authorisation. An organisation that has a culture with a strong sense of mission (Denison 2000) will be better able to use information to make brand-aligned decisions. And a participatory structure helps the flow of knowledge both inside the organisation and also where the organisation meets its customers.

ORGANISING FOR MANAGEMENT DECISION-MAKING

In tune with Kaplan and Norton's strategic mapping process, the determinant of where to make investments within the assemblage should be based on the overall organisational objectives and the customer objectives and strategy. If, for example, the customer objective is customer intimacy then the organisational emphasis should be on getting close to customers and building long-term, trusting relationships. Working back from this, managers need to determine the best use of resources in terms of investments in leadership, HR drivers, organisational culture and marketing and communications. This sounds simple, but the reality is far more complex.

First, the fulfilment of the organisational objectives needs to take into account stakeholders other than customers. Suppliers, government, local communities, investors and employees all need to be considered and it may be that their needs conflicts with those of customers. Trade-offs may have to be made.

Secondly, we might deduce that to achieve customer intimacy we should ensure that we have the best managers and employees but this still leaves open the question of whether to invest in current or new employees, to develop better recruitment processes or fund better training systems. Organisations might like to think that all of these things are good to have, but choices always have to be made about priorities.

Thirdly, it is often difficult to know whether an idea works or doesn't because of the concept itself or its execution.

Finally, as the marketplace is dynamic, a decision to make an investment in a certain type of marketing activity might be made redundant by a competitor move or a change in consumption habits.

The only way such judgements can be made is if there is a historical and accessible source of information that can be utilised. This is the rationale behind the need for acquiring robust information over time that indicates the results of investment decisions. Figure 8.1 depicts the branding governance process which connects planning, structuring, executing and evaluating.

1. Market intelligence and organisational performance data is gathered, inputted and used to help formulate the brand objective and strategy.

Figure 8.1   Assemblage branding decision-making process

2. The brand objective and strategy are determined by the needs of the overall organisational strategy and if executed effectively help to deliver that strategy.

3. The performance in delivering the strategy is collected into the brand governance system which provides feedback to the organisational strategy.

4. If the governance system works and communicates effectively it then provides insight for organisational members into the organisation and the external environment.

5. The way the world is viewed by organisational members determines which elements are emphasised in setting up the brand governance system.

The process as described can thus be used in the formulation of plans, in the emergence of strategies as data impacts on thinking, in conducting experiments, as a guide to investment decisions and as a point of accountability.

To ensure the strategic relevance of decisions about the assemblage, some organisations establish high-level branding governance groups. These groups are known by a variety of names but their role is to ensure that the different parts of the organisation are linked together in the delivery of value. Ideally, these groups should comprise people who can represent the totality of the assemblage: marketing director, head of market research, head of advertising, head of strategy, HR director, IT director, finance director and in some cases the CEO. Depending on the nature of the organisation, other key representatives should be included such as the leaders from key geographies if the structure is international and key operational heads in larger organisations.

The most important role is for people to put aside their own agendas in pursuit of a well-connected assemblage that is an effective resource allocator and communicates both upwards to the board of directors and downwards to management and employees. The effective functioning of this governance group is determined by the quality and integration of information. As the Head of Brand Strategy at a global bank observed,

> we spend large sums on research. Everything has to be shown to have an impact on business performance. Brand development and management must be fact based, so we look to understand the return on brand investment. We need to show that investments are effective, so we emphasise measurement which is rigorous and global.

In many organisations, however, fact-based management is undermined by the lack of unity in measurement. When we have conducted research with more decentralised organisations, we have found a plurality of measurement systems that could not be easily integrated. An effective branding governance system should ideally combine the separate systems into an integrated software program that runs off a single database so that departments can more easily share information and communicate with each other in a common language. Thus, it is possible to frame various data into one screen to see relationships between trends inside the organisation with developments in brand equity scores and financial results.

Based on 25 interviews with marketing managers we also found a positive attitude towards implementing tighter branding governance through the combination and display of organisational, marketing and finance information. In such a system, data on brand-building investments, advertising campaigns and price discounts, brand equity data like awareness, associations and the brand story, and sales and financial results were thought to provide the following potential benefits:

1. possible to reduce costs by 10–30% or to re-allocate the budget and to improve the effectiveness by investing about 1% of an annual budget in integrated data capture and analysis

2. save time and enhance consistency in delivering common presentations and brand history overviews, especially as an input in briefing

3. understand quickly the impact of investments in both the internal and external markets and to help make decisions that are effective and profitable

4. improve the effectiveness of strategies and campaigns

5. reduce time in learning and training

6. ensure independency from agencies and other advisors by having a complete brand history available in-house

7. strengthen the knowledge capital and improve the basis of decision-making

BRANDING GOVERNANCE: THE ASSEMBLAGE BRANDING ELEMENTS

The assemblage branding model (Figure 8.2) determines the elements that need to be included in the branding governance process. The assemblage is both a representation of a current state and a picture of potentiality. At any given moment in time we can fix an image of the organisation in terms of its performance in such specific areas as HR, organisational culture and leadership and we can determine the overall brand equity and brand value. Yet we cannot be sure of what the organisation is capable, nor how external events and internal pressures are changing as we evaluate. In discussing such intensive processes, Deleuze talks about 'speeds of becoming and capacities to become' (Delanda 2004: 101). This is important because in complex systems, where there is emergence and adaptation the shape of the assemblage changes all the time not only in response to managerial decisions, but because the organisational culture delivers self-generated responses from people inside the organisation. To appreciate this, just think of Quiksilver and its rapid free-flow entrained way of

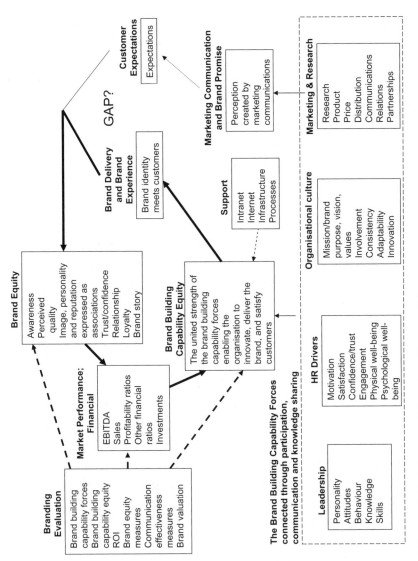

Figure 8.2   The assemblage branding model

working. The wants and needs of its board sports consumers are changing constantly and consequently the Quiksilver assemblage needs to adapt to meet them. This is not to say that everything changes at once, because as we have observed there needs to be a balance of territorialisation and de-territorialisation in the system.

Although we can never know the full potential of an assemblage we can get a sense of it through trend data that show the movement within the brand-building forces and by conducting experiments. Also by benchmarking the data, the organisation can compare itself to best in class performers and spot the potential gaps where improvements can be made. However, the organisation has to recognise its individuality. It might appear that in a given industry success is achieved by organisations that are externally focused and highly flexible, but there might also be other niches that are more appropriate to a certain set of competencies and organisational culture. We should also recognise that potential is not only hidden within the forces, but more importantly in the connecting arrows. How well aligned are the brand building forces and how well connected are they? If an organisation has a marketing policy based on a desire to achieve customer intimacy while HR and the culture emphasises process improvement and evaluation is focused on profitability, the forces could all be strong in themselves but at odds with the goal of delivering value to customers.

It is one of the key roles of leadership to ensure alignment in the assemblage; to generate a focus to activities that is driven in turn by the organisational objectives and strategy. A well-fused and entrained structure that emphasises connectivity is also more likely to achieve both the internal linkages between different areas and the external linkage with customers and other stakeholders. The challenge here is that the volume of 'noise' creates a problem of potential overload, which is dealt with by organisational members cutting out things that seem unimportant. This always creates the danger that something might be missed that is important, but as observed in Chapter 6, organisational culture dictates to a large extent what we pay attention to and it is only by questioning and occasionally challenging the culture that other factors outside the norms are considered.

When the organisation is well connected it does create the potential for a stronger brand equity. If the organisation relies overly on marketing communication as a brand equity builder, it may well generate awareness and positive associations, but the expectations created by communication may not be fulfilled if the experience of the product or service does not meet those expectations. As observed earlier in this book, this tends to be the case when there is a lack of unity in the 4Ps and when there is organisational siloisation. When there is a good linkage then marketing communication generates appropriate expectations which are then matched by the reality of delivery, thereby enhancing the potential loyalty of customers (see Figure 4.6).

Finally while the assemblage model conveys high level attributes, we should recognise that it is possible to drill down into the data. Providing the data is entered into the software system, when there are movements in awareness or customer satisfaction for example, we can then look at the causes of the change and draw inferences as to the cause and effect. As a specific instance, take one division of software services company, Visma, which observed an improvement in one element of its brand equity – customer service – from a rating of 3.5 to 4.2. Drill down into the data and the reason for the improvement was the management decision, based on research into the determinants of customer satisfaction, to train people to prioritise answering the phone more quickly. By reducing the average time by nearly two-thirds, customers became more positive.

HOW CAN BRAND EQUITY AND
MARKETING EFFORTS BE MEASURED?

In the context of an entrained way of thinking, the goal of marketing expenditure should be to bring the organisation and the customer closer together. One aspect of this process is advertising, which has the potential to communicate both a functional and emotional message. The argument is that advertising can create awareness (either high or low involvement), it can predispose people to try a product or service and that it can reinforce post-purchase feelings towards the brand. Yet as we have argued, advertising has limitations. Customers have become cynical towards it, media fragmentation inhibits effectiveness (at least for mass market brands) and it is largely a medium of distance. It may entertain us, but it is the organisation that is sending the message rather than a customer asking for it. Also if our goal is to achieve customer loyalty, we have to rely on other mechanisms to deliver this. Advertising should be seen as an element in the brand-building process, but only an element.

Rather than communicating to customers, organisations should be thinking of ways to build closer connections by creating direct contacts, well-targeted direct mail, club-based initiatives and genuine involvement in product innovation, testing and usage. Beyond this we would also argue that in an entrained approach the emphasis should be getting the product to be inspiring, fulfilling and interesting. As the designer, Peter Saville says, 'the best brands are constantly morphing packages'.[2] When an organisation pays attention to its product in this way the potential to build a bond of trust is enhanced. The brand becomes a subject of word-of-mouth discovery, not through some attempt at manipulation, but because the brand has something real and relevant to offer. It is debatable whether this language of 'loyalty', 'relationships' and 'love' is appropriate for brand relationships, but we can see that people who are involved with the brands they use can have some depth of relationship (Smit, Tolboom and Franzen 2004).

More than a hundred years ago, American retailer, John Wanamaker said: 'I know half of my advertising is wasted, I just don't know which half.' Al Ries subsequently claimed that he thought three-quarters was wasted. To provide an insight into the performance of marketing investments, it is possible to track the impact of expenditure on awareness (recall and recognition); perceived quality; image, personality, and reputation expressed as associations; trust/confidence in; relationship; loyalty; and brand story. These are both qualitative and quantitative measures but what can be observed in Figures 8.3 and 8.4 is the quantitative relationship between marketing activity, investments, brand equity impacts and financial performance. It is possible to drill down into this data so that in Figure 8.4 we can see the effect of TV expenditure on performance. We can also insert other variables, such as changes in pricing and distribution and we can insert tags that notify the viewer of changes in the product, competitor actions or service delivery and qualitative research findings. The combination of this trend data enable us to see the performance of marketing investments, so that there is a far better indication as to whether money is being well spent. Also by combining this insight with measures from the other forces described below a sense of the whole assemblage performance emerges.

HOW CAN HR DRIVERS BE MEASURED IN BRANDING GOVERNANCE?

It has been our argument in this book that the talent inside an organisation is fundamental to its performance, yet as with marketing, the human resources function is often underplayed because HR managers are seen to be insufficiently strategic in their thinking and approach. Part of the potential benefit of an

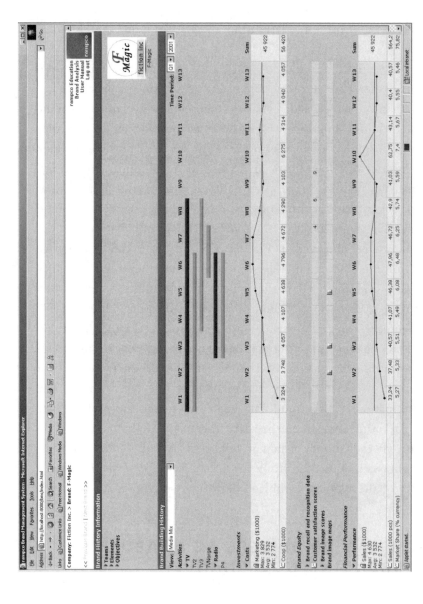

Figure 8.3   Relationship between marketing investments, brand equity and financial performance
(1)

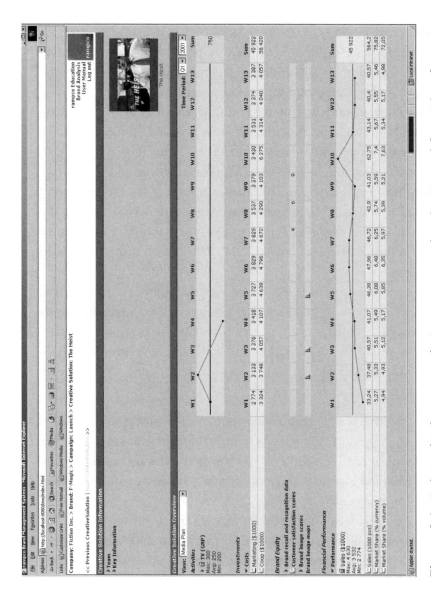

Figure 8.4 Relationship between marketing investments, brand equity and financial performance (2)

integrated brand governance system is that it brings to the fore the importance of the role of talent in performance. Some writers have argued that all customer facing employees are potential brand ambassadors, but we would argue that *all* employees can contribute towards the brand building potential of the organisation. However, the potential is only realised if the brand (in terms of vision and values) is understood and incorporated into people's behaviour so that they can contribute to profitable relationships with external customers and fulfil the organisation's brand promise. This indicates that a good understanding of the brand enables employees' to see how their actions can enhance the brand, particularly though the delivery of customer service (Thomson et al. 1999). It is an employee's motivation, engagement and competence that determines the ability to deliver good service. Providing good service requires a strong empathy with customers, which is part of the rationale for bringing the customer inside the organisation and achieving entrainment. There are other important critical factors when it comes to the ability to deliver customer service (Chenet et al. 2000):

- effective teams: requires harmony in the group, commitment to the group, and participation in decision making, together with a common sense of success; here critical factors are collaboration versus competition and personal involvement and commitment
- the employee's qualification and ability to do the job
- understanding and adoption of the vision and values
- the technological support that enables employees to do their job
- perceived control related to the relationship between individual reactions to stress and the opportunity to control these situations; rules and procedures and the organisational culture can be critical factors

All of these functional and emotional attributes can be measured using quantitative and qualitative research. As well as measures that cover actual facts such as competence development expenditure, absenteeism, hours spent in training, employee qualifications, indices can be developed for example to determine employee perceptions of:

- the importance of the job for the individual
- understanding of the brand
- relevance of the brand to day-to-day work – ability to translate vision and values
- satisfaction with job
- degree of identification
- degree of internalisation of brand
- degree of involvement and commitment
- freedom of action – potential for self-organisation
- quality of support – training, development, technology
- connectedness with other parts of the organisation
- importance of organisational environment
- ability to deliver high standard of customer service
- quality of leadership
- quality of communication – feedback from external and internal audiences
- opportunity for creative expression and self-actualisation
- trust in the organisation

This sort of data, if maintained and updated regularly along-side data from the other brand-building forces, can create a picture of the organisational talent and how it impacts on other forces such as leadership and culture. We can also explore specific correlations to determine whether there are linkages between employee satisfaction and the delivery of customer satisfaction.

What the organisation actually measures should be determined by the needs of the organisational strategy. Some measures such as satisfaction, brand understanding and usage should be consistent, but others such as creativity and freedom may vary in the way they are interpreted by different organisations. The value of the HR data by itself is that it provides a measure of the human resource inside the organisation and its degree of connectivity with the identity. When allied with the data from the other brand-building forces it indicates the capability of the organisation to enhance brand equity and the specific role of people in so doing. This is valuable both in planning new integrated strategies, as a diagnostic tool in pinpointing gaps in performance (when connected to customer research) and in building internal consensus for correcting areas where there is non-alignment.

HOW CAN ORGANISATIONAL CULTURE BE MEASURED IN BRANDING GOVERNANCE?

Several researchers have found that there are close links between a strong organisational culture and efficiency and business performance. However, while a 'strong organisational culture' might be valuable, it is understood in many different ways (Denison and Mishra 1995, Van der Post, de Coning and Smith 1997, Dellana and Hauser 1999, Cooper et al. 2001). We might characterise a strong culture as one that has a powerful and engaging mission, but sometimes these messianic cultures are impervious to changes in the environment because they are too rigid and lack adaptability. Similarly we might characterise an adaptive culture as strong because it is potentially receptive to movement, but it can also suffer from a lack of clear direction. In other words, a strong culture must exhibit both freedom and order or, as Denison (2000) would argue, it must work through the tensions inherent in adaptability and mission.

But we can also look at organisational culture in other ways. As suggested in Chapter 6, we can categorise cultures as either fulfilling or not. Does the culture provide the potential for fulfilment for most organisational members? When the culture creates fulfilment for people, it helps to deliver a coherent brand story for customers – a narrative that is defined by the brand and manifested in employees who share in a common cause. A fulfilling organisational culture is also communicated in the myths of charismatic leaders and heroes – the inspirational brand ambassadors who determine clear expectations for themselves and their colleagues.

In terms of measuring culture, it can be argued that it requires the sort of depth that only qualitative analysis can provide, but there are also quantitative tools that can be used. Cameron and Quinn's OCAI (1999) creates a matrix that allocates the organisational culture to either a predominantly internal or external bias and either a flexibile and individualistic orientation or a stable, controlled one. These categorisations which they call clan, adhocracy, hierarchy and market, largely mirror Denison's categories. Denison and Mishra's (1995) measurable definition of organisational culture suggests four main dimensions:

- involvement (empowerment, team orientation, and capability development)
- congruency and consistency (core values, agreement, and co-ordination and integration)
- adaptability (creating change, customer focus, and organisational learning)
- a clear and acknowledged mission (strategic directions and intent, goals and objectives, and vision)

Denison and Mishra categorise the involvement and consistency dimensions as internally focused and adaptability and mission as externally focused. The virtue of the Denison approach is that the perspective it has derived from implementing the model aligns with many of the arguments we have made in this book, specifically:

- effective organisations are good at encouraging participation, at building teams and developing people's potential throughout the organisation

- people are encouraged to be self-organising
- the organisation invests in developing the skills of its members
- people know the values of the organisation and understand the implications for the way they behave
- linked to the point above, organisational members are good at working across boundaries to achieve common goals
- organisations that are adaptable are driven by their customers, take risks and learn from what they do
- adaptable organisations 'usually experience sales growth and increased market share'
- successful organisations have a strong sense of mission and are able to express a sense of the future
- clear goals and objectives can be linked to the mission, vision and strategy

(Denison, 2000)

In a study of a Scandinavian business school which used the Denison scales plus research into employee satisfaction and employee trust/confidence in top management, the scores were very low compared with other comparable organisations. For instance, employees found the organisational culture insufficiently inclusive because of limited opportunities to participate in the decision-making process. Further, the majority of the employees did not consider the culture as consistent because the core values seemed to have little meaning and influence on employee behaviour. The scores on adaptability and organisational learning were low, which is particularly disappointing for a knowledge producing organisation. Also, there seemed to be little support for long-term objectives and the vision. Thus, it was difficult to motivate employees to take collective action and move the organisation towards common goals.

However, employees seemed to be satisfied in a general sense, particularly in the academic faculty. This result can be explained largely by academic individualism in that the most appreciated aspect of a faculty job is the ability to pursue one's own academic interests. Predictably the trust/confidence in top management was very low. The somewhat poor scores on the main four organisational culture dimensions reflect a shortage of emotional and social capital and in particular relationships may be weak. Finally, the organisational culture seemed somewhat fragmented and there were indications of sub-cultures. This would suggest that the culture of this business school is not strong and is an inhibitor to building a coherent brand.

By way of contrast, by applying Denison's scales to a large newspaper publisher we see a different cultural type emerge. Here employee understanding and support for the core values was weak, despite a real interest in the values themselves. However, mission and involvement seemed relatively strong in comparison. By dividing employees and mangers into two groups, some significant differences emerge, in terms of trust/confidence, job satisfaction, mission, vision, values, involvement and consistency. While qualitative research suggested that there would be differences in departmental responses, this did not prove to be the case. Further investigation of the data confirmed that trust/confidence and job satisfaction are strongly correlated and the dimensions of mission, consistency and involvement have the biggest impact on job satisfaction as a dependent variable. The dimensions of job satisfaction, mission, and involvement have greatest influence on trust/confidence in. Using these results, it is clear that there is a need to enhance involvement as a precursor to strengthening both job satisfaction and trust/confidence in top management.

The Denison model works well as a diagnostic tool for identifying cultural issues within an organisation. Its virtue is that it doesn't force categorisations onto cultures, but rather recognises that organisations are never purely one thing or another. Rather they exhibit tendencies to be more dominantly aligned with the different dimensions. These tendencies can be conducive to achieving organisational goals or they can represent a barrier. By creating a cultural score, the issues can be identified and remedial action thought through in terms of working with the culture and the other brand-building forces. Further, by using tracking data, progress towards better alignment can be monitored and actions developed as necessary.

HOW CAN LEADERSHIP BE MEASURED?

Organisational culture, HR drivers and leadership are so clearly connected in the quest to enhance the brand-building capability of the organisation that the measurement of one force is inevitably linked to the others (Figure 8.5). Certain leadership qualities are necessary to develop and maintain a consistent approach to HR drivers and a strong, positive organisational culture especially once we accept the fluidity of the assemblage and the needs of internal and external participation. Given the dominant qualities of leaders that we stressed in Chapter 7 – analytical, good at listening, communicative, committed, self-knowledgeable, emotionally intelligent, adaptive, decisive, ability to express values, ability to express oneness – it should be evident as to the type of qualities needed for managers to lead and manage brands. Managers can be evaluated on these qualities qualitatively, but also quantitatively through web-based or print evaluations by employees on a regular basis. The results can then be integrated in the branding governance software system. Thus, it is possible to see how satisfaction with leaders and management is linked to other results and performances such as organisational culture and the various HR drivers. Poor scores should lead to a diagnosis of the problem and investments in management training and development programmes.

The idea of quantitatively measuring management attributes is a relatively new one. In 1987 Schleh wrote about ROM (return on management) but the term didn't get much uptake in terms of specific ROM techniques until Simons and Davila (1998) in a *Harvard Business Review* article elaborated on the issue. The

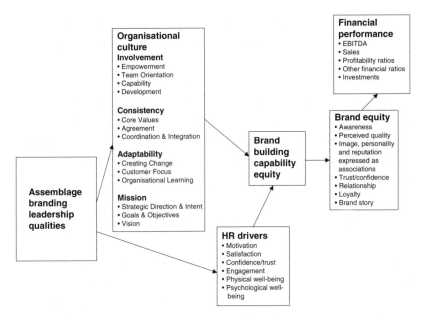

Figure 8.5 The connection between leadership, culture, HR drivers and brand building

authors stressed that managerial energy is an organisation's most important and most scarce resource, and it must be channelled into implementing strategies and into the right projects or issues. Simons and Davila presented a new business ratio that indicated a qualitative measure based on whether an organisation was getting the maximum pay back from investments in implementing business strategy. Return on management was expressed by them in the following equation:

$$\text{ROM} = \frac{\text{Productive organisational energy released}}{\text{Management time and attention invested}}$$

The challenge for managers with this idea of ROM is the need to construct estimates of magnitude where both the numerator and the denominator in the ratio are qualitative. ROM then is perhaps a useful mental model – a way of thinking that each manager can train herself/himself to follow. The equation encourages management discipline in terms of how time is spent and what is achieved.

A more robust way of looking at the issue is to develop another ratio that incorporates investments in management development and output of those investments. The numerator would be documented results of management development and the denominator would be the actual costs. Thus, we can present return on investments in management development (ROIMD) as:

$$\text{ROIMD} = \frac{\text{Results of management development}}{\text{Actual costs}}$$

For example, Aker Kværner has invested worldwide approximately €3.5 million in corporate level management development programmes. The 200 or so corporate managers can take part in a number of programmes at the Aker Kværner Academy, but most are involved in two different leadership programmes: (1) Business Leadership Program; (2) Developing Your Leadership. To measure progress and deviations from objectives, 360 degrees leadership evaluations are completed. The ultimate objective is to strengthen and maintain a positive and effective leadership culture. There is also an annual review between all employees and their managers where personal business contracts (PBCs) are discussed. In such meetings the manager and the employee agree on the challenges for the next year in terms of health, culture/environment, and security. When there is a meeting between a manager and her/his superior, there is also a review of skills in developing people/employees and contribution to the organisational culture. The success of managers is therefore measured on how well employees are developed (results are provided by the annual employee satisfaction measure/organisational climate study). Thus if the denominator is €3.5 million, the numerator is derived from the scoring of managers on the metrics that matter most to the organisation.

PRESENTING THE DATA

In our assemblage and participatory branding philosophy we encourage leaders to understand the organisation's inner life (the link between leadership qualities, the strength of HR drivers and organisational culture characteristics) and its influence on customer satisfaction and financial performance. The only way to understand the possible co-variations and fluctuations across these dimensions and parameters is to create robust measures that are both timed and timely, to enter the data into one integrated system and to create the opportunity to review the data in one graphical interface (Figure 8.6). The overall responsibility for branding governance strategy is in the hands of the CEO and top management. Senior managers should concentrate not only on an understanding of their own specific area of interest or competence, but also on the linkages between the different areas, because a movement in the HR force, for example, impacts on culture, marketing, leadership and all the elements that contribute to brand building.

The challenge is to create an IT system and an application that pulls data from different storage areas and servers to compare and display the figures within one framework. Another possibility is to transfer all raw data to one server where different applications can gather the data and transform it for presentation. If the data remains fragmented, thinking is likely to be similar. When everything is linked the inter-relationships become clearer and managers are encouraged to recognise that actions in one area of the assemblage will have implications for other areas. Figure 8.6 presents trend data relating expenditures on different forces to results. This big picture gives us a sense of how the assemblage is moving either in response to internal investment decisions or, by using markers on the data, in response to external events. It is difficult to find an appropriate metaphor, but rather than thinking in a linear way (which is a silo way of thinking of cause and

Costs and
investments and
performance/results

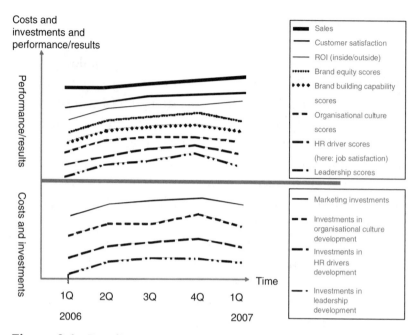

Figure 8.6   Branding governance graphics

effect), we should imagine the assemblage as like a moon jellyfish. A stimulus causes the whole assemblage to wobble and then reach some new equilibrium. To make sure we capture the wobbles, data should be organised in such a way that statistical software programs can be used to investigate correlations between the various variables. For instance sales can be defined as the dependent variable while HR drivers' scores, organisational culture scores and marketing investment can be used as independent variables that may explain sales fluctuations.

Equally while recognising the interlinked nature of the data, we may also want to go deeper into the data to explore the underlying intensities. We have argued throughout this book that when we start to see numbers we tend to start forgetting people. We need to remind ourselves in looking at the data generated through evaluation that we need to explain the meaning behind the numbers. As Deleuze would argue, it is in the correct structuring of problems that we find truth. To achieve this we may need to look at specific data, conduct qualitative research, work with customers to explore implications or conduct experiments to see the impact of new ways of doing things. And we finally need to remind ourselves that we bring our own prejudices to these challenges. In evaluating the assemblage in a certain way, we bring our preconceptions to the process. We need to remind ourselves of that and to keep questioning our approach. If we can do that and we can make some sense of the messiness of the assemblage, we will see new ways of making connections and bringing value to customers. As Manuel Delanda writes of the non-linear approach, we can 'define a world capable of surprising us through the emergence of unexpected novelty, a world where there will always be something else to explain and which will therefore remain forever problematic' (Delanda 2000: 155).

CONCLUSION

This chapter on evaluation brings together all the elements of the assemblage. While we have looked at the assemblage elements separately in this book, it should be clear that there are strong overlaps between all the different elements and a connectivity between the organisation and its customers. The argument for encouraging the linkage of the assemblage is that it is through a unification of the parts that value is delivered. When siloisation prevails, investment decisions lack coherence as the different forces in the assemblage head off in different directions, often sustained by a disconnected analysis of performance. Achieving unity is a major challenge in most organisations, because divisionalised structures encourage identification with immediate units rather than the organisational whole. Unity is a project that must be continually worked at. It requires

- a strong and clearly articulated sense of purpose – a focus (what Denison would call mission) that inspires and motivates organisational members
- a strong customer presence so that the point of accountability is the delivery of value to the customer
- a cultural fluidity that encourages people to self-organise across departmental boundaries
- evaluation mechanisms that stress both the connectivity of metrics and the end purpose of the business

Thus we argue for measurement of the assemblage as a continuous process not because of an obsession with measurement itself, but rather because without an integrated evaluation process we lose organisational connectivity. This is of value when we develop strategies, when we diagnose how well we're doing in executing those strategies, when we need an internal currency for discussion, when we experiment with new products and services and when we need to identify our strengths and weaknesses. Yet we must exercise caution here and remind ourselves that the data we generate must be interpreted carefully. We must dig below the surface of what we find and seek out the underlying intensities that drive change.

NOTES

1. When Gerstner arrived at IBM he found that there were 339 different satisfaction surveys being conducted with different methodologies. Also research data indicated that customer satisfaction was good (in spite of the fact that the company was losing market share) – this was because the sales force were asked to pick the research respondents and not surprisingly they chose their happiest and best customers.
2. Interview at Belgrade design and branding week, 20 May 2006.

REFERENCES AND BIBLIOGRAPHY

Aaker, D.A. (1991) *Managing Brand Equity: Capitalizing on the Value of a Brand Name.* New York: The Free Press.

Aaker, D.A. (1996) *Building Strong Brands.* New York: The Free Press.

Aaker, D.A. and Joachimsthaler, E. (2000) *Brand Leadership.* New York: The Free Press.

Aaker, D.A., Kumar, V. and Day, G.S. (2001) *Marketing Research,* 6th edn. New York: John Wiley & Sons, Inc.

Amabile, T.M. (2001) Beyond talent. *American Psychologist* 56(4) Apr: 333.

Amabile, T.M., Patterson, C., Mueller, J., Wojcik, T., Odomirok, P., Marsh, M. and Kramer, S. (2001) Academic-practitioner collaboration in management research: a case of cross-profession collaboration. *Academy of Management Journal* 44(2) Apr: 418–31.

Ambler, T. and Barrow, S. (1996) The employer brand. *Journal of Brand Management* 4: 185–206.

Andersen, N. (2003) Polyphonic Organisations. In T. Bakken and T. Hernes (eds) *Autopoietic Organization Theory: Drawing on Niklas Luhmann's Social Systems Perspective.* Oslo: Abstrakt Forlag AS.

Argyris, C. (1970) *Intervention Theory and Method.* Reading, Mass: Addison Wesley.

Argyris, C. and Schön, D. (1978) Organizational learning. In D. Pugh (ed.) *Organization Theory.* London: Pelican, 352–71.

Ashforth, B.E. (1985) Climate formation: issues and extensions. *Journal of Management Review* 10(4): 837–45.

Ashforth, B. (1998) Epilogue: what have we learned and where do we go from here. In D. Whetten and P. Godfrey (eds) *Identity in Organizations: Building Theory through Conversations.* Thousand Oaks, CA: Sage.

Ashforth, B.E. and Mael, F. (1989) Social identity theory and the organization. *Academy of Management Review* 14(1): 20–39.

Ashkanasy, N. and Tse, B. (2000). Transformational leadership as management of emotion: a conceptual review. In N.M. Ashkanasy, C.E.J. Hartel and W.J. Zerbe (eds.) *Emotions in the Workplace: Research, Theory, and Practice.* Westport, CT: Quorum Books.

Ashkanasy, N.M., Wilderom, P.M.C. and Peterson, M.F. (2000) *Handbook of Organizational Culture and Climate.* Thousand Oaks: Sage Publications, Inc.

Azoulay, A. and Kapferer, J.N. (2003) Do brand personality scales really measure brand personality? *Journal of Brand Management* 11(2) Nov: 143–55.

Backhaus, K.B. (2004) An exploration of corporate recruitment descriptions on monster.com. *Journal of Business Communication* 41(2): 115–36.

Baecker, D. (2003) Management within the system. In T. Bakken and T. Hernes (eds) *Autopoietic Organization Theory.* Oslo: Abstrakt Forlag, 183–212.

Bakan, J. (2004) *The Corporation: The Pathological Pursuit of Profit and Power.* London: Constable.

Baker, A.C., Jensen, P.J., Kolb, D.A. and Associates (2002) *Conversational learning: An Experiential Approach to Knowledge Creation.* Westport, CT: Quorum.

Bakken, T. and Hernes, T. (2003) *Autopoietic Organization Theory: Drawing on Niklas Luhmann's Social Systems Perspective.* Oslo: Abstrakt Forlag AS.

Bang, H. (1998) *Organisasjonskultur i praksis. Verktøy for kartlegging, utvikling og endring av organisasjonskultur.* Oslo: Tano Aschehoug.

Barley, S.R. (1983) Semiotics and the study of occupational and organisational cultures. *International Studies of Management and Organisation* 28, 393–413.

Bar-On, R. (2000) Emotional and social intelligence: insights from the Emotional Quotient Inventory. In Ed. R. Bar-On and J.D.A. Parker (eds) *Handbook of Emotional Intelligence*. San Francisco: Jossey-Bass, 363–88.

Barry, D. and Elmes, M. (1997) Strategy retold: toward a narrative view of strategic discourse. *Academy of Management Review* 22(2): 429–52.

Bass, B.M. (1985) *Leadership and Performance Beyond Expectations*. New York: Free Press.

Bass, M.R. (1990) *Bass & Stogdill's Handbook of Leadership: Theory, Research and Managerial Applications*. New York: The Free Press.

Bass, B.M. and Avolio, B.J. (1993). Transformational leadership and organizational culture. *Public Administration Quarterly* 17(1), 112–21.

Belova, O. (2006) Listening to the other: polyphony and dialogue in organisational research. *Narrative in Management Science*. Barcelona.

Bennis, W. (1997) Becoming a leader of leaders. In R. Gibson (ed.) *Rethinking the Future*. London: Nicholas Brealey, 148–63.

Berle, A. and Means, G.C. (1932) *The Modern Corporation and Private Property*. New York: Commerce Clearing House.

Berlin, I. (2005) *Liberty* (H Hardy ed.). Oxford: Oxford University Press.

Beverland, M.B. (2006) The 'real thing': brand authenticity in the luxury wine trade. *Journal of Business Research* 59(2): 251–8.

Bjerke, R., Gopalakrishna, P. and Sandler, D. (2005) A cross-national comparison of Scandinavian value orientations: from value segmentation to promotional appeals. *Journal of Promotion Management* 12(1), 35–56.

Bloom, H. (2001) *How to Read and Why*. London: 4th Estate.

Bohm, D. (2004) *On Creativity*. Abingdon: Routledge Classics.

Bono, J.E. and Judge, T.A. (2004) Personality and transformational and transactional leadership: a meta-analysis. *Journal of Applied Psychology* 89(5) Oct: 901–10.

Booth, H. (2003) An inward-facing outlook. *Design Week* 18(26), 9.

Breen, B. (2002) BMW: driven by design. *Fast Company* 62, Sep: 122–35.

Brønn, P. (2003) Intervju per mail om organisasjonskultur. Oslo: BI Norges Markedshøyskole, 20 November.

Brown, R. and Williams, J. (1994) Group identification: the same thing to all people? *Human Relations* 37(7), 547–64.

Brown, J.S. and Paul, D. (2000) *The Social Life of Information*. Cambridge MA: Harvard Business School Press.

Brown, S., Kozinets, R.V. and Sherry, J.F. Jr (2003) Teaching old brands new tricks: retro branding and the revival of brand meaning. *Journal of Marketing* 67(3): 19–33.

Boxx, W.R., Odom, R.Y. and Dunn, M.G. (1991) Organizational values and value congruency and their impact on satisfaction, commitment, and cohesion: an empirical examination with the public sector. *Public Personnel Management* Vol 20, Issue 2.

Bungay, S. (2003) *Alamein*. London: Aurum.

Burmann, C. and Zeplin, S. (2005) Building brand commitment: a behavioural approach to internal brand management. *Journal of Brand Management* 12(4): 279–300.

Business Week (2004) Coke: Wooing the TiVo Generation. *Business Week*, 1 Mar.

Cameron, K. and Quinn, R. (1999) *Diagnosing and Changing Organizational Culture*. First published by Addison-Wesley. Revised edition (2006) San Francisco: Jossey-Bass.

Cameron, K. and Quinn, R. (2006) *Diagnosing and Changing Organizational Culture*. San Francisco: Jossey-Bass.

Carter, P. and Jackson, N. (2004) Gilles Deleuze and Felix Guattari: A 'minor' contribution to organization theory. In S Linstead (ed.), *Organization Theory and Postmodern Method*. London: Sage.

Chan Kim, W. and Mauborgne, R. (2003a) Fair process: managing in the knowledge economy. *Harvard Business Review* 81(1).

Chan Kim, W. and Mauborgne, R. (2003b) Tipping point leadership, *Harvard Business Review* 81(4): 60–9.

Chatman, J.A. (1989) Improving interactional organizational research: a model of person–organization fit. *Academy of Management Review* Vol 14.

Chatman, J.A. (1991) Matching people and organizations: selection and socialization in public accounting firms. *Administrative Science Quarterly* 36(3), 459–84.

Chatwin, B. (1987) *The Songlines.* London: Viking Press.

Chenet, P., Tynan, C. and Money, A. (2000) The service performance gap: testing the redeveloped causal model. *European Journal of Marketing* 34(3/4): 472–95.

Collins, J. (2001) *Good to Great.* London: Random House.

Collins, J. and Porras, J. (1998) *Built to Last: Visionary Habits of Successful Companies.* London: Random House.

Cooper, C.L., Cartwright, S. and Earley, P.C. (2001) *The International Handbook of Organizational Culture and Climate.* New York: John Wiley & Sons, Ltd.

Cornelissen, J.P. (2005) Beyond compare: metaphor in organization theory. *Academy of Management Review* 30(4): 751–64.

de Chernatony, L. (1993) Categorizing brands: evolutionary process underpinned by two key dimensions. *Journal of Marketing Management,* 9(2), 173–88.

de Chernatony, L. (1998) *Brand Management.* Darmount Publications.

de Chernatony, L. (2001) *From Brand Vision to Brand Evaluation: Strategically Building and Sustaining Brands.* Oxford: Butterworth Heinemann.

de Chernatony, L. and Dall'Olmo Riley, F. (1998a) Defining a 'brand': beyond the literature with experts' interpretations. *Journal of Marketing Management* 14: 417–43.

de Chernatony, L. and Dall'Olmo Riley, F. (1998b) Modelling the components of the brand. *European Journal of Marketing* 32(11/12): 1074–90.

de Chernatony, L. and Dall'Olmo Riley, F. (1999) Experts' views about defining services brands and the principles of services branding. *Journal of Business Research* 46(2), 181–92.

de Chernatony, L. and McDonald, M. (1998) *Creating Powerful Brands: in Consumer, Service and Industrial Markets.* 2nd edn. Oxford: Butterworth Heinemann.

de Chernatony, L. and Segal-Horn, S. (2003) The criteria for successful services brands. *European Journal of Marketing* 37(7/8): 1095–18.

Debray, R. (2000) Transmitting Culture. Trans. Eric Rauth. New York: Columbia University Press (*Transmettre*, 1997, Editions Odile Jacob).

Delanda, M. (2003) *A Thousand Years of Nonlinear History.* New York: Swerve.

Delanda, M. (2004) *Intensive Science and Virtual Philosophy*. London: Continuum.

Deleuze, G. (1968) *Difference and Repetition*. (*Différence et Répétition*, Paris: Presses Universitaires de France). Trans. P. Patton. London: Continuum, 2004.

Deleuze, G. (2002) *Desert Islands and Other Texts, 1953–1974*. (Paris: Les éditions de Minuit). Ed. D. Lapoujade, trans. and M. Taormina. Semiotext(e) Foreign Agents Series, Los Angeles, 2004.

Deleuze, G. and Guattari, F. (1980) *A Thousand Plateaus: Capitalism and Schizophrenia*. (*Mille Plateaux*, Paris: Les éditions de Minuit). Trans. B Massumi. London: Continuum, 2004.

Deleuze, G. and Guattari, F. (1991) *What Is Philosophy?* (*Qu'est-ce que la philosophie?* Paris: Les éditions de Minuit). Trans. G. Burchell and H. Tomlinson, London, New York: Verso, 2003.

Dellana, S.A. and Hauser, R.D. (1999) Toward defining the quality culture. *Engineering Management Journal* 11(2) June: 11.

Denison, D.R. (1990) *Corporate Culture, and Organizational Effectiveness*. New York: John Wiley.

Denison, D.R. (2000) Organizational culture: can it be a key lever for driving organizational change? In S. Cooper and C. Cartwright (eds) *The Handbook of Organizational Culture*. London: John Wiley & Sons.

Denison, D.R. (2001) Bringing corporate culture to the bottom line. *Organizational Dynamics* 13(2): 5–23.

Denison, D.R. and Mishra, A. (1995) Toward a theory of organizational culture and effectiveness. *Organization Science* 6(6): 204–23.

Denning, S. (2001) *The Springboard: How Storytelling Ignites Action in Knowledge-Era Organizations*, Boston, MA: Butterworth-Heinemann.

Dostoyevsky, F. (1864) *Notes from Underground* (*Zapiski iz Poolpolya*). Trans. J Coulson, Penguin, 2003, p. 31.

Douglas, M. (1966) *Purity and Danger*. London: Routledge & Kegan Paul. (Repr. Routledge Classics, 2004.)

Drucker, P. (1993) *The New Organization*. SEI Distinguished Lecture. SEI Center for Advanced Studies in Management, The Wharton School.

Drucker, P. (1998) Management's new paradigms. *Fortune*, 5 Oct.

Dunbar, R. (1992) Neocortex size as a constraint on group size in primates. *Journal of Human Evolution* 20, 469–93.

Dutton, J. and Dukerich, J. (1991) Keeping an eye on the mirror: image and identity in organizational adaptation. *Academy of Management Journal* 34(3): 517–54.

Eco, U. (1997) *Kant and the Platypus: Essays on Language and Cognition.* (*Kant e L'ornitorinco*). Trans. A. McEwen. London: Secker & Warburg, 1999.

Economist (2004) Marketing in the spotlight: what people really think of marketing. *The Economist.* Marketing Directors' Summit, March.

Edvinsson, L. and Malone, M. (1997) *Intellectual Capital.* London: Piatkus.

Ehrenreich, B. (2002) *Nickel and Dimed: Undercover in Low-Wage USA.* London: Granta.

Ehrenzweig, A. (2000) *The Hidden Order of Art.* (First published in 1967 by Weidenfeld & Nicolson) London: Phoenix Press.

Ellsberg, D. (2002) *Secrets: A Memoir of the Vietnam and the Pentagon Papers.* New York: Viking.

Feldwick, P. (1991) Defining a Brand. In D. Cowley (ed.) *Understanding Brands.* London: Kogan Page.

Flint, J. (1997) Chrysler. *Forbes Magazine*, 13 Jan: 84.

Ford, C.M. and Gioia, D.A. (2000) Factors influencing creativity in the domain of managerial decision making. *Journal of Management*, 26(4): 705–32.

Foucault, M. (2002) *Power: Essential Works of Foucault 1954–1984, vol 3.* J.D. Faubian (ed.) London: Penguin 2002.

Fukuyama, F. (2000) Social capital. In L. Harrison and S.P. Huntington (eds) *Culture Matters.* New York: Basic Books.

Gad, T. (2001) *4d Branding.* London: FT Prentice Hall.

Gaddis, J.L. (2005) Grand strategy in the second term. *Foreign Affairs*, January/February.

Gagliardi, P. (2002) The role of humanities in the formation of new European elites. Annual Meeting of the European Academy of Management – keynote speech. Stockholm.

Gagliardi, P. (2006) Exploring the aesthetic side of organizational life. In S. Clegg, C. Hardy, T. Lawrence and W. Nord (eds) *The Sage Handbook of Organization Studies.* Thousand Oaks, California: Sage.

Gainer, B. and Padanyi, P. (2005) The relationship between market-oriented activities and market-oriented culture: implications for the development of market orientation in non-profit service organizations. *Journal of Business Research* 58(6) June: 854–62.

Gallup (2002) Employee engagement index survey research at www. gallup.com

Gerstner, L. (2002) *Who Says Elephants Can't Dance?* New York: Harper Collins.

Gladwell, M. (2000) *The Tipping Point.* New York: Little Brown.

Godin, S. (ed.) and the Group of 33. (2005) *The Big Moo: Stop Trying to be Perfect and Start Being Remarkable.* New York: Portfolio.

Goleman, D. (1995) *Emotional Intelligence: Why It Can Matter More Than IQ.* London: Bloomsbury.

Grönroos, C. (1994) From marketing mix to relationship marketing: towards a paradigm shift in marketing. *Management Decision* 32(2), 4–20.

Gratton, L. (2004) *The Democratic Enterprise.* UK: Pearson Education.

Greenley, G.E. Hooley, G.J. and Rudd, J.M. (2005) Market orientation in a multiple stakeholder orientation context: Implications for marketing capabilities and assets. *Journal of Business Research* 58, 1483–94.

Guignon, C. (2004) *On Being Authentic.* Abingdon: Routledge.

Hampton, G.M. and Hampton, D.L. (2004) Relationship of professionalism, rewards, market orientation and job satisfaction among medical professionals: the case of certified nurse-midwives. *Journal of Business Research* 57(9): 1042–53.

Handy, C. (2001) The citizen company. In J. Henry (ed.) *Creative Management.* London: Sage, 240–1.

Harris, P. (2005) To see with the mind and think through the eye: Deleuze, folding architecture and Simon Rodia's Watts Towers. In G. Lambert and I. Buchanan (eds) *Deleuze and Space.* Edinburgh: Edinburgh University Press, 36–60.

Hatch, M.J. and Schultz, M. (2002) Scaling the Tower of Babel: relational differences between identity, image and culture in organizations. In M. Schultz, M.J. Hatch and M.H. Larsen (eds), *The Expressive Organization: Linking, Identity, Reputation and the Corporate Brand.* Oxford: Oxford University Press.

Hegel (1975) *Hegel's Aesthetics: Lectures on Fine Art 1975.* T.M. Knox (Trans) London: Oxford University Press.

Henry, J. (2001) *Creative Management.* Sage, London.

Herbst, P. (1976) *Alternatives to Hierarchies.* Leiden: Nijhoff.

Hertz, N. (2001) *The Silent Takeover: Global Capitalism and the Death of Democracy.* London: Arrow.

Herzberg, F. (2003) One more time: how do you motivate employees? *Harvard Business Review* 81(1): 86.

Herzberg, F., Mausner, B. and Snyderman, B.B. (1959) *The Motivation to Work*. London: John Wiley & Sons. (New edition in 2003, New Brunswick, NJ: Transaction Publishers.)

Hofstede, G. (1980) *Culture's Consequences*. Calif: Sage.

Hofstede, G. (1991) *Cultures and Organizations. Intercultural Cooperation and Its Importance for Survival*. London: McGraw-Hill International.

Hofstede, G., Neyguijen, B., Ohayv, D.D. and Sanders, G. (1990) Measuring organizational cultures: a qualitative and quantitative study across twenty cases. *Administrative Science Quarterly* 35(2): 286–316.

Hoskin, K., Macve, R. and Stone, J. (1997) The historical genesis of modern business and military strategy: 1850–1950. Paper submitted to *Interdisciplinary Perspectives on Accounting Conference*. Manchester, July.

Hutton, J.G. (1996) Integrated marketing communications and the evolution of marketing thought. *Journal of Business Research* 37(3), 155–62.

Ind, N. (1997) *The Corporate Brand*. Macmillan, Basingstoke.

Ind, N. (1998) An integrated approach to corporate branding. *Journal of Brand Management* 5(5): 323–9.

Ind, N. (2001) *Living the Brand: How To Transform Every Member of Your Organization into a Brand Champion*. London: Kogan Page.

Ind, N. (2003) *Beyond Branding: How the New Values of Transparency and Integrity Are Changing the World of Brands*. London: Kogan Page.

Ind, N. and Watt, C. (2004) *Inspiration: Capturing the Creative Potential of Your Organisation*. Basingstoke, Hants: Palgrave.

Ind, N. and Watt, C. (2006) Brands and breakthroughs: how brands help focus creative decision making. *Journal of Brand Management* 13(4/5): 330–8.

International Survey Research (2002) Employee commitment study: 'Employee satisfaction in the world's 10 largest economies: globalisation or diversity?' at www.isrinsight.com

Janis, I. (1982) *Group Think*. Boston: Houghton Mifflin.

Jaworski, B. and Kohli, A. (1993) Market orientation: antecedents and consequences. *Journal of Marketing* 57: 53–70.

Kant, I. (2004) *Groundwork of the Metaphysics of Morals*. Trans. M. Gregor. Cambridge: Cambridge University Press.

Kapferer, J.N. (1997) *Strategic Brand Management: Creating and Sustaining Brand Equity Long Term.* 2nd edn. London: Kogan Page.

Kaplan, R. and Norton, D. (2000) Having trouble with your strategy? Then map it. *Harvard Business Review* 3–11.

Kao, J. (1996) *Jamming: the Art and Discipline of Business Creativity.* New York: Harper Business.

Karp, P. (2006) Edelman, Wal-Mart and the loss of control in media. *Publishing 2.0.* Article written 15-10-06; downloaded 16-10-06. http://publishing2.com/2006/10/15/edelman-wal-mart-and-the-loss-of-control-in-media.

Katz, D. (1964) The motivational basis of organizational behaviour. V. Vroom and E. Deci (eds), *Management and Motivation.* London: Penguin, 265–92.

Kee-hung, L. and Cheng, E. (2005) Effects of quality management and marketing on organizational performance. *Journal of Business Research* 58)(4) Apr: 446–56.

Keller, K.L. (1993) Conceptualizing, measuring, managing customer-based brand equity. *Journal of Marketing* 57(1): 22.

Keller, K.L. (2003) *Strategic Brand Management: Building, Measuring, and Managing Brand Equity.* 2nd edn. Upper Saddle River, New Jersey: Prentice Hall.

Keller, K.L. (2005) Branding shortcuts. *Marketing Management,* 14(5) Sep/Oct: 18–23.

Kelley, T. (2001) *The Art of Innovation.* New York: Doubleday.

Kelly, E., Leyden, P. and GBN (2002) *What's Next? Exploring the New Terrain for Business.* Cambridge, Mass: Perseus.

Klein, N. (2000) *No Logo.* London: Flamingo/Harper Collins.

Kluth, A. (2006) Among the audience: a survey of new media. *The Economist,* 22 Apr.

Koestenbaum, P. and Block, P. (2001) *Freedom and Accountability at Work: Applying Philosophic Insight to the Real World.* San Francisco: Jossey-Bass/Pfeiffer.

Kohli, A.K. and Jaworski, B.J. (1990) Market orientation: the construct, research propositions, and managerial implications. *Journal of Marketing* 54: 1–18.

Korten, D.C. (2001) *When Corporations Rule the World.* Bloomfield, CT: Kumarian Press.

Kotler, P. (1984) *Marketing Management: Analysis, Planning and Control,* 5th edn. New York: Prentice Hall.

Kotler, P. and Armstrong, G. (1987) *Marketing: An Introduction*. Englewood Cliffs, NJ: Prentice Hall.

Kotler, P., Jain, D.C. and Maesincee, S. (2002) *Marketing Moves: A New Approach to Profits, Growth & Renewal*. Boston, Mass: Harvard Business School Press.

Lawer, C. and Knox, S. (2006) Customer advocacy and brand development. *Journal of Product & Brand Management* 15(2): 121–9.

Leoncini, P.M. (2002) Make your values mean something. *Harvard Business Review* 80(7): 113–17.

Letiche, H. (2004) Jean-François Lyotard. In S. Linstead (ed.) *Organization Theory and Postmodern Thought*. London: Sage.

Levine, R., Locke, C., Searls, D. and Weinberger, D. (2000) *The Cluetrain Manifesto*. Cambridge, Mass: Perseus.

Levitt, T. (1960) Marketing myopia. *Harvard Business Review* 38(4): 45–56.

Lévy, P. (1997) *Collective Intelligence: Mankind's Emerging World in Cyberspace*. R. Bononno (trans.). Cambridge, Mass: Perseus Books.

Lichtenthal, J.D. and Wilson, D.T. (1992) Becoming market oriented. *Journal of Business Research* 24(3) May: 191–207.

Liker, J. (2004) *The Toyota Way: 14 Management Principles from the World's Greatest Manufacturer*. New York: McGraw Hill.

Lings, I.N. (2004) Internal market orientation: construct and consequences. *Journal of Business Research* 57(4) Apr: 405.

Lorraine, T. (2005) Ahab and becoming-whale: the nomadic subject in smooth space. In G. Lambert and I. Buchanan (eds) *Deleuze and Space*. Edinburgh: Edinburgh University Press.

Luhmann, N. (2003) Organization. In T. Bakken and T. Hernes (eds) *Autopoietic Organization Theory*. Oslo: Abstrakt Forlag, 31–52.

Lyotard, J.-F. (1979) *The Postmodern Condition: A Report on Knowledge*. G. Bennington and B. Massumi (Trans.) Manchester: Manchester University Press. (Originally published (1979) as *La Condition Post-Moderne: Rapport sur le Savoir*, Paris: Les editions de Minuit.)

McCarthy, E.J. (1960) *Basic Marketing: A Managerial Approach*, 13th edn, Irwin, Homewood Il, 2001.

Macrae, C. (2003) Brand, dynamic valuation and transparent governance of living systems. In N. Ind (ed.) *Beyond Branding*. London: Kogan Page.

McGovern, G. and Quelch, J.A. (2004) The fall and rise of the CMO. *Strategy and Business* 37, Special report, p. 5.

McGregor, D. (1960) *The Human Side of Enterprise*. New York: McGraw-Hill.

Mack, A. (2004) The Cathedral and the Bazaar. In: Nicholas Ind Inspiration Newsletter #001 at http://www.nicholasind.com/newsletter/001.html (13-10-2004).

McMurray, A.J. (2003) The relationship between organizational climate and organizational culture. *Journal of American Academy of Business* 3(1/2), 1–8.

Maister, D. (2001) *Practice What You Preach! What Managers Must Do to Create a High Achievement Culture*. New York: The Free Press.

Mann, F. (1957) Studying and creating change: a means to understanding social organisation. In C. Arensberg et al. (eds) *Research in Industrial Human Relations: A Critical Appraisal*. New York: Harper and Bros.

Manning, P. (1979) Metaphors of the field: varieties of organisational discourse. *Administrative Science Quarterly* 24(x), 660–71.

Manville, B. and Ober, J. (2003) *A Company of Citizens*. Boston, Mass: Harvard Business School Press.

Marketing (2004) Marketers on the board: board or boring. *Marketing* 8 Sep.

Maslow, A.H. (1943) A theory of human motivation. *Psychological Review* 50, 370–96.

Marshall, G. and Howard Morgan, H. (2004) Leadership is a contact sport. *Strategy and Business*. Fall.

Maslow, A. (1962) *Toward a Psychology of Being*. Princeton, NJ: Van Nostrand.

Maslow, A. (1998) *Maslow on Management*. New York: John Wiley and Sons Ltd.

Matsunoa, K., Mentzer, J. and Rentz, J. (2005) A conceptual and empirical comparison of three market orientation scales. *Journal of Business Research* 58: 1–8.

May, T. (2005) *Gilles Deleuze: An Introduction*. Cambridge: Cambridge University Press.

Mayer, J.D. and Salovey, P. (1997) What is emotional intelligence? In D. Sluyten and P. Salovey (eds) *Emotional Development and Emotional Intelligence: Implications for Educators*. New York: Basic, 3–34.

Merleau-Ponty, M. (1945) *Phenomenology of Perception* (*Phénomenologie de la perception*, Gallimard). Trans. C. Smith. Abingdon: Routledge, 2005.

Merleau-Ponty, M. (1993) Cézanne's doubt. In G.A. Johnson (ed.) *The Merleau-Ponty Aesthetics Reader: Philosophy and Painting* Evanston, IL: Northwestern University Press, 63–4.

Meyers, D. (2003) Whose brand is it anyway? In N. Ind (ed.) *Beyond Branding*. London: Kogan Page,

Mintzberg, H., Ahlstrand, B. and Lampel, J. (1998) *Strategy Safari*. Harlow, Essex: FT Prentice Hall.

Mitchell, A. (2000) *Right Side Up: Building Brands in the Age of the Organized Consumer.* New York: Harper Collins Business.

Mitchell, A. (2003) Beyond brand narcissism. In N. Ind (ed.) *Beyond Branding*. London: Kogan Page, 36–55.

Moore, J. (2003) Authenticity. In N. Ind (ed.) *Beyond Branding*. London: Kogan Page, 104–21.

Morgan, G. (1997) *Imaginazation: New Mindsets for Seeing, Organizing and Managing.* London: Sage.

Morgan, R.M. and Hunt, S. (1994) The commitment–trust theory of relationship marketing. *Journal of Marketing* 58, 20–38.

Morner, M. (2003) The emergence of open-source software projects: how to stabilise self-organizing processes in emergent systems. In T. Bakken and T. Hernes (eds) *Autopoietic Organization Theory.* Oslo: Abstrakt Forlag, 259–71.

Morris, P. (ed.) (2003) *The Bakhtin Reader: Selected Writings of Bakhtin, Medvedev, Voloshinov.* London: Arnold.

Morse, G. (2003) Why we misread motives – we think people are more mercenary than they really are. *Harvard Business Review* 81(1): 18.

Muniz, A.M. Jr and O'Guinn, T.C. (2001) Brand community. *Journal of Consumer Research*, 27(4) Mar: 412–32.

Muniz, A.M. and O'Guinn, T.C. (2005) Marketing communications in a world of consumption and brand communities. In A.J. Kimmel (ed.) *Marketing Communication: New Approaches, Technologies and Styles.* Oxford: Oxford University Press.

Murdoch, I. (1994) *Metaphysics as a Guide to Morals.* London: Penguin.

Nancy, J.-L. (1996) *Being Singular Plural (Etre Singulier Pluriel,* Editions Galilée). Trans. R. Richardson and A. O'Byrne. Stanford, California: Stanford University Press.

Nancy, J.-L. (1997) *Hegel: The Restlessness of the Negative (Hegel: L'inequiétude de négatif.* Hachette Littératures). Trans. J. Smith and S. Miller. Minneapolis: University of Minnesota Press, 2002.

Nancy, J.-L. (2005) The insufficiency of 'values' and the necessity of 'sense'. *Journal for Cultural Research* 9(4) Oct.

Narver, J.C. and Slater. S.F. (1990) The effect of a market orientation on business profitability. *Journal of Marketing* 54(4) Oct., 20–35.

Nietzsche, F. (1974) *The Gay Science*. Trans. W. Kaufmann. New York: Vintage Books.

Nunnally, J.C. and Bernstein, I.H. (1994) *Psychometric Theory. 3rd edition*. New York: McGraw-Hill.

O'Reilly, C., Chatman, J. and Caldwell, D. (1991) People and organizational culture. *Academy of Management Journal* 34(3): 487–516.

Organ, D.W. (1988) *Organizational Citizenship Behaviour: The Good Soldier Syndrome*. Lexington, Mass: DC Heath.

Orwell, G. (1981) *A Collection of Essays*. New York: Harvest Books.

Parker, C.P., Baltes, B.B., Young, S.A., Altmann, R., LaCost, H., Huff, J. and Roberts, J.E. (2003) Relationships between psychological climate perceptions and work outcomes: a meta-analysis review". *Journal of Organizational Behaviour*, 24: 389–416.

Parr, A. (2005) *The Deleuze Dictionary*. Edinburgh: Edinburgh University Press.

Patterson, M.G., West, M.A., Lawthom, R. and Nickell, S. (1997) *Impact of People Management Practices on Business Performance*. London: The Institute of Personnel and Development.

Peterson, R.A. (2005) In search of authenticity, *Journal of Management Studies* 42(5): 1083–98.

Pfeffer, J. (1998) *The Human Equation: Building Profits by Putting People First*. Boston, Mass: Harvard Business School Press.

Pfeffer, J. (2002) To build a culture of innovation, avoid conventional management wisdom. In F. Hesselbein, M. Goldsmith and I. Somerville (eds) *Leading for Innovation*. San Francisco: Jossey-Bass.

Pfeffer, J. and Sutton, R.I. (2006) Evidence based management. *Harvard Business Review* 84(1) Jan: 62–74.

Podsakoff, P.M., MacKenzie, S.B., Paine, J.B. and Bachrach, D.G. (2000) Organizational citizenship behaviors: a critical review of the theoretical and empirical literature and suggestions for future research. *Journal of Management* 26(3): 513–63.

Popper, K. (2002) *The Open Society and its Enemies*. London: Routledge.

Porter, M. (1980) *Competitive Strategy: Techniques for Analyzing Industries and Competitors*. New York: The Free Press.

Pringle, H. and Gordon, W. (2001) *Brand Manners: How to Create the Self Confident Organization to Live the Brand.* Chichester: John Wiley & Sons.

Raymond, E.S. (1999) *The Cathedral and the Bazaar: Musings on Linux and Open Source by an Accidental Revolutionary.* O'Reilly.

Reichheld, F.F. (1996) *The Loyalty Effect: The Hidden Force Behind Growth, Profits and Lasting Value.* Boston, Mass: Harvard Business School Press.

Research International (2004) Marketing in the spotlight: what people really think of marketing. The Economist Directors' Summit, March 2004, www.research-int.com

Rezania, D., Lingham, T. and Dolan, S. (2006) Team development: the significance and relationship of team awareness and action. *Narrative in Management Science.* Barcelona.

Ricoeur, P. (1975) *The Rule of Metaphor: The Creation of Meaning in Language (La Métaphore Vive).* Trans. R. Czerny, K. McLaughlin and J. Costello. London: Routledge Classics, 2003.

Ries, A. and Trout, J. (1981) *Positioning: the Battle for Your Mind.* New York: McGraw-Hill.

Rokeach, M. (1973) *The Nature of Human Values.* New York: Free Press.

Ronell, A. (2005) *The Test Drive.* Urbana and Chicago: University of Illinois Press.

Rosenthal, E.C. (2005) *The Era of Choice: The Ability to Choose and Its Transformation of Contemporary Life.* Cambridge, Mass: MIT Press.

Rousseau, D.M. (1990) New hire perceptions of their own and their employer's obligations: a study of psychological contracts. *Journal of Organizational Behaviour* 11, 389–400.

Rubin, R.S., Munz, D.C. and Bommer, W.H. (2005) Leading from within: the effects of emotion recognition and personality on transformational leadership behavior. *Academy of Management Journal* 48(5) Oct: 845–58.

Rucci, A., Kirn, S. and Quinn, R. (1998) The employee-customer-profit chain at Sears. *Harvard Business Review* Jan/Feb, 82–97.

Sadri, G. and Lees, B. (2001) Developing corporate culture as a competitive advantage. *Journal of Management Development* 20(9/10) Dec: 853.

Sartre, J.-P. (1960) *Critique of Dialectical Reason, Vol. 1* (Critique de la raison dialectique, Paris: Editions Gallimard) Trans. A Sheridan-Smith. London: Verso, 2004.

Saxenian, A. (1994) Lessons from Silicon Valley. *Technology Review* 97(5).

Schacter, D. (2001) *The Seven Sins of Memory*. New York: Houghton Mifflin.

Schein, E.J. (1985) *Organizational Culture and Leadership*. San Francisco: Jossey-Bass.

Schirmacher, W. (2005) 'Homo Generator in Artificial Life: From a Conversation with Jean-François Lyotard'. *Poiesis* 7: 86–99.

Schleh, E.C. (1984) *How to Boost Your Return on Management*. New York: McGraw-Hill.

Schlosser, E. (2001) *Fast Food Nation: The Dark Side of the All-American Meal. New York: Houghton-Mifflin.*

Schneider, B. and Reichers, A. (1983) On the etiology of climates *Personnel Psychology* 36(1), 19–39.

Schumacher, E.F. (1988) *Small Is Beautiful: A Study of Economics as If People Mattered*. London: Abacus. (First published 1973)

Schwartz, S.H. (1992) Universals in the content and structure of values: theoretical advances and empirical tests in 20 countries. In M.P. Zanna (ed.) *Advances in Experimental Social Psychology*. San Diego: Academic Press, 1–65.

Seidl, D. (2003) Organisational identity in Luhmann's theory of social systems. In T. Bakken and T. Hernes (eds) *Autopoietic Organization Theory*. Oslo: Abstrakt Forlag, 123–50.

Senge, P. (1998) *The Fifth Discipline: The Art and Practice of the Learning Organization*. London: Century Business.

Shotter, J. (2005) Peripheral vision. *Organization Studies* 26(1): 113–35.

Shotter, J. and Cunliffe, A. (2002) Managers as practical authors: everyday conversations for actions. In D. Thorpe and R. Holman (eds) *Management and Language: The Manager as Practical Author*. London: Sage, 15–37.

Siguaw, J.A. and Diamantopoulos, A. (1995) Measuring market orientation: some evidence on Narver and Slater's three-component scale. *Journal of Strategic Marketing*, 3(2) June.

Siguaw, J.A., Simpson, P.M. and Baker, T.L. (1998) Effects of supplier market orientation on distributor market orientation and the channel relationship: the distributor perspective. *Journal of Marketing* 62(3), 99–111.

Simons, R. and Davila, A. (1998) How high is your return on management. *Harvard Business Review.* Jan–Feb: 70–80.

Simons, T., Walsh, K. and Sturman, M. (2001) Service from the heart: the relative influence of job satisfaction and affective commitment on service quality and employee turnover. Presented at AOM Conference, 2001.

Sjödin, H. (2006) Dirt! an interpretive study of negative opinions about a brand extension. *European Advances in Consumer Research* 7: 92–6.

Sjödin, H. and Ind, N. (2006) Metaphor in brand extension. *Narrative in Management Science.* Barcelona.

Slater, S.F. and Narver, J.C. (1994a) Does competitive environment moderate the market orientation-performance relationship? *Journal of Marketing* 58, Jan: 46–55.

Slater, S.F. and Narver, J.C. (1994b) Market orientation, customer value, and superior performance. *Business Horizon.* Mar–Apr: 22–8.

Slater, S.F. and Narver, J.C. (1995) Market orientation and the learning organization. *Journal of Marketing* 59(3) July.

Smidts, A., Van Riel, C.B.M. and Pruyn, A.Th.H. (2001) The impact of employee communication and perceived external prestige on organizational identity. *Academy of Management Journal* 44(5), 1051–62.

Smit, E., Tolboom, M. and Franzen, G. (2004) Your brand loves you, but do you love your brand? *3rd International Conference on Research in Advertising.* Oslo.

Smith, A. (1998) *An Inquiry into the Nature and Causes of the Wealth of Nations.* Ed. K. Sutherland. Oxford: Oxford University Press. (First published 1776)

Spinoza, B. de (1677) *Ethics*, trans. E. Curley, London: Penguin Books, 1996, p. 67 (II/135)

Sturges, J., Conway, N., Guest, D. and Liefooghe, A. (2005) Managing the career deal: the psychological contract as a framework for understanding career management, organizational commitment and work behavior. *Journal of Organizational Behaviour* 26: 821–38.

Surowiecki, J. (2005) *The Wisdom of Crowds: Why the Many are Smarter than the Few and How Collective Wisdom Shapes Business, Economies, Societies and Nations.* Doubleday.

TEMO Group (2002) for Stockholm Södra published in *Svenska Dag-bladet Närinsliv*, 19 August.

Thompson, L. and Brajkovich, L.F. (2003) Improving the creativity of organizational work groups. *Academy of Management Executive* 17(1), 96–112.

Thomson, K. and Hecker, L.A. (2000) The business value of buy-in: how staff understanding and commitment impact on brand and business performance. R. Varey and B. Lewis (eds) *Internal Marketing: Directions for Management*. London: Routledge.

Thomson, K., de Chernatony, L., Arganbright, L. and Khan, S. (1999) The buy-in benchmark: how staff understanding and commitment impact brand and business performance. *Journal of Marketing Management* 15(8), 819–36.

Thyne, M. (2001) The importance of values research for nonprofit organizations: the motivation-based values of museum visitors. *International Journal of Nonprofit and Voluntary Sector Marketing* 6(2) May: 116–30.

Thyssen, O. (2003) Luhmann and management: a critique of the management theory in 'Organisation Und Entscheidung'. In T. Bakken and T. Hernes (eds) *Autopoietic Organization Theory*. Oslo: Abstrakt Forlag, 213–34.

Tirole, J. (2006) *The Theory of Corporate Finance*. Princeton: Princeton University Press.

Tsoukas, H. and Chia, R. (2002) On organizational becoming: rethinking organizational change. *Organization Science* 13(5): 567–82.

Turban, D. and Greening, D. (1996) Corporate social performance and organizational attractiveness to prospective employees. *Academy of Management Journal* 40(3): 658–72.

Van Maanen, J. (1977) The fact of fiction in organisational ethnography. *Administrative Science Quarterly* 24, 539–50.

van Os, H. (2002) Preface to 'Een collectie: selected works from the collection of the ABN AMRO Bank'. Amsterdam.

Van der Post, W.Z., de Coning, T.J. and Smith, E. (1997) An instrument to measure organizational culture. *South African Journal of Business Management* 28 (4): 147–69.

Van Riel, C. (1999) *Ten Years of Research 1988–1998 of the Corporate Communication Centre, Erasmus University, Rotterdam*. Special Issue on Communication Research in Belgium and the Netherlands.

Weick, K.E. (2003) Organizational design and the Gehry experience. *Journal of Management Enquiry* 12(1): 93–7.

Weick, K.E., Sutcliffe, K.M. and Obstfeld, D. (2005) Organizing and the process of sensemaking. *Organization Science* 16(4): 409–21.

Whetten, D. and Godfrey, P. (1998) *Identity in Organizations: Building Theory through Conversations*. Thousand Oaks, Calif: Sage.

Williams, C.C. (2005) Trust diffusion: the effect of interpersonal trust on structure, function, and organizational transparency. *Business & Society* 44(3) Sep: 357–68.

Wilson, A.M. (2001) Understanding organisational culture and the implications for corporate marketing. *European Journal of Marketing* 35(3/4), 353–67.

Wise, J.M. (2005) Assemblage. In C.J. Sivale (ed.) *Gilles Deleuze: Key Concepts*. Chesham, Bucks: Acumen, 77–87.

Woodward, B. (2006) *State of Denial*. New York: Simon & Schuster.

INDEX